# Understanding &Trading Futures

## REVISED EDITION

*A Hands-On
Study Guide
for Investors
and Traders*

**Carl F. Luft**

**IRWIN**
*Professional Publishing*®
Chicago • London • Singapore

This publication is designed to provide accurate and authoritative information in regard to the subject matter covered. It is sold with the understanding that the author and the publisher are not engaged in rendering legal, accounting, or other professional service.

ISBN 1-55738-570-X

Printed in the United States of America

BB

CTV/BJS

2 3 4 5 6 7 8 9 0

*This book is dedicated to my wife, Norine,
and to my kids: Maggie, Carl, and Joey.*

# CONTENTS

# PREFACE

The purpose of this book is to educate the conservative investor about futures contracts. It is assumed that the reader knows nothing about the futures markets, or futures contracts, but is eager to learn. These contracts are not for everybody. It is true that they can be extremely risky, and that some strategies are rather complex. However, it is also true that there are some basic, futures-oriented strategies that can be used to lower the risk of either a long or short position in a given asset.

This book is only one of many futures books that are available to today's investor. However, it is unique in that it provides the reader with detailed trading examples and worksheets that address the very real issues of cash management in various trading strategies. It is hoped that after reading this book, the prudent investor will be able to recognize those situations where futures contracts are an appropriate strategy, and then capitalize on them.

The book is organized as follows. Chapter One provides a general introduction to futures markets and contracts. First, the reasons for the existence and growth of futures markets are discussed. Next, the mechanics of futures trading are presented.

Chapter Two focuses on the properties and behavior of futures prices, and their relationship to cash market prices. Chapter Three discusses both fundamental and technical analysis of futures contract prices. Chapters Four through Seven deal with specific trading strategies for soybeans, Treasury Bonds, Standard and Poor's 500 Index, and foreign currency futures contracts. These strategies are explained through actual market examples and worksheets. The goal is to present the various futures-oriented strategies as clearly as possible. The worksheets are designed to minimize the strategies' complexity, in addition to providing the reader with the opportunity to implement them. Finally, the book concludes with several appendices.

I am deeply grateful to all those individuals who have made this book possible. It could not have been written without the wonderful people at Probus and my colleagues and friends at DePaul, particularly Geoff Hirt and Corey Von Allmen. However, I am most grateful to my wife, Norine, and to my kids, Maggie, Carl, and Joey for supporting me in this project and giving me the time to get it finished.

# Chapter 1

# INTRODUCTION TO FUTURES CONTRACTS

## THE NEED FOR FUTURES MARKETS

Understanding risk is the key to understanding futures markets and contracts. The need to manage the risk associated with changing prices always has existed. Since many assets are subject to this price risk, virtually all market participants are affected by it in some way. For example, suppose that a wheat farmer can cover the costs of producing a bushel of wheat and earn a fair profit at a price of $4.00 per bushel. Also, suppose that a baker can earn a fair profit on a loaf of bread if a bushel of wheat costs no more than $4.00. Finally, with wheat at a price of $4.00 per bushel, assume that the consumer pays $.25 for a loaf of bread. All parties are subject to the risk that the price of wheat will change. The farmer runs the risk of a price drop, which will result in less income and a shrinking profit. At worst, the farmer will be unable to cover the production costs and may have to declare bankruptcy. The baker faces the risk of rising wheat prices, which means that the price of bread must rise if the baker wants to maintain the profit margin. However, the baker may not sell as much bread after the price increase, and thus will suffer a loss in revenue. If the baker is willing to accept lower profits in order to preserve sales volume, then it is unlikely that the price of bread will rise. In either case the baker is forced to accept less income due to the higher cost of wheat. Finally, if the price of wheat rises and causes the price of bread to increase, then the consumer will have to spend more for the

same quantity of bread. Consequently, consumers will probably purchase less bread, and thus lower their standard of living. Of course, if
the price of wheat remains stable, then no one suffers. But there is no
guarantee that wheat prices will remain stable. It is this price instability which defines price risk.

The above example shows clearly the effects of price instability,
and illustrates how it affects different market participants. Rising
prices are beneficial to the commodity producer, but are harmful to
the end users. Conversely, falling commodity prices benefit users,
but hurt producers. Those market participants who are able to eliminate the unwanted price risk, and its harmful effects, are deemed
hedgers. Both the producer and user can hedge price risk by transferring it to someone who is willing to accept it, i.e., a speculator. Speculators are willing to assume price risk in return for the opportunity to
earn large profits. The behavior of both hedger and speculator is
consistent with economic theory. In the hedger's case, price risk is
traded for smaller, yet more stable profits. On the other hand, the
speculator is willing to bear large amounts of risk since it is virtually
impossible to earn large profits without assuming comparable
amounts of risk.

From the above, it is obvious that hedgers and speculators differ
according to the amount of risk each is willing to assume. Equally
important in distinguishing between the two is each one's relationship to the underlying asset. Hedgers always have a need for the
underlying asset in the normal course of business, and thus take
positions in the asset based upon their business requirements. Speculators have no need for the underlying asset, and any positions taken
are motivated strictly by the expectations of a price change.

In the wheat example, the farmer, or producer, is in the business of
growing wheat for a profit, and thus has a long position in wheat.
The long position results from having possession of the physical asset, the wheat. Conversely, the normal course of business for the
baker, or user, is to take the wheat and transform it into bread. Since
the baker does not possess the wheat until it is time to make the
bread, the baker has a short position in wheat. Suppose that the
farmer and baker expect the price of wheat to be quite unstable. Both
would like to eliminate the price risk associated with their positions.
Enter the speculators, who neither produce nor use wheat as a matter
of course. Suppose that one speculator anticipates a rise in the price
of wheat, and that another speculator expects the price of wheat to
drop. The farmer can guarantee a fair profit today by selling the

wheat for future delivery at $4.00 per bushel to a speculator who expects the price to rise above $4.00 per bushel. Similarly, the baker can guarantee a fair profit for a loaf of bread today by agreeing to purchase the wheat, and then take delivery for $4.00 per bushel, from a speculator who believes that the price will fall below $4.00 per bushel. Thus the farmer offsets the existing long position by selling the asset for future delivery, and the baker offsets the existing short position by purchasing the asset for future delivery. Each hedger's offsetting position is made possible by a speculator who is willing to assume a position in the underlying asset based upon the expectation of a price change. At this point, both hedgers have established a price of $4.00 per bushel of wheat, while the speculators have open positions which will generate profits or losses based on the change in the price of wheat.

If the price of wheat rises to $5.00 per bushel, then the speculator who has purchased the wheat from the farmer earns a $1.00 per bushel profit, and the speculator who sold the wheat to the baker suffers a $1.00 per bushel loss. The reverse happens if the price of wheat drops to $3.00 per bushel. That is, the speculator who has purchased the wheat from the farmer suffers a $1.00 per bushel loss, and the speculator who sold the wheat to the baker enjoys a $1.00 per bushel gain.

Not all speculators earn huge profits. Many of them suffer the consequences of bearing large amounts of risk: the loss of all of their wealth. It is not true that speculators manipulate markets, or that they are inherently dishonest. It is true that speculators perform two vital economic functions. First, they provide the opportunity for hedgers to transfer unwanted price risk. Without speculators, hedgers would not be able to avoid the risk associated with unstable prices. Secondly, speculators help provide the liquidity necessary for a smoothly functioning market. By putting their own capital at risk for the chance to earn commensurate profits, speculators provide a pool of funds which facilitate the transfer of assets. Thus, hedgers need speculators, and speculators need hedgers. For without hedgers, speculators would be unable to assume the levels of risk necessary to achieve large profits.

The third market participant, the arbitrager, ranks equally with the hedger and speculator in importance. Basically, the pure arbitrager earns a guaranteed profit by transacting in assets that are mispriced while avoiding price risk. The pure arbitrager is similar to the speculator, since neither has a need for the underlying commodity in the normal course of business. However, the pure arbitrager differs from the speculator in that the speculator earns a profit only if risk is assumed, while the arbitrager assumes no risk, yet earns a guaranteed profit. Since there is no risk of loss for the pure arbitrager it makes him or her similar to the hedger, but unlike the hedger the pure arbitrager is able to reap superior profits. Essentially, the pure arbitrager has found a free lunch.

According to economic theory it is arbitrage activity that keeps prices at their fair, or equilibrium, values. As long as there exists an opportunity to earn a guaranteed profit without assuming risk, there will be those who will act to take advantage of the situation. For example, suppose that an investor observes that IBM common stock is trading in New York for $100 per share, and that identical shares of IBM common stock are trading in Chicago for $102.50 per share. This price discrepancy can be exploited by purchasing shares of IBM in New York for $100 each, and then simultaneously selling each share for $102.50 in Chicago. The result is that the investor is guaranteed a profit of $2.50 per share, without having to bear any price risk. Given this situation, other investors will have an incentive to buy shares of IBM common stock in New York and then sell them immediately in Chicago. As more investors act to profit from the price discrepancy, the demand in New York for IBM shares, relative to the available supply, will increase and IBM's share price will rise. However, as the supply of IBM shares, relative to their demand, increases in Chicago, the price of IBM common stock will drop. These price adjustments will continue until the supply of IBM shares equals the demand for IBM shares in both New York and Chicago. When supply equals demand the market is said to be in equilibrium, and the incentive to arbitrage disappears. Consequently, the resulting price is defined as the equilibrium, or fair, price. In this example the equilibrium price is $101 per share of IBM.

Successful arbitragers are institutions that have extremely low borrowing costs, and extremely fast computer programs that allow them to transact in various markets with only minimal delay in order execution if there is an opportunity to earn a risk-free, guaranteed profit. This is neither wrong nor illegal. It is an economic fact of life. Furthermore, it is virtually impossible for the small investor to be a successful arbitrager since the competition is so fierce. Even though the small investor cannot arbitrage successfully, it is important to understand the arbitrage mechanism because it is such an integral part of the price determination process in every market.

## THE DEVELOPMENT OF FUTURES MARKETS

The practice of buying and selling various commodities for future delivery is not new. The first such transactions involved agricultural commodities. Producers, i.e., farmers, sold their crops for delivery in the forward market; while users, i.e., processors, agreed to purchase the crops in the forward market. The forward market was characterized by a buyer and seller entering into a contract where it was agreed that delivery would occur at some point in the future, for a specified price. The seller was bound by the contract to deliver the physical commodity to the buyer, who was contractually bound to take delivery of the physical commodity. No money changed hands until delivery occurred. Nothing was standardized, and everything was negotiable in the forward market: the commodity's quantity, quality, delivery date, and price. However, the forward market was rather cumbersome for speculators since it was impossible to transfer the contract once an agreement had been reached. Furthermore, it was the responsibility of each market participant to locate a trading partner. Frequently, these trading partners proved to be less than trustworthy when it came time to make or take delivery of the commodity. Both producers and processors reneged on their obligations.

In addition to these clumsy trading practices, the forward market was plagued by severe fragmentation. The lack of a centralized trading location hampered the flow of funds and caused severe liquidity problems. Clearly, a better method of trading agricultural commodities was needed. Thus, a group of Chicago merchants banded together and formed the Chicago Board of Trade in 1848. Their primary purpose was to provide a centralized location for the trading of forward contracts. This proved to be successful for a number of years; however, the fact that forward contracts were not standardized highlighted the need for a more efficient trading system. In 1865 the Chicago Board of Trade responded to this need by creating agricultural commodity futures contracts which traded via a system of margins.

Although some people believe that futures margins are too complex to understand, there is nothing mysterious about the futures margin concept. Basically, futures margins guarantee that the contract will be honored by both buyer and seller. Each party must post a good faith deposit which is equal to a small fraction of the contract's face value. The logic is that the commodity's daily price change is expected to be less than or equal to some amount. Thus, the appropriate margin level is determined according to the commodity's expected daily price change. If the commodity price drops during the day, then the futures contract buyer, the long position, suffers a loss, and the futures contract seller, the short position, experiences a gain. At the end of the trading day, an amount equal to the commodity's price change is deducted from the long position's margin account, and is added to the short position's margin account. Conversely, a commodity price rise during the day results in the short position's, i.e., the futures contract seller's, account being deducted an amount equal to the price rise, while the long position, i.e., the futures contract buyer, has the amount of the day's price change added to the margin account. If the commodity's price does not change during the day, then nothing happens to either margin account since neither party experiences a gain or loss. This process is called marking-to-market and insures that each market participant is able to meet their contractual obligation.

Futures contracts exhibited two important differences from forward contracts. First, the futures contract terms were standardized according to a given commodity's quantity, quality, delivery date, and delivery procedures. Recall that everything was negotiable for forward contracts. Second, futures market gains and losses were taken incrementally, while all forward contract gains and losses occurred when the commodity changed hands. Both of these features rendered futures contracts more attractive to speculators and hedgers than forward contracts, and resulted in an extremely liquid market where the obligation to make or take delivery of various agricultural commodities, and the associated price risk, were transferred quite easily.

In addition to transferring price risk, futures contracts and markets performed another important function: price discovery. The price of any good in any market is determined by the interaction of supply and demand forces. Since futures contracts are obligations to make or take delivery of some commodity at some later date, their prices provide important information concerning the underlying commodity's expected levels of supply and demand. Therefore, current futures contract prices reflect the market's consensus, or forecast, of the prices which are expected to prevail when the contract matures. If a commodity's supply is expected to be extremely large relative to its demand, then the current futures price will be relatively low. On the other hand, if the commodity's supply is expected to be scarce relative to its demand, then the current futures price will be relatively high.

These economic relationships were true during the 19th century when the Chicago Board of Trade was in its infancy, and the only futures exchange in existence; and they are just as true today. However, the Chicago Board of Trade now has been joined by 11 other futures exchanges. These 12 futures exchanges have been designated by the federal government as organized futures exchanges. Their purpose is to provide a forum for the trading of futures contracts. All futures contracts must be traded by exchange members, and guaranteed by clearing members.

Clearing members belong to the clearing association, or clearinghouse, and have the primary responsibility of guaranteeing each contract's performance. The clearinghouse also oversees the collection of margin and the marking-to-market process. This is accomplished by the clearinghouse matching each futures contract that has been bought with an identical futures contract that has been sold. This matching process occurs at the end of the trading day and allows the clearinghouse to take the opposite side of each trade. Thus, the clearinghouse becomes the buyer for every seller, and the seller for every buyer. With the clearinghouse as the opposite party to each trade, the individual does not have to worry about contract performance, and it relieves the individual from having to seek out a trading partner who is willing to take the opposite side of a given position. The presence of the clearinghouse fosters market liquidity since it becomes easy for an individual to unilaterally open or close a position. While the clearinghouse is the guarantor of each trade, there is no direct contact between it and the individual investor. It is the individual's brokerage house that will clear all trades through the clearinghouse. Figure 1-1 illustrates the clearing structure.

It is obvious from Figure 1-1 that there are more market participants than clearing members and retail customers. Brokerage houses, institutions, and floor traders are also quite active in the futures market. Perhaps the least understood of these is the floor trader. Basically, floor traders can be divided into two groups: commission brokers and market makers. Many brokerage houses choose to use floor traders who are exchange members and who execute the brokerage house's customer trades for a standard fee, or commission. Such floor traders are called commission brokers. However, not all brokerage houses use commission brokers. Some large brokerage houses serve as clearing members and also employ their own traders

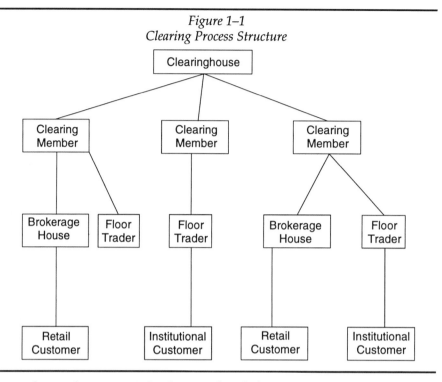

*Figure 1–1*
*Clearing Process Structure*

in order to better satisfy the needs of their institutional and retail customers. The second group of floor traders, market makers, trade for their own accounts and provide liquidity to the market. The term "local" is used synonymously with "market maker."

The futures markets and various futures exchanges always have been subject to some form of regulation. From the middle of the 19th century until just after the World War I, the futures industry operated under a patchwork, self-regulation system. Each exchange was responsible for enforcing its own regulations. This included the mechanical trading practices such as margin and delivery, as well as the conduct of its members. In 1922 Congress passed the Grain Futures Act, which established that futures trading must occur on federally licensed exchanges. The act used the threat of license revocation as an incentive for the exchanges to enforce their regulations against unethical trading practices, such as fraud and market manipulation, by their members. The Grain Futures Act was replaced in 1936 by the Commodity Exchange Act, which broadened the federal government's regulatory powers and placed all agricultural commodity futures contracts under the jurisdiction of the United States Department of Agriculture. The Commodity Exchange Act was in effect until 1974, when Congress passed the Commodity Futures Trading Commission Act. This act completely revised the 1936 Commodity Exchange Act and created an independent commission, the Commodity Futures Trading Commission (CFTC), which was given regulatory authority over all futures contracts and markets. The act authorizes the commission's existence for only four years at a time, but since 1974 Congress has reauthorized the commission in 1978, 1982, 1986, and 1989. In 1992, Congress reauthorized the commission for two years. The latest reauthorization petition requests a five-year authorization for the commission.

One of the provisions of the CFTC act empowers the CFTC to create registered futures associations. In September of 1981 the Commodity Futures Trading Commission approved the creation of the National Futures Association (NFA), an association designed to continue the tradition of self-regulation in the futures industry. Although the NFA is an industry association, it assists the CFTC in enforcing industry standards. This assistance takes various forms. The NFA handles the licensing and registration of futures industry professionals. Compliance with CFTC financial requirements is administered by the NFA. Customer and member arbitration is also an important function of the NFA. Finally, the NFA can prohibit a member from trading because of fraudulent or unethical practices. However, if criminal prosecution is warranted, it must be initiated by the CFTC; the NFA cannot prosecute members for criminal practices.

## THE MECHANICS OF FUTURES TRADING

Before one can trade a futures contract, one should understand how the prices are reported in the financial press. Most investors will follow futures contract price changes in either *The Wall Street Journal* or *Barron's*. Price quotes from *The Wall Street Journal* are presented in Figure 1-2, while Figure 1-3 provides futures price quotes from *Barron's*. The publications are similar in that they both provide the same basic information regarding futures prices. They differ in that *The Wall Street Journal* reports daily price changes in the futures markets, while *Barron's* shows the futures price activity on a weekly basis.

Figure 1-2 shows futures price quotes for a variety of commodities traded on various futures exchanges as of the close of trading on Friday, March 4, 1994. Information regarding the futures contracts of each commodity is presented in a standardized format. This format conveys such information as the trading location of the futures con-

*Figure 1-2*
## Futures Prices

Friday, March 4, 1994.

Open Interest Reflects Previous Trading Day.

| | Open | High | Low | Settle | Change | Lifetime High | Lifetime Low | Open Interest |
|---|---|---|---|---|---|---|---|---|

### GRAINS AND OILSEEDS

**CORN (CBT)** 5,000 bu.; cents per bu.

**OATS (CBT)** 5,000 bu.; cents per bu.

**SOYBEANS (CBT)** 5,000 bu.; cents per bu.

**SOYBEAN MEAL (CBT)** 100 tons; $ per ton.

**SOYBEAN OIL (CBT)** 60,000 lbs.; cents per lb.

### FOOD AND FIBER

**COCOA (CSCE)** – 10 metric tons; $ per ton.

**COFFEE (CSCE)** –37,500 lbs.; cents per lb.

**SUGAR—WORLD (CSCE)** – 112,000 lbs.; cents per lb.

**SUGAR—DOMESTIC (CSCE)** – 112,000 lbs.; cents per lb.

**COTTON (CTN)** – 50,000 lbs.; cents per lb.

**ORANGE JUICE (CTN)** – 15,000 lbs.; cents per lb.

### METALS AND PETROLEUM

**COPPER-HIGH (CMX)** – 25,000 lbs.; cents per lb.

**GOLD (CMX)** – 100 troy oz.; $ per troy oz.

**PLATINUM (NYM)** –50 troy oz.; $ per troy oz.

**PALLADIUM (NYM)** 100 troy oz.; $ per troy oz.

**SILVER (CMX)** –5,000 troy oz.; cents per troy oz.

tracts; the size and unit cost of the commodity futures contracts; the contracts' price changes; and the quantity of contracts traded and held by market participants.

For example, the corn quotes show that corn futures contracts are traded on the Chicago Board of Trade, where each contract controls 5,000 bushels of corn, prices are quoted in cents per bushel, and maturities follow a quarterly cycle of December, March, June, and September. Trading is active in nine corn futures contracts maturing between March of 1994 and December of 1995. The "Open" column shows that the March 1994 contract began the trading day at a price of 278¾, or $2.78¾ per bushel. During the day, the highest price for March 1994 corn was 279½, or $2.79½ per bushel, while the lowest price was 277⅜, or $2.77⅜ per bushel. These levels are indicated by the "High" and "Low" columns respectively. The "Settle" column denotes that the March 94 corn futures contract closed, or settled, at a price of 278¼, or $2.78¼ per bushel, at the end of the trading day. The –½ in the "Change" column shows that the settlement price for the March '94 contract fell ½¢ from the prior day's close. The three dots in the "Change" column for the May and July '94 contracts indicate that there was no change in the May and July 1994 corn futures contracts' settlement prices from the prior trading day, Thursday, March 3, 1994. The "Lifetime High and Low" columns show that since it began trading, the March '94 corn contract has ranged in value from $3.11¾ per bushel to $2.32¾ per bushel. The last column, "Open Interest," reveals that there are 5,785 long positions in March 1994 corn futures contracts which are outstanding. Since every futures contract requires both a buyer and seller, the clearinghouse computes the open interest for a particular contract by summing all the outstanding long positions. "Est vol 48,000" indicates that Friday's estimated trading volume was 48,000 for all corn futures contracts, while "vol Thur 96,990" shows that Thursday's actual volume was 96,990 corn futures contracts. Finally, the total open interest for all corn futures contracts is 330,201, which is 581 contracts less than the previous trading day's open interest as indicated by "open int 330,201, –581."

The Barron's data, Figure 1-3, are similar to The Wall Street Journal data. The data are grouped by commodity, and are arranged to show the contracts' "Season," or lifetime, "High" and "Low," followed by the week's "High" price, "Low" price, closing price, net change in price, and open interest. "Fri. to Thurs. sales," and "Total open interest" provide the total contract volume and sales for the most recent

## Figure 1-3
### Commodities and Financial Futures

BARRON'S • MARKET WEEK

# COMMODITIES AND FINANCIAL FUTURES

Commodities, or futures, contracts originally called for delivery of physical items, such as agricultural products and metals, at a specified price at a specified future date.

Increasingly, these contracts have come to apply also to Treasury bills, notes and bonds, certificates of deposit, major market indices and major currencies.

## FOREIGN EXCHANGE

Friday, March 4, 1994

The New York foreign exchange selling rates below apply to trading among banks in amounts of $1 million and more, as quoted at 3 p.m. Eastern time by Bankers Trust Co. Retail transactions provide fewer units of foreign currency per dollar.

## CRB INDEX

## Interest Rate

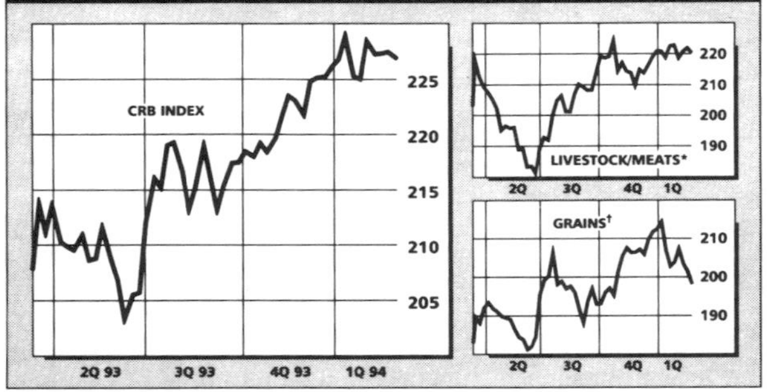

The Commodity Research Bureau's Futures Price Index (1967 = 100) represents an unweighted average of 21 prices: *Cattle, Cocoa, Coffee, Copper, †Corn, Cotton, Crude Oil, Gold, Heating Oil, *Hogs, Lumber, Orange Juice, Platinum, *Pork Bellies, Silver, †Soybean Meal, Soybean Oil, Soybeans, Sugar #11, Unleaded Gasoline, †Wheat.

*= LIVESTOCK / MEATS, †= GRAINS.

# Figure 1-3

## *Commodities and Financial Futures (continued)*

| | | | | |
|---|---|---|---|---|
| **Mexico** (Peso) | | | | |
| Floating rate .......... | .3076923 | 3.2500 | .3208728 | 3.1165 |
| **Netherlands** (Guilder) | .5182 | 1.9299 | .5209 | 1.9196 |
| **New Zealand** (Dollar) | .5741 | 1.7419 | .5780 | 1.7301 |
| **Norway** (Krone) ........ | .1343 | 7.4441 | .1349 | 7.4149 |
| **Pakistan** (Rupee) ...... | .0330 | 30.33 | .0330 | 30.30 |
| **Peru** (New Sol) ......... | .4759 | 2.10 | .4759 | 2.10 |
| **Philippines** (Peso) ..... | .03670 | 27.25 | .03663 | 27.30 |
| **Poland** (Zloty) .......... | .00004554 | 21959.00 | .00004538 | 22038.00 |
| **Portugal** (Escudo) .... | .005682 | 176.01 | .005749 | 173.95 |
| **Saudi Arabia** (Riyal) . | .26702 | 3.7450 | .26666 | 3.7501 |
| **Singapore** (Dollar) .... | .6309 | 1.5850 | .6318 | 1.5828 |
| **Slovak Rep.** (Koruna) | .0301841 | 33.1300 | .0301841 | 33.1300 |
| **South Africa** (Rand) | | | | |
| Commercial Rate ... | .2875 | 3.4783 | .2881 | 3.4715 |
| Financial Rate ....... | .2169 | 4.6100 | .2121 | 4.7150 |
| **South Korea** (Won) .... | .0012385 | 807.40 | .0012375 | 808.10 |
| **Spain** (Peseta) .......... | .007094 | 140.96 | .007171 | 139.45 |
| **Sweden** (Krona) ........ | .1247 | 8.0216 | .1247 | 8.0182 |
| **Switzerland** (Franc) .. | .6942 | 1.4405 | .7009 | 1.4268 |
| 30-Day Forward .... | .6938 | 1.4414 | .7004 | 1.4278 |
| 90-Day Forward .... | .6936 | 1.4417 | .7001 | 1.4284 |
| 180-Day Forward .... | .6943 | 1.4402 | .7002 | 1.4281 |
| **Taiwan** (Dollar) ........ | .037756 | 26.49 | .037779 | 26.47 |
| **Thailand** (Baht) ........ | .03954 | 25.29 | .03943 | 25.36 |
| **Turkey** (Lira) ........... | .0000513 | 19474.50 | .0000547 | 18278.70 |
| **United Arab** (Dirham) | | | | |
| ................................ | .2723 | 3.6725 | .2723 | 3.6725 |
| **Uruguay** (New Peso) | | | | |
| Financial ............... | .211864 | 4.72 | .218818 | 4.57 |
| **Venezuela** (Bolivar) | | | | |
| Floating rate .......... | .00896 | 111.59 | .00901 | 110.98 |
| **SDR** ........................ | 1.38723 | .71570 | 1.39569 | .71649 |
| **ECU** ........................ | 1.12600 | .... | 1.13210 | .... |

Special Drawing Rights are based on exchange rates for the U.S., West German, British, French and Japanese currencies. Source: International Monetary Fund.

European Currency Unit is based on a basket of community currencies. Source: European Community Commission.

z-Not quoted.

## BARRON'S GOLD MINING INDEX

| 12-month High | 12-month Low | | 3/03 | 2/24 | | % Chg. |
|---|---|---|---|---|---|---|
| 929.31 | 562.47 | Gold mining | 782.25 | 785.72 | – | .44 |

## FUTURES

## Metals and Petroleum

**GOLD**
**100 troy oz.; dollars per troy oz.**

| | | | | | | | |
|---|---|---|---|---|---|---|---|
| 398.30 | 375.60 | Mar | 381.00 | 375.60 | 377.60 | –1.00 | 1 |
| 418.50 | 335.20 | Apr | 383.60 | 374.00 | 378.60 | –1.20 | 71,255 |
| ..... | ..... | May | ..... | ..... | 379.70 | .... | 11 |
| 417.20 | 339.40 | Jun | 385.50 | 376.30 | 380.80 | –1.00 | 34,743 |
| 415.00 | 341.50 | Aug | 387.40 | 379.70 | 383.10 | –1.00 | 5,315 |
| 417.00 | 344.00 | Oct | 390.00 | 382.00 | 385.60 | –.90 | 4,113 |
| 426.50 | 343.00 | Dec | 392.60 | 383.50 | 388.10 | –.90 | 12,200 |
| 411.00 | 363.50 | Feb | 395.00 | 387.00 | 390.90 | –.80 | 2,611 |
| 417.00 | 364.50 | Apr | 397.00 | ..... | 393.70 | –.70 | 3,475 |
| 428.50 | 361.20 | Jun | 396.00 | ..... | 396.50 | –.60 | 3,982 |
| 412.50 | 380.50 | Aug | ..... | ..... | 399.50 | –.50 | 497 |
| 413.30 | 410.20 | Oct | ..... | ..... | 402.60 | –.40 | 264 |
| 429.00 | 402.00 | Dec | 429.00 | 403.00 | 405.80 | –.20 | 3,221 |

Fri. to Thurs. sales 156,733.
Total open interest 145,954

**HI GRADE COPPER**
**25,000 lbs.; cents per lb.**

| | | | | | | | |
|---|---|---|---|---|---|---|---|
| 107.50 | 73.00 | Mar | 89.80 | 85.25 | 89.50 | +4.05 | 5,449 |
| 90.10 | 74.50 | Apr | 89.50 | 85.70 | 89.45 | +3.85 | 1,074 |
| 102.20 | 73.60 | May | 90.00 | 85.50 | 89.55 | +3.75 | 32,853 |
| 89.50 | 74.10 | Jun | 86.40 | 86.00 | 89.40 | +3.50 | 845 |
| 102.95 | 74.20 | Jul | 89.45 | 85.75 | 89.20 | +3.20 | 8,586 |
| 103.30 | 74.90 | Sep | 89.50 | 86.00 | 89.20 | +3.00 | 3,537 |
| 101.90 | 75.75 | Dec | 89.80 | 86.50 | 89.30 | +2.70 | 3,741 |
| 89.70 | 76.90 | Jan | 88.35 | ..... | 89.40 | +2.65 | 88 |
| 99.00 | 73.00 | Feb | 88.70 | ..... | 89.50 | .... | 12 |
| 89.70 | 62.70 | Mar | 89.45 | 87.30 | 89.60 | +2.50 | 1,320 |
| 89.80 | 76.85 | May | 89.45 | 87.90 | 89.90 | +2.45 | 443 |
| 89.90 | 78.00 | Jul | 88.50 | 87.90 | 90.20 | +2.40 | 417 |
| 88.70 | 75.30 | Aug | ..... | ..... | 89.20 | +3.10 | 388 |
| 90.30 | 79.10 | Sep | 89.95 | 88.90 | 90.50 | +2.35 | 277 |
| 88.30 | 75.20 | Oct | ..... | ..... | 89.25 | +2.95 | 139 |
| 88.30 | 77.75 | Nov | 86.50 | ..... | 89.25 | +2.80 | 175 |
| 90.90 | 88.30 | Dec | 89.40 | ..... | 90.90 | +2.25 | 188 |
| ..... | ..... | Jan | ..... | ..... | 91.20 | .... | |

Fri. to Thurs. sales 42,550.
Total open interest 59,532

**LIGHT SWEET CRUDE**
**1,000 bbl.; dollars per bbl.**

| | | | | | | | |
|---|---|---|---|---|---|---|---|
| 20.88 | 14.08 | Apr | 14.83 | 14.41 | 14.57 | .... | 109,498 |
| 20.80 | 14.30 | May | 14.97 | 14.60 | 14.72 | –.02 | 61,361 |
| 21.05 | 14.58 | Jun | 15.15 | 14.80 | 14.86 | –.08 | 64,750 |
| 20.78 | 14.83 | Jul | 15.33 | 14.99 | 15.01 | –.12 | 26,543 |
| 20.78 | 15.07 | Aug | 15.50 | 15.20 | 15.18 | –.15 | 14,982 |
| 20.78 | 15.28 | Sep | 15.69 | 15.35 | 15.36 | –.17 | 18,483 |
| 20.73 | 15.54 | Oct | 15.82 | 15.56 | 15.53 | –.19 | 13,685 |
| 20.69 | 15.71 | Nov | 16.01 | ..... | 15.68 | –.20 | 10,126 |
| 20.80 | 15.80 | Dec | 16.20 | 15.83 | 15.83 | –.21 | 20,445 |
| 17.38 | 15.98 | Jan | 16.35 | 15.98 | 15.99 | –.23 | 7,942 |
| 19.60 | 16.32 | Feb | 16.50 | 16.32 | 16.15 | –.23 | 8,333 |
| 20.66 | 16.30 | Mar | 16.68 | 16.30 | 16.28 | –.24 | 8,233 |
| 19.68 | 16.61 | Apr | 16.68 | 16.63 | 16.41 | –.25 | 2,671 |
| 19.23 | 16.70 | May | 16.80 | 16.75 | 16.53 | –.25 | 3,203 |
| 20.30 | 16.65 | Jun | 16.95 | 16.70 | 16.63 | –.25 | 16,805 |
| 17.73 | 16.85 | Jul | 16.97 | 16.85 | 16.72 | –.25 | 1,446 |
| 18.90 | 17.16 | Aug | ..... | ..... | 16.81 | –.25 | |
| 19.84 | 17.08 | Sep | 16.97 | ..... | 16.90 | –.25 | 5,515 |
| 20.80 | 17.25 | Dec | 17.50 | ..... | 17.20 | –.26 | 13,010 |

Fri. to Thurs. sales 355,189.
Total open interest 437,799

**HEATING OIL**
**42,000 gal; cents per gal**

| | | | | | | | |
|---|---|---|---|---|---|---|---|
| 58.75 | 42.85 | Apr | 46.30 | 44.40 | 44.89 | –.34 | 48,566 |
| 57.50 | 42.30 | May | 44.45 | 43.00 | 43.45 | –.23 | 45,747 |
| 58.00 | 42.60 | Jun | 44.10 | 43.00 | 43.30 | –.28 | 27,956 |
| 57.00 | 43.20 | Jul | 44.70 | 43.70 | 43.85 | –.33 | 19,324 |
| 55.60 | 44.35 | Aug | 45.30 | 44.65 | 44.60 | –.33 | 8,331 |
| 57.17 | 45.40 | Sep | 46.40 | 45.70 | 45.65 | –.33 | 7,025 |
| 57.30 | 46.45 | Oct | 47.65 | 46.65 | 46.65 | –.33 | 4,526 |
| 58.30 | 47.45 | Nov | 48.35 | ..... | 47.60 | –.33 | 3,663 |
| 59.00 | 48.40 | Dec | 49.40 | 48.65 | 48.55 | –.33 | 6,748 |
| 62.25 | 43.25 | Jan | 50.00 | 49.40 | 48.95 | –.33 | 2,382 |
| 58.75 | 49.45 | Feb | 50.40 | 49.45 | 48.90 | –.28 | 1,393 |
| 57.50 | 48.40 | Mar | 49.75 | 49.00 | 48.00 | –.28 | 418 |
| 55.00 | 47.10 | Apr | 48.75 | ..... | 47.25 | –.28 | 342 |
| 51.50 | 47.40 | May | 48.00 | ..... | 47.00 | –.28 | 252 |
| 51.00 | 47.90 | Jun | 48.00 | ..... | 47.00 | –.28 | 249 |
| 50.26 | 48.48 | Jul | 48.48 | ..... | 47.50 | –.28 | 356 |
| ..... | ..... | Aug | ..... | ..... | 49.90 | .... | |

Fri. to Thurs. sales 187,111.
Total open interest 177,278

**UNLEADED GASOLINE**
**42,000 gal; cents per gal**

| | | | | | | | |
|---|---|---|---|---|---|---|---|
| 62.50 | 43.85 | Apr | 46.25 | 44.70 | 45.13 | –.72 | 36,348 |
| 61.30 | 44.70 | May | 46.80 | 45.55 | 45.83 | –.62 | 39,596 |
| 61.00 | 45.35 | Jun | 47.35 | 46.05 | 46.40 | –.60 | 18,016 |
| 60.50 | 45.75 | Jul | 47.45 | 46.30 | 46.62 | –.53 | 5,775 |
| 60.00 | 45.75 | Aug | 47.10 | 46.35 | 46.52 | –.53 | 5,088 |
| 54.00 | 45.85 | Sep | 46.70 | ..... | 46.37 | –.58 | 2,511 |
| 46.15 | 44.80 | Oct | 46.15 | 45.05 | 45.07 | –.53 | 1,816 |
| 48.00 | 43.90 | Nov | 44.60 | 44.00 | 44.32 | –.33 | 2,094 |

Fri. to Thurs. sales 145,124.
Total open interest 111,244

| | | | | | | | |
|---|---|---|---|---|---|---|---|
| 2.235 | 1.975 | Jun | 2.160 | 2.110 | 2.124 | – 46 | 933 |
| 2.180 | 1.978 | Jul | 2.175 | 2.110 | 2.134 | – 41 | 584 |
| 2.205 | 2.068 | Aug | 2.185 | 2.130 | 2.154 | – 41 | 1,180 |
| 2.230 | 2.170 | Sep | 2.230 | 2.170 | 2.189 | – 41 | |

Fri. to Thurs. sales 64,635.
Total open interest 116,222

**PLATINUM**
**50 troy oz.; dollars per troy oz.**

| | | | | | | | |
|---|---|---|---|---|---|---|---|
| 428.50 | 335.00 | Apr | 397.80 | 385.80 | 395.30 | +1.90 | 13,226 |
| 428.00 | 357.00 | Jul | 398.90 | 387.00 | 396.50 | +3.10 | 3,759 |
| 408.50 | 368.00 | Oct | 398.40 | 388.00 | 397.00 | +3.30 | 1,120 |
| 410.00 | 374.80 | Jan | 399.00 | 390.00 | 397.40 | +3.30 | 528 |
| 401.00 | 390.00 | Apr | 400.00 | 390.00 | 398.50 | +3.40 | 505 |

Fri. to Thurs. sales 13,913.
Total open interest n.a.

**PALLADIUM**
**100 troy oz; dollars per oz**

| | | | | | | | |
|---|---|---|---|---|---|---|---|
| 143.50 | 99.00 | Mar | 136.00 | 129.00 | 130.50 | –4.95 | 69 |
| 138.75 | 114.00 | Jun | 137.40 | 128.00 | 130.50 | –5.85 | 4,197 |
| 137.75 | 118.00 | Sep | 137.50 | 128.40 | 130.00 | –6.10 | 402 |
| 136.75 | 122.50 | Dec | 136.00 | ..... | 129.50 | –6.35 | 169 |

Fri. to Thurs. sales 4,772.
Total open interest 4,837

## Livestock and Meat

**CATTLE**
**40,000 lbs.; cents per lb.**

| | | | | | | | |
|---|---|---|---|---|---|---|---|
| 82.75 | 73.20 | Apr | 77.27 | 76.17 | 77.20 | +.25 | 38,349 |
| 75.10 | 71.25 | Jun | 75.07 | 74.35 | 74.97 | –.03 | 20,739 |
| 73.87 | 70.20 | Aug | 73.65 | 73.00 | 73.25 | –.35 | 11,937 |
| 74.00 | 71.07 | Oct | 73.95 | 73.45 | 73.67 | –.28 | 9,690 |
| 74.30 | 72.35 | Dec | 74.10 | 73.82 | 73.95 | –.17 | 2,048 |
| 74.25 | 73.00 | Feb | 73.75 | 73.57 | 73.57 | –.08 | 821 |
| 75.10 | 73.20 | Apr | 74.90 | ..... | 74.82 | –.10 | 59 |

Fri. to Thurs. sales 65,676.
Total open interest 83,643

**FEEDER CATTLE**
**50,000 lbs.; cents per lb.**

| | | | | | | | |
|---|---|---|---|---|---|---|---|
| 85.35 | 79.52 | Mar | 82.47 | 81.67 | 82.42 | +.20 | 3,520 |
| 85.00 | 79.20 | Apr | 81.90 | 80.85 | 81.72 | +.30 | 2,968 |
| 84.40 | 78.70 | May | 81.60 | 80.50 | 81.55 | +.50 | 2,712 |
| 83.00 | 79.55 | Aug | 82.15 | 81.40 | 82.12 | +.05 | 2,117 |
| 81.70 | 79.50 | Sep | 81.70 | 81.10 | 81.67 | +.05 | 367 |
| 81.35 | 79.30 | Oct | 81.35 | 80.70 | 81.35 | +.10 | 499 |
| 88.00 | 77.45 | Nov | 81.85 | ..... | 81.85 | +.05 | 163 |
| 80.90 | 79.00 | Jan | 80.90 | 80.62 | 80.80 | –.05 | 11 |

Fri. to Thurs. sales 3,516.
Total open interest 12,357

**HOGS**
**40,000 lbs.; cents per lb.**

| | | | | | | | |
|---|---|---|---|---|---|---|---|
| 51.92 | 39.57 | Apr | 49.70 | 48.12 | 48.67 | –1.20 | 13,132 |
| 56.27 | 45.27 | Jun | 55.07 | 53.92 | 54.62 | –.55 | 9,169 |
| 55.37 | 45.30 | Jul | 54.40 | 53.37 | 53.95 | –.50 | 3,244 |
| 53.40 | 46.35 | Aug | 52.80 | 51.75 | 52.02 | –.65 | 2,690 |
| 49.75 | 43.60 | Oct | 48.80 | 48.05 | 48.22 | –.38 | 1,500 |
| 50.50 | 45.30 | Dec | 49.60 | 49.00 | 49.15 | +.05 | 1,274 |
| 50.80 | 48.80 | Feb | 49.85 | 49.45 | 49.65 | –.17 | 233 |
| 48.80 | 40.90 | Apr | 48.00 | 47.30 | 47.70 | –.37 | 63 |
| 51.50 | 51.00 | Jun | 51.35 | ..... | 51.45 | +.45 | 3 |

Fri. to Thurs. sales 27,717.
Total open interest 31,308

**PORK BELLIES**
**40,000 lbs.; cents per lb.**

| | | | | | | | |
|---|---|---|---|---|---|---|---|
| 60.90 | 38.60 | Mar | 57.00 | 54.85 | 56.65 | +.68 | 439 |
| 61.80 | 40.50 | May | 58.10 | 56.10 | 57.40 | –.02 | 5,858 |
| 62.00 | 39.30 | Jul | 58.45 | 56.30 | 57.70 | +.18 | 2,424 |
| 59.50 | 42.00 | Aug | 55.90 | 54.05 | 55.00 | +.08 | 455 |
| 61.15 | 39.10 | Feb | 60.00 | 58.50 | 59.60 | –.32 | 17 |
| 59.90 | 59.25 | Mar | 59.90 | ..... | 58.65 | –.60 | 3 |
| 61.00 | 60.00 | May | 61.00 | ..... | 60.90 | +.65 | 4 |

Fri. to Thurs. sales 12,325.
Total open interest 9,200

| | | | | | | | |
|---|---|---|---|---|---|---|---|
| 96.80 | 96.22 | May | 96.40 | 96.22 | 96.25 | –.09 | 1,273 |
| 96.67 | 96.02 | Jul | 96.17 | 96.02 | 96.02 | –.12 | 269 |
| 96.58 | 95.90 | Aug | 95.98 | ..... | 95.92 | –.12 | 169 |
| 96.44 | 95.93 | Sep | 95.84 | ..... | 95.76 | –.14 | 269 |
| 96.00 | 96.00 | Dec | ..... | ..... | 95.28 | –.14 | |
| 96.72 | 96.10 | Jun | 96.27 | 96.10 | 96.12 | –.10 | 1,581 |

Last index 3.26, up 0.01
Fri. to Thurs. sales 9,834.
Total open interest 10,082

## Currency

**AUSTRAL. DOLLAR**
**$ per dlr; 1 point equals $0.0001**

| | | | | | | | |
|---|---|---|---|---|---|---|---|
| .7294 | .6380 | Mar | .7170 | .7020 | .7154 | – 35 | 6,331 |
| .7269 | .6395 | Jun | .7160 | .7010 | .7139 | – 31 | 493 |
| .7210 | .6645 | Sep | ..... | ..... | .7124 | – 27 | 21 |
| .6975 | .6975 | Dec | .6975 | ..... | .7109 | .... | 1 |

Last spot .7150
Fri. to Thurs. sales 6,343.
Total open interest 6,846

**BRITISH POUND**
**$ per pound; 1 point equals $0.0001**

| | | | | | | | |
|---|---|---|---|---|---|---|---|
| 1.5384 | 1.4000 | Mar | 1.4992 | 1.4824 | 1.4894 | + 18 | 30,618 |
| 1.5150 | 1.4474 | Jun | 1.4950 | 1.4760 | 1.4852 | + 26 | 13,988 |
| 1.4950 | 1.4440 | Sep | 1.4900 | ..... | 1.4826 | + 38 | 460 |
| 1.4950 | 1.4500 | Dec | ..... | ..... | 1.4810 | + 50 | 18 |

Last spot 1.4885
Fri. to Thurs. sales 95,202.
Total open interest 45,084

**CANADIAN DOLLAR**
**$ per dlr; 1 point equals $0.0001**

| | | | | | | | |
|---|---|---|---|---|---|---|---|
| .8712 | .7345 | Mar | .7422 | .7345 | .7365 | – 35 | 29,562 |
| .7805 | .7340 | Jun | .7420 | .7340 | .7360 | – 34 | 15,112 |
| .7740 | .7345 | Sep | .7411 | ..... | .7354 | – 37 | 766 |
| .7670 | .7315 | Dec | .7398 | .7344 | .7348 | – 39 | 567 |
| .7605 | .7365 | Mar | .7380 | ..... | .7339 | – 43 | 174 |
| .7522 | .7374 | Jun | .7333 | ..... | .7329 | – 50 | 13 |

Last spot .7369
Fri. to Thurs. sales 49,830.
Total open interest 46,194

**EURODOLLARS**
**$1 million;pts of 100 pct.**

| | | | | | | | |
|---|---|---|---|---|---|---|---|
| 96.250 | 90.280 | Mar | 96.250 | 96.070 | 96.110 | –100 | 307,672 |
| 95.890 | 90.400 | Jun | 95.890 | 95.600 | 95.660 | –160 | 450,965 |
| 95.570 | 90.360 | Sep | 95.570 | 95.230 | 95.290 | –210 | 363,356 |
| 95.180 | 90.710 | Dec | 95.180 | 94.790 | 94.840 | –260 | 267,780 |
| 94.990 | 90.240 | Mar | 94.990 | 94.600 | 94.650 | –250 | 239,491 |
| 94.730 | 90.710 | Jun | 94.730 | 94.360 | 94.420 | –240 | 188,580 |
| 94.520 | 91.310 | Sep | 94.520 | 94.150 | 94.210 | –240 | 148,140 |
| 94.280 | 91.180 | Dec | 94.280 | 93.910 | 93.970 | –220 | 117,003 |
| 94.220 | 90.750 | Mar | 94.220 | 93.870 | 93.910 | –230 | 98,916 |
| 94.080 | 93.730 | Jun | 94.080 | 93.730 | 93.780 | –220 | 75,197 |
| 94.300 | 93.560 | Sep | 93.920 | 93.590 | 93.640 | –210 | 68,388 |
| 94.830 | 93.390 | Dec | 93.720 | 93.390 | 93.430 | –210 | 53,623 |
| 93.690 | 93.070 | Mar | 93.690 | 93.360 | 93.400 | –220 | 48,462 |
| 93.570 | 91.890 | Jun | 93.570 | 93.230 | 93.270 | –230 | 41,055 |
| 93.460 | 92.100 | Sep | 93.460 | 93.130 | 93.170 | –230 | 38,749 |
| 93.270 | 92.120 | Dec | 93.270 | 92.940 | 92.980 | –230 | 32,824 |

Fri. to Thurs. sales 2,745,035.
Total open interest 2,663,860

**GERMAN MARK**
**$ per mark; 1 point equals $0.0001**

| | | | | | | | |
|---|---|---|---|---|---|---|---|
| .6205 | .5642 | Mar | .5900 | .5804 | .5814 | – 31 | 107,937 |
| .6133 | .5607 | Jun | .5870 | .5774 | .5785 | – 30 | 34,428 |
| .6065 | .5600 | Sep | .5837 | .5760 | .5766 | – 28 | 2,417 |
| .5790 | .5590 | Dec | ..... | ..... | .5757 | – 27 | 76 |

Last spot .5915, up 58
Fri. to Thurs. sales 287,244.
Total open interest 144,858

trading week. Any differences that occur are due to the *Barron's* data encompassing a week's worth of trading, while *The Wall Street Journal* data are reported daily. Finally, the *Barron's* price data include a decimal point, while some of *The Wall Street Journal* data do not. This is most prevalent in the grain quotes.

In the earlier discussion, several important concepts were introduced: price risk, long positions, short positions, margin, and marking-to-market. The following examples will illustrate and reinforce these concepts. Brokerage costs and commissions will be ignored in the following examples because they can vary widely among brokers. Be sure to consult your broker about specific costs.

Suppose that a three-month corn futures contract is trading at $2.20 per bushel, and an average small investor believes that corn prices are going to rise dramatically during the next week because of huge impending grain purchases by various foreign countries. The obvious strategy is to purchase corn futures contracts so as to profit from the expected price increase. Assume that this investor's broker requires an initial margin of $800 per corn futures contract, and a maintenance margin of $500 per contract. Furthermore, this investor will open the futures position on the morning of the first trading day, and will close out the position on the morning of the sixth trading day.

The earlier margin discussion introduced the concept of both the buyer and seller posting a good faith deposit, and the concept of taking gains or losses on a daily basis via the margin account, i.e., marking-to-market. The following examples are more sophisticated in that they distinguish between initial margin and maintenance margin. Initial margin is the amount that the market participant must deposit with the broker when a futures position is established. The maintenance margin is the minimum amount that must remain in the margin account at all times. Since prices change, the margin account's value will change too, via the marking-to-market process. The account will be credited if the position is realizing daily gains. However, if the position is suffering daily losses, then the account will be debited. As losses accumulate the maintenance level will be reached, and the broker will require the market participant to restore the margin account to the initial level. If the participant does not have the resources to restore the margin account to the initial level, then the position will be liquidated by the broker.

If the investor in this example has a total of $2,500 in cash, then he or she will instruct the broker to purchase two corn futures contracts. Pursuing such a course of action makes this investor a speculator. Recall that if one has no need for the underlying commodity in the normal course of business, then one has neither a long nor short position in the commodity's cash market. Since there is no position in the cash market, any futures market position that is initiated becomes a speculative position rather than a hedge position. As a speculator, this investor is providing liquidity for some hedger as well as absorbing the risk of a corn price decline. By purchasing two corn futures contracts at $2.20 per bushel, and depositing $1,600 in cash with the broker, the investor is speculating with 10,000 bushels of corn, worth $22,000, for a small fraction of their face value. This is a highly leveraged position with the potential to produce huge profits and losses, since leverage magnifies the effect of price changes. Indeed all speculative futures positions are highly leveraged positions which can result in huge profits or losses. The daily trading activity is tabulated in Figure 1-4.

Figure 1-4 may be interpreted as follows. Column 1 represents the trading day; column 2 provides the number and type of contract in the position; column 3 is the initial value of the investor's position; column 4 shows the price at which the contract settled each day, or when the position was liquidated; column 5 denotes the position's settlement value; column 6 gives the daily gain or loss in the total position; column 7 shows the effects of marking-to-market on a daily basis; column 8 shows the investor's cumulative gain or loss.

The results presented in Figure 1-4 indicate that this investor was correct in anticipating a rise in corn prices. The long position resulting from the purchase of two corn futures contracts experienced a $200 gain during the first day (i.e., $200 divided by 10,000 bushels, or $.02 per bushel). Notice that the position's settlement price is $22,200, versus the position's initial value of $22,000. At the end of the first trading day the investor's margin account is marked-to-market with a credit which brings the margin account balance up to $1,800. A similar event occurs on the second day. The investor's margin account is marked-to-market with a position gain of $300, resulting in a margin account balance of $2,100, and a cumulative gain of $500. On the third day the position's settlement price was $22,300, a $200 decline from the previous trading day. Thus the investor suffered a $200 loss. The $200 was withdrawn from the margin account when it was marked-to-market on the third trading day, and the position's

## Figure 1-4
### Profitable Margin Example

| Day | Position | Position Initial Value | Unit Settle Price | Position Settle Price | Daily Gain or (Loss) | Margin Account Balance | Cumulative Gain (Loss) |
|-----|----------|------------------------|-------------------|-----------------------|----------------------|------------------------|------------------------|
| 1 | +2 Corn | $22,000 | $2.220 | $22,200 | $200 | $1,800 | $200 |
| 2 | +2 Corn | $22,000 | $2.250 | $22,500 | $300 | $2,100 | $500 |
| 3 | +2 Corn | $22,000 | $2.230 | $22,300 | ($200) | $1,900 | $300 |
| 4 | +2 Corn | $22,000 | $2.240 | $22,400 | $100 | $2,000 | $400 |
| 5 | +2 Corn | $22,000 | $2.280 | $22,800 | $400 | $2,400 | $800 |
| 6 | +2 Corn | $22,000 | $2.270 | $22,700 | ($100) | $2,300 | $700 |

+ indicates a long position
- indicates a short position

cumulative gain was reduced to $300. Corn prices rose on the fourth and fifth trading days, to $2.24 and $2.28 per bushel respectively, resulting in gains to the investor and credits to the margin account when it was marked-to-market.

On the morning of the sixth trading day, the investor decided to liquidate the long position in the two corn futures contracts by selling them at the current market price. Figure 1–4 shows that corn was trading for $2.27 per bushel, and that the position was worth $22,700 when the contracts were sold, a decline of $.01 per bushel from its $2.28 settlement value of the prior day. This price decline resulted in the margin account being debited $100 before the investor was allowed to withdraw all remaining funds in the margin account. Once the investor has offset the open futures position, there is no longer any reason to leave the funds in the margin account.

The investor in this example was rewarded to the tune of $700 over six trading days for speculating that grain prices would rise in the near future, and thus increased the total cash amount to $3,200. Although the investor suffered some losses on the third and sixth days, the losses were not large enough to drive the margin account below the $1,000 maintenance level, or $500 per contract. The trading activity shown in Figure 1–5 tells a different story. Figure 1–5 uses the same initial data: six trading days, long two corn futures contracts, $800 initial margin per contract, $500 maintenance margin per contract, and an initial price of $2.20 per bushel. However, in this example, the corn price drops dramatically, resulting in a large enough loss to warrant a margin call.

The columns in Figure 1–5 carry the same interpretation as the columns in Figure 1–4. Figure 1–5 shows that this investor was incorrect in anticipating a rise in corn prices. The long position in corn futures suffered a $250 loss, or $.025 per bushel, during the first day. Notice that the position's settlement price is $21,750, versus the position's initial value of $22,000. At the end of the first trading day the investor's margin account is marked-to-market with a $250 debit, which puts the margin account balance at $1,350. On the second day, the investor's margin account is marked-to-market with a position gain of $50, resulting in a margin account balance of $1,400, but a cumulative loss of $200. On the third day the position's settlement price was $22,550, a $250 decline from the previous trading day, and another $250 loss. The $2,500 was withdrawn from the margin account when it was marked-to-market on the third trading day, and the position's cumulative loss rose to $450. Corn prices continued to

## Figure 1-5
## Losing Margin Example

| Day | Position | Position Initial Value | Unit Settle Price | Position Settle Price | Daily Gain or (Loss) | Margin Account Balance | Cumulative Gain (Loss) |
|---|---|---|---|---|---|---|---|
| 1 | +2 Corn | $22,000 | $2.175 | $21,750 | ($250) | $1,350 | ($250) |
| 2 | +2 Corn | $22,000 | $2.180 | $21,800 | $50 | $1,400 | ($200) |
| 3 | +2 Corn | $22,000 | $2.155 | $21,550 | ($250) | $1,150 | ($450) |
| 4 | +2 Corn | $22,000 | $2.125 | $21,250 | ($300) | $850 | ($750) |
| 5 | +2 Corn | $22,000 | $2.110 | $21,100 | ($150) | $1,450 | ($900) |
| 6 | +2 Corn | $22,000 | $2.100 | $21,000 | ($100) | $1,350 | ($1,000) |

+ indicates a long position
- indicates a short position

fall on the fourth day. The $.03 per bushel drop to $2.125 resulted in the position's value settling at $21,250, and a margin account balance of only $850; $150 below the $1000 maintenance level. This investor must deposit $750 in the margin account to bring it back to the initial level of $1,600, or $800 per contract. Thus, at the beginning of the fifth trading day the margin account stands at $1,600. However, the price of corn dropped another $.015 per bushel by the end of the day to $2.11, causing the position to lose another $150 and the margin account to be debited when it was marked-to-market. The $150 debit reduces the margin balance to $1,450, and increases the cumulative loss to $900 at the end of the fifth day.

On the morning of the sixth trading day, the investor liquidated the long position in the two corn futures contracts by selling them at the current market price. Figure 1-5 shows that corn was trading for $2.10 per bushel, and the position was worth $21,000 when the contracts were sold, a decline of $.01 per bushel from its $2.11 settlement value of the prior day. This price decline resulted in the margin account being debited another $100 before the investor was allowed to withdraw the remaining $1,350 in the margin account.

During the six days the investor suffered a total loss of $1,000, and was left with only $1,500 in cash. One might ask: what went wrong? Corn prices were supposed to rise due to an impending grain purchase by foreigners. In fact, for this investor the grain purchase did not materialize, and prices fell rather than rose. The key to understanding this example is to realize that corn prices were not *guaranteed* to rise, they were *expected* to rise. Since the investor was speculating, nothing out of the ordinary happened. Any speculator who bears price risk always faces the prospect of losing all of his or her wealth.

There is one final point in this example that warrants discussion. Recall that the investor began the speculative strategy with a total of $2,500 in cash. No doubt there are those who question the purchase of only two corn futures contracts when the investor had more than enough to meet the initial margin requirement of $2,400 for three corn futures contracts. Purchasing three contracts would have left only $100 in reserve for margin calls. In rising markets, such as those depicted in Figure 1–4, this would have been sufficient since the position was profitable from the beginning and did not suffer any margin calls. However, in sharply falling markets, disaster would have resulted because of insufficient liquidity. If the investor did not have enough cash to meet the margin call when the margin account fell below the maintenance level, then the brokerage house would have liquidated enough of the position to cover the trading losses and restore the margin account to an appropriate initial level. This situation is depicted in Figure 1–6.

At the end of the fourth trading day the margin account has dropped below the $1,500 maintenance level ($500 per contract for three contracts). The investor must bring the account up to its initial level of $2,400, $800 per contract for three contracts. Thus the investor must deposit $1,125 in cash to satisfy the margin requirement—the $2,400 requirement less the current margin balance of $1,275. However, the investor has a severe liquidity problem since there is only a $100 reserve. Since the investor does not have enough cash to satisfy the margin call, the brokerage house will sell two of the corn futures contracts, bringing the position down to long one corn futures contract with an initial margin requirement of only $800. Since there was a balance of $1,275 in the margin account at the end of the fourth day, the investor had more than enough to satisfy the margin requirements for one corn futures contract. Therefore, the investor withdrew the $475 excess. Now the investor had $575 cash on hand, the $475 excess coupled with the $100 remaining after the purchase of the three corn futures contracts. If all of the contracts in the position had to be liquidated to cover the losses, then that is what the brokerage house would have done. One never should trade futures contracts without having sufficient liquidity. One rule of thumb is to have enough liquidity to cover five consecutive days of losses. Failure to have sufficient liquidity will result in a quick exit from the futures markets.

Note that at the end of the fifth trading day the investor was long only one corn futures contract, and that the margin account had dropped to a level of $725. This drop in corn futures prices to $2.11 per bushel caused another $75 debit to the margin account and increased the total loss to $1,200. Finally, the $.01 per bushel drop on the sixth trading day prior to final liquidation resulted in another $50 loss ($.01 times 5,000 bushels), a margin account balance of only $675, and a cumulative loss of $1,250. At this point the investor had a total of $1,250: $675 from the margin account and $575 cash on hand. Onehalf of the original $2,500 had been lost because corn prices did not move as anticipated.

If one is to understand completely the mechanics of futures trading, then it is imperative that one have a firm grasp of the order process. All orders to buy and sell futures contracts are executed by

## Figure 1-6
### Losing Margin Example

| Day | Position | Position Initial Value | Unit Settle Price | Position Settle Price | Daily Gain or (Loss) | Margin Account Balance | Cumulative Gain (Loss) |
|---|---|---|---|---|---|---|---|
| 1 | +3 Corn | $33,000 | $2.175 | $32,625 | ($375) | $2,025 | ($375) |
| 2 | +3 Corn | $33,000 | $2.180 | $32,700 | $75 | $2,100 | ($300) |
| 3 | +3 Corn | $33,000 | $2.155 | $32,325 | ($375) | $1,725 | ($675) |
| 4 | +3 Corn | $33,000 | $2.125 | $31,875 | ($450) | $1,275 | ($1,125) |
| 5 | +1 Corn | $11,000 | $2.110 | $10,550 | ($75) | $725 | ($1,200) |
| 6 | +1 Corn | $11,000 | $2.100 | $10,500 | ($50) | $675 | ($1,250) |

+ indicates a long position
- indicates a short position

Futures Commission Merchants (FCMs) in a trading pit on the floor of a federally designated exchange, via a system of face-to-face trading where prices are determined by open outcry. Futures Commission Merchants are registered exchange members whose purpose is to conduct futures-related business for their customers. The average retail customer will use the FCM to execute orders and manage margin accounts. The orders most likely to be used by the retail customer and executed by the FCM are: the market order, the market-if-touched order, the limit order, the stop order, the stop limit order, and the spread order. The market order carries no contingencies with regard to time or price. The market-if-touched order, the limit order, the stop order, and the stop limit order are all conditional orders, however.

The most straightforward order is the market order, which is illustrated in Figure 1–7. When placing a market order the customer instructs the broker, who is employed by an FCM brokerage house, to either buy or sell a given number of futures contracts at the market

*Figure 1–7*
*Order Process*

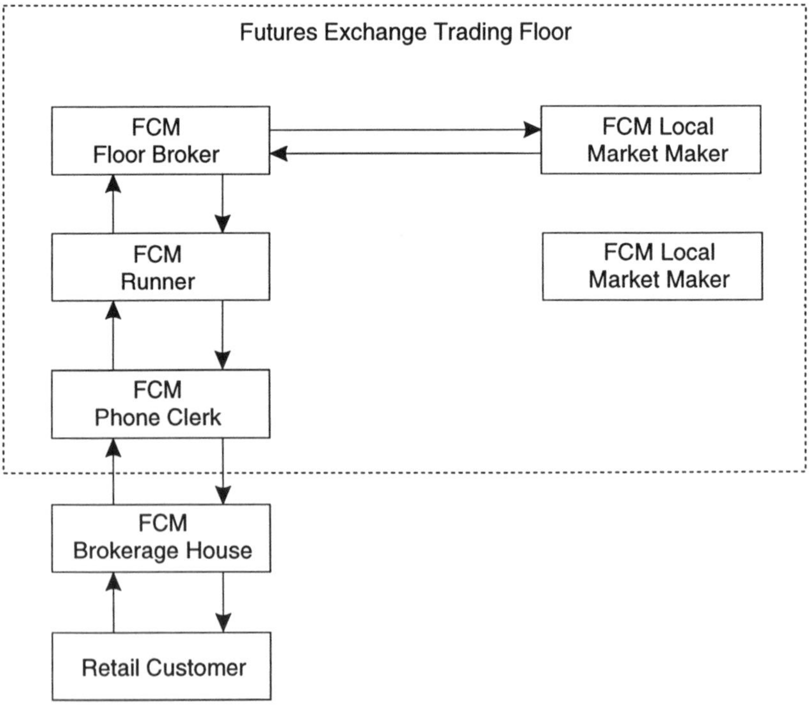

price. The order is relayed to the trading floor, where a brokerage house clerk time stamps the order and passes it to a runner. The runner takes the order to the commodity's trading pit and gives it to the brokerage house's trader. Since this is a market order it will be executed immediately at the prevailing market price. Once the order has been executed, its confirmation is handed to the runner, who carries it back to the clerk, where it is time stamped. The clerk then relays the order confirmation to the broker in the brokerage house office. Then the broker informs the retail customer that the order has been executed and verbally confirms the price, quantity, maturity, and type of position (long or short). Written confirmation is sent the next day.

Usually, the price at which the market order is executed is slightly different from the price which was in effect when the customer placed the order. This discrepancy is caused by the short time lag between the order's receipt and execution. The time lag is a fact of life and cannot be avoided when trading futures contracts. However, the elapsed time from the retail customer's order placement until confirmation is less than ten minutes for agricultural commodities, and less than five minutes for financial futures.

The market-if-touched order is a conditional order and is executed only if some market level is reached. A market-if-touched order to buy will be executed if the market price of the commodity drops below a certain level, while a market-if-touched order to sell will be executed if the market price of the commodity rises above a certain level. Once the price has reached the specified level the order is executed at the prevailing market price even if the market price is above or below the specified level.

The limit order also is a conditional order. The customer specifies a certain price or time which governs when the order can be executed. A price limit order requires that the order be executed at that price or better. A price limit order to buy means that the FCM broker must execute the purchase of the futures contract at the limit price or lower. A price limit order to sell requires that the FCM broker execute the sale of the futures contract at the limit price or higher. A time limit order determines how long the FCM broker has to execute the order. Unless stated otherwise, all orders are assumed to be day orders, that is, good until the end of the day's trading session. If a day order is not executed during the trading session, then it expires. However, a good-till-cancelled order remains in effect until the cus-

tomer instructs the FCM broker to cancel the order or until the futures contract expires.

The third type of conditional order is the stop order. When a customer places a stop order, he or she directs the broker to execute the
trade as soon as a specific price level is reached. A sell stop means
that the customer wants to sell futures contracts at the prevailing
market price once the market price quote drops to the specified price
level. A buy stop connotes that the customer wants to purchase futures contracts at the prevailing market price once the market price
quote rises to the specified price level. Once the specified price level
has been reached, the stop order becomes an unrestricted market
order. Many speculators use stop orders to protect open positions
when markets are moving against them. For example, a speculator
who is short futures contracts will put a buy stop in at a level that is
slightly higher than the price at which the short was established.
Then, if the price begins to rise, the short position will be offset without too great a loss. Conversely, a speculator who is long futures
contracts will establish a sell stop at a level that is slightly lower than
the price at which the long position was established. There is no
guarantee that the stop order will be executed at the specified price,
since in a fast market the specified price level may be penetrated very
quickly, and the FCM broker may not be able to get the order executed until the market price is much higher or lower than the specified price level.

The basic difference between a stop order and a market-if-touched
order is that the market-if-touched order becomes an unrestricted
market order if a specific price level is reached, and if a trade occurs
at that level; while a stop order becomes an unrestricted market order
if a specific price level is reached—it is not necessary for a trade to
occur at that level. The difference between the limit order and the
market-if-touched and stop orders is that the limit order must be
executed at the specified limit or better; the market-if-touched and
stop orders can be executed at any market price once their specific
conditions have been met.

The final conditional order is the stop limit order, which combines
the attributes of the stop and limit orders. This order goes into effect
once the market price reaches a designated level; as with a stop order, no trade has to occur. Once this level has been reached the order
must be executed at that level or better, as per the limit portion of the
order. Buy stop limit orders can be used by market participants who
are short futures contracts to protect themselves in rising markets,

and sell stop limit orders can be used by market participants who are short futures contracts to protect themselves in falling markets. However, this strategy is more risky than simply using stop orders because a stop limit order cannot be executed at a price level which is less advantageous than the specified level. If the market has moved away from the specified limit and continues in the same direction, then the market participant is powerless to avoid further losses.

The spread order is used to take both a long and a short futures position. There are two basic types of spreads: the intracommodity spread and the intercommodity spread. The intracommodity spread establishes simultaneous long and short positions in futures contracts of the same commodity, but at different maturities. The intercommodity spread establishes simultaneous long and short positions in futures contracts of different commodities, most often with the same maturity. When a spread order is executed by the FCM broker for the retail customer, the entire spread is bought or sold for the difference between the prices of the two positions. It is always more advantageous for the retail customer to buy or sell the spread itself because spread commissions are lower than the commissions charged for individual contract positions.

## SUMMARY

This chapter has provided an introduction to futures markets and futures contracts. The need for futures markets and contracts was explained within the context of price risk and then related to the concepts of hedging, speculating, and arbitrage. The development and evolution of the futures markets was traced from the first forward-contracting transactions in the 19th century through the more sophisticated futures contract trading practiced by the large futures exchanges today. The organization and regulation of the futures exchanges, and of the industry in general, was discussed to familiarize the reader with the safeguards that have been established over the years. Finally, the mechanics of trading futures contracts was explained to help the retail customer understand what can and cannot be expected to happen when participating in the futures markets.

This chapter is intended to serve as a basic overview of the futures markets and to provide a foundation for the remaining chapters. Many specific questions relating to the futures industry, the futures markets, and futures contracts have not been dealt with. If you are serious about futures trading, then make sure to seek out knowledgeable advisors. This book can be used as a reference guide, and as an introduction to more sophisticated literature. It should not be used as a definitive source for complex futures trading strategies.

# Chapter 2

# THE PROPERTIES OF FUTURES PRICES

## THE UNDERLYING LOGIC OF PRICE DETERMINATION

Prices for goods and services are determined by the interaction of the forces of supply and demand. Economic theory holds that the market clearing mechanism for any good or service is the price. A smoothly functioning market is not plagued by shortages or surpluses, and the price is allowed to fluctuate freely in response to changing levels of supply and demand. If demand for a good or service increases relative to its supply, then the price will rise until all those who are willing to pay the higher price for the good or service are satisfied. Conversely, if the supply of a good or service increases relative to its demand, then the price will drop until at some point it will not pay to produce the good or service since the price will not be high enough for the producer to cover costs and provide a fair profit. At this point, those responsible for the production of the good or service will quit providing it.

If the pricing mechanism is tampered with, then severe disruptions can occur. Perhaps the most familiar (but certainly not the only) example is when oil prices in the United States were controlled and the Organization of Petroleum Exporting Countries (OPEC) instituted the oil embargo of the 1970s. Since OPEC restricted the supply of oil and the United States did not allow prices to rise, the pricing mechanism was not allowed to function properly, and markets did not clear. The artificially low prices provided no incentive for U.S. oil producers to increase production in response to the smaller supply of OPEC oil. Furthermore, the artificially low prices did little to change oil consumption patterns in the United States. The factors of a diminished supply, high demand, and artificially low prices combined to make life miserable for many people; severe shortages and long lines to buy gas were the result. However, once oil prices were deregulated and oil prices were allowed to fluctuate freely, markets cleared. Consumption patterns changed, domestic production increased, and there was ample oil, albeit at higher prices, for the United States.

In Chapter One the existence of futures markets and futures contracts was explained within a risk-management framework. If a commodity's price was set at some arbitrary level and then not allowed to fluctuate, there would be no uncertainty regarding the commodity's price in the future. Thus, there would be no price risk, and no need for either the commodity's producer or user to hedge the effects of changing prices. Such a market would require an institution that would have to be ready, willing, and able to purchase any excess supply at the given price to prevent a surplus, and to provide the market with the commodity at the given price to prevent a shortage. This institution would perform the market clearing function at the stated price, and would guarantee price stability over the long run. The fact is that governments are the only institutions that have both sufficient resources and the inclination to perform the market clearing function. As long as a government is willing to perform the market clearing function there will not be a need for a futures market or a futures contract in that commodity. However, if the government ceases to clear markets, then prices will change in response to market forces, and the need for a futures market—and the associated futures contract—becomes clear.

Gold is a good example of a commodity whose price was controlled for many years by a government, but then allowed to fluctuate freely in the world market. The price of gold used to be guaranteed by the United States government until the early 1970s, when international economic pressures forced the United States to discontinue the practice of redeeming dollars in gold. Once the United States abandoned the gold standard, the price of gold rose dramatically, and then fluctuated in response to the changing forces of supply and demand. This meant that gold producers and users needed to hedge price risk. Thus, on December 31, 1974, gold futures contracts began trading on several U.S. futures exchanges.

## SPOT PRICES

The examples above illustrate that commodity prices in general will fluctuate in response to changing supply and demand factors. Now it becomes necessary to distinguish between spot prices and futures prices since both will respond to changing supply and demand conditions. A commodity's spot price represents the price at which the commodity will pass from the seller to the buyer immediately, or on the spot. Frequently the term "cash price" is used synonymously with the term "spot price." A commodity's futures price is the price at which the commodity will pass from the seller to the buyer when the contract matures.

It is generally true that spot prices are determined by supply and demand forces in the cash market. However, the forces of supply and demand may be manifested differently in different commodity markets. For example, the determinants of the spot price for soybeans are different from the pricing determinants of Treasury Bonds and stock indexes.

Cash soybean prices are determined by grain elevator operators who deal in soybeans. These dealers purchase beans from farmers, take delivery, and then resell the beans to processors. It is important to understand that unprocessed soybeans are useful only as seed and dairy cattle feed. However, once processed into meal and oil, soybeans become much more valuable. Soybean meal carries a very high protein content and is quite desirable as livestock feed. But it is possible to use other sources of protein, such as cottonseed cake and corn, to fatten slaughter animals. Thus, the cash price of soybeans relies in part upon the demand generated by the amount of livestock that are being prepared for slaughter (i.e., cattle, hogs, and poultry) and the supply of protein substitutes. Soybean oil is used widely in edible oil products such as margarines and cooking oils. However, since soybean oil competes with various other animal and vegetable oil products, such as butter and coconut oil, the cash price for soybeans depends upon both the demand for edible oils and the supply of close substitutes.

United States Treasury Bonds differ dramatically from soybeans. T-Bonds are not an agricultural commodity; they are a debt instrument issued by the federal government. The bonds carry a stated maturity and coupon rate and entitle the holder to semiannual coupon payments during the bond's life and full payment of the redemption, or face, value at the bond's maturity. Treasury Bond maturities range from 15 to 30 years, and each bond's coupon rate is commensurate with the market's required yield at the time of issue. For example a newly issued 20-year bond may have a redemption value of $1,000, and carry a coupon rate of 10 percent if the market is pricing existing 20-year Treasury Bonds at a 10 percent yield to maturity. This new issue will come to the market at par, or 100 percent of its $1,000 redemption value, and will provide payments of $50 every 6 months for the next 20 years. Then at maturity the bondholder will receive the final $50 interest payment as well as the $1,000 redemption value. Given these cash flows and yield to maturity, the T-Bond spot price is relatively easy to calculate. It is simply the discounted present-day value of all the future cash flows.

The interaction of the forces of supply and demand is captured in the bond's yield to maturity, the only parameter that fluctuates. Thus, it is imperative that one understands the relationship between bond prices and yields. Since all of the bond's other parameters—the time to maturity, the coupon rate, and the redemption value—are fixed, the bond price will change in response to changing yields to maturity. If interest rates, or yields, rise then bond prices will fall. Conversely, if interest rates, or yields, fall then bond prices will rise. This inverse relationship can be seen quite clearly in Figure 2–1.

Equation (1) in Figure 2–1 is the general debt instrument pricing equation and is based on the fact that a dollar received today is worth more than a dollar that will be received at some point in the future. The longer one has to wait, the less valuable the dollar. The equation shows that the spot price of an N period debt instrument is found by discounting each period's coupon rate of c, and the redemption value of R, by the bond's current, or spot, yield to maturity of y. Each period's cash flow is discounted, or divided, by the instrument's compound yield to maturity to move money through time and put all the cash flows on an equal footing. The longer-term cash flows must be worth less than the near-term cash flows.

Equations (2) through (5) use a 9 percent coupon rate, a $1,000 face value, and a 9 percent yield to maturity for a 3- period bond to determine the $1,000 bond price. Note that since the bond's price is equal to its redemption value it is selling at par. This occurs because the bond's spot yield to maturity equals the bond's coupon rate. When the spot yield to maturity changes, the bond price changes as well. Equations (6) through (9) show that if the bond's spot yield to maturity falls from 9 percent to 8 percent, then the bond's price will

*Figure 2.1*
*Debt Instrument Pricing Equations*

$$\text{Price} = \frac{C}{(1+y)^{t=1}} + \frac{C}{(1+y)^{t=2}} + \frac{C}{(1+y)^{t=3}} + \ldots + \frac{C}{(1+y)^{t=N}} \tag{1}$$

$$\text{Price} = \frac{\$90}{(1.09)^1} + \frac{\$90}{(1.09)^2} + \frac{\$90}{(1.09)^3} + \frac{\$1,000}{(1.09)^3} \tag{2}$$

$$\text{Price} = \$82.56 + \$75.74 + \$69.50 + \$772.20 \tag{3}$$

$$\text{Price} = \$227.80 + \$772.20 \tag{4}$$

$$\text{Price} = \$1,000.00 \tag{5}$$

$$\text{Price} = \frac{\$90}{(1.08)^1} + \frac{\$90}{(1.08)^2} + \frac{\$90}{(1.09)^3} + \frac{\$1,000}{(1.08)^3} \tag{6}$$

$$\text{Price} = \$83.33 + \$77.16 + \$71.44 + \$793.80 \tag{7}$$

$$\text{Price} = \$231.93 + \$793.80 \tag{8}$$

$$\text{Price} = \$1,025.73 \tag{9}$$

$$\text{Price} = \frac{\$90}{(1.10)^1} + \frac{\$90}{(1.10)^2} + \frac{\$90}{(1.10)^3} + \frac{\$1,000}{(1.10)^3} \tag{10}$$

$$\text{Price} = \$81.82 + \$74.38 + \$67.62 + \$772.20 \tag{11}$$

$$\text{Price} = \$223.82 + \$751.30 \tag{12}$$

$$\text{Price} = \$975.12 \tag{13}$$

rise to a value of $1,025.73. On the other hand, if spot interest rates rise from 9 percent to 10 percent, then the bond's price will drop to $975.12.

Common stocks are similar to bonds in that both provide periodic cash flows. But there are certain differences that exist between stocks and bonds which must be considered. Common stocks differ from bonds in that they provide the owner with a proportionate share of ownership in the firm, while bonds result in the owner being a lender to the firm that issues the debt. Debt matures, but common stock does not. Most common stocks pay dividends which can change from period to period; bonds pay the same fixed amount of interest each period. A stock's dividend payments are made at the discretion of the board of directors, but a bond's interest, or coupon, payments are not subject to such discretion. For example, if a board of directors decides not to pay a dividend during a given quarter, then no contract has been breached and that is the end of it. However, if a board of directors fails to make a coupon payment on the firm's debt, then the bond indenture agreement has been violated and the firm is in default.

Since their dividends are uncertain, and their lives are infinite, spot prices of common stock are much more difficult to determine than are the spot prices of Treasury Bonds. However, the concept of present value can be extended from debt instruments (bonds), to equity instruments (common stocks) in a straightforward manner. The logic is the same in both cases: determine the discounted present value of all future cash flows. Figure 2–2 illustrates the equity pricing model.

Equation (1) presents the cash flows in the form of dividends ($D_t$) from today (t=0) until infinity t=∞). Each of these cash flows is discounted, or divided, by the firm's required rate of return, k. This equation shows that one must discount each dividend that occurs to price a share of stock. This is extremely tedious, cumbersome, and impossible to do for an infinite number of dividend payments. However, equation (1) can be reduced to a much more manageable equation (2) by assuming that k is constant, and that the firm's earnings and dividends grow at some constant long-run average rate, g. In this equation only three values are needed to obtain an estimate for the share price: the dividend amount that is expected to occur next period, t=1; the firm's required rate of return, k; and the long- run growth rate of the firm's earnings and dividend stream. These equations are known as the constant growth valuation model. Equations (3) and (4) illustrate the share valuation process using the constant growth model.

In equation (3) it is assumed that the most recently observed cash dividend, $D_0$, is $1.00; the firm's required rate of return, k, is 15

---

*Figure 2–2*
*Equity Instrument Pricing Equations*

$$\text{Price} = D_0 + \frac{D_1}{(1+k)^{t=1}} + \frac{D_2}{(1+k)^{t=2}} + ... + \frac{D_\infty}{(1+k)^{t=\infty}} \tag{1}$$

$$\text{Price} = \frac{D_1}{k-g} \tag{2}$$

$$\text{Price} = \$1.00 + \frac{\$1.04}{(1.15)^{t=1}} + \frac{\$1.0816}{(1.15)^{t=2}} + ... + \frac{D_\infty}{(1.15)^{t=\infty}} \tag{3}$$

$$\$9.45 = \frac{\$1.04}{.15 - .04} \tag{4}$$

percent; and that the long-run average growth rate for earnings and dividends, g, is 4 percent. Given these data it is easy to see that the expected dividend next period, $D_1$, is \$1.04, and the expected dividend in two periods, $D_2$, is \$1.0816, which reflects a 4 percent growth in the \$1.04 dividend. If taken to infinity, the dividend would become infinitely large. However, the discount factor, $(1.15)^{t=\infty}$ would also become infinitely large, resulting in an extremely small term at infinity. In this valuation model the later terms have virtually no impact on the share price. This simply reflects the fact that near-term cash flows are more valuable than longer-term cash flows in a present value framework. Equation (4) takes these data and expresses them in a much more manageable format to achieve the share price of \$9.45.

The constant growth model may be simple, but it is also a powerful aid to understanding changing share prices. Clearly, investors will choose not to hold shares of a given company if they think that the company will do badly in the future. This unfavorable outlook about the company's prospects will have an effect on the shares' supply and demand. On the supply side, the gloomy outlook will cause investors to sell shares and avoid the adverse effects of poor performance. Share demand will drop because investors will be unwilling to purchase shares that are expected to perform poorly in the future. The constant growth model can capture this shareholder sentiment and its effect on share supply and demand through a lower long-run growth rate, g, and a higher required rate of return, k. If the growth rate, g, declines it means smaller future dividend payments. The threat of lower long-run growth and a smaller dividend stream causes investors to perceive the firm as being more risky. To compensate for this greater risk, investors will demand a higher rate of return from the firm. Thus, the differential between the firm's required rate of return, k, and g, the firm's long-run growth rate, increases and translates to a larger denominator. The combination of smaller future dividends, the model's numerator, and a larger differential between k and g, the model's denominator, combine to force the share price downward.

The discussion above dealt with declining growth rates. However, if long-run growth is expected to increase, then future dividends can be expected to rise, and the differential between the required rate of return, k, and the growth rate, g, will decrease. Now the larger numerator and smaller denominator reflect an increase in share demand relative to the supply, and thus a share price increase. Once again, the constant growth model has been able to capture and reflect shareholder sentiment.

From above it is clear that share prices are quite sensitive to changing growth rates. However, for the analysis to be complete it is important to examine the effects of changes in k, the firm's required rate of return. The role of k in the equity valuation model is similar to that of y in the bond valuation model. Both perform the function of discounting a stream of cash flows, i.e., moving money through time, and both quantify the market's perception of a given instrument's risk. The effects of a changing y in the debt valuation model are clear-cut: bond prices move inversely to interest rates. The effects of a changing k are not always predictable. The reason is that k captures only part of the change in the supply and demand factors, while g captures the rest. Therefore g must always be considered in relation to k when one is attempting to forecast the effects of changing interest rates on share prices. It is quite possible that share prices actually will rise when interest rates are rising because the economy is very robust and growth rates are rising by more than the increase in interest rates. Conversely, it is possible that share prices will decline when interest rates are dropping because the economy is in a recession and a company is not expected to grow as rapidly as in the past. This relationship between k, the firm's required rate of return, and g, the firm's long-run growth rate, makes it difficult to predict share price movement accurately. Nevertheless, it would be virtually impossible to understand how cash market prices for shares are formed if one had no idea of how these variables interact.

Stock indexes are portfolios which are composed of many companies' shares. Different indexes have different values because of the composite shares' performance, and also because of how the shares are weighted in the index. The S&P 500 Index is a value weighted combination of 500 different companies, representing approximately 80 percent of the value of all the shares traded on the New York Stock Exchange, where each company's weight in the index is determined by its relative market importance. The S&P 500 Index values are computed by multiplying each company's number of outstanding shares of common stock by the share's current cash market price. These values then are summed and compared to a 1941-1943 base period. Since the cash market prices for the common shares, or equities, of the S&P 500 Index components rely on the relationship between k and g, then the same must be true of the S&P 500 Index. Therefore, changing cash market values of the S&P 500 Index will reflect the overall market supply and demand factors. These factors can be captured and represented by the interaction between a market-wide required rate of return and a market-wide long-run growth rate in earnings and dividends.

## *FUTURES PRICES*

Futures prices for a given commodity are similar to the spot prices for that commodity in that both are influenced in the same way by the same supply and demand factors. However, the futures prices for a commodity will differ from its spot prices in that the futures prices are subject to two additional influences, carrying costs and arbitrage. As the name implies, carrying costs are those costs incurred by a market participant who is long the physical commodity and carries it through time until physical delivery occurs. These costs include the cost of storing, insuring, and transporting the commodity, as well as the foregone interest that could have been earned on the funds that were invested in the physical commodity. The second additional factor, arbitrage, is the process that links the spot price and carrying costs to the futures price. This linkage is easy to grasp if one remembers that people are rational and will act in their best interests. Recall that the pure arbitrager will transact to earn a guaranteed profit without assuming any risk. This arbitrage activity insures that prices will be at equilibrium.

The relationship of carrying costs, spot prices, and arbitrage is best understood in relation to physical commodities. If a commodity's futures contract price is greater than the sum of its spot price and carrying charges, then market participants will purchase the commodity in the cash market and simultaneously sell the commodity for the relatively high futures price by selling, or shorting, the futures contract. Purchasing the physical commodity in the spot market, storing it, and delivering it to satisfy the short futures position will be financed by borrowing. At delivery, the commodity will be sold for the futures price, which is greater than the cost of purchasing the commodity in the spot market, carrying it, and then delivering it. The difference between the revenue from the short futures position and the cost of the long spot position is an arbitrage profit since it was guaranteed by the relatively high price of the futures contract. This transaction will be undertaken by market participants as long as it is profitable to do so. The arbitrage opportunity will disappear once the futures price falls to a level that is equal to the spot price plus the carrying costs. Thus, the presence and activity of arbitragers in the market will cause the futures price of a given commodity to be no greater than the commodity's spot price plus the carrying cost.

This arbitrage process is called a cash and carry transaction and can be illustrated quite clearly using soybeans. Suppose that the spot price of soybeans is $5.80 per bushel, and that the storage, insurance, and transportation costs per bushel are $.05 per month. Furthermore, suppose that the borrowing cost is 10 percent per year. Given these data, the one-year soybean futures contract price should be no higher than $6.98 per bushel. The computations are as follows. First, if a bushel of beans was purchased in the spot market it would cost $5.80. The cost of physically carrying this bushel of beans for one year is $.60, $.05 per month times 12 months, payable at the end of the year when the grain is removed from the storage facility. Thus, if one did not have any cash and had to borrow enough to purchase a bushel of beans in the spot market the loan amount would be $5.80. Since the one-year borrowing rate is 10 percent, the amount that must be repaid at the end of the year is $6.38; the $5.80 principal plus the interest cost of $.58, i.e., 10 percent times $5.80. Summing the year-end loan value, $6.38, and the physical carrying costs, $.60, yields a value of $6.98.

Now, suppose that the observed price for a one-year soybean futures contract is $7.25 per bushel. Given the spot price and carrying cost, this futures contract is overpriced. Thus, there is an opportunity to arbitrage. Assume that a market participant decides to capitalize on the mispricing by performing a cash and carry arbitrage using 10,000 bushels of beans, which translates to two soybean futures contracts. The first step is to borrow an amount equal to the spot price of 10,000 bushels of beans, $58,000, for one year at 10 percent. Next, the beans should be purchased in the spot market for $58,000. At the same time that the beans are purchased, two soybean futures contracts, maturing in one year, should be sold for the current futures price of $7.25 per bushel. Once the beans' $7.25 per bushel selling price is established, a profit of $.27 per bushel, or $2,700 for the 10,000 bushel position, is guaranteed. Specifically, during the year the investor will incur a $500 per month charge to cover the physical carrying costs of 10,000 bushels of soybeans. At the end of the year a total of $6,000 will have to be paid for carrying the 10,000 bushels of beans until they are delivered to satisfy the short position in two soybean futures contracts. When the beans are delivered they will change hands for an effective price of $7.25 per bushel, or $72,500; $63,800 of which will be used to pay off the one-year loan, and $6,000 of which will be paid to cover the physical carrying costs. This leaves a risk-free $2,700 profit. This set of transactions will be performed again and again until the futures price falls to its equilibrium level, that is, the price level that makes it unprofitable to undertake these transactions. In this example that price is $6.98 per bushel.

In the above example the equilibrium futures price was determined via the arbitrage process. An alternative way of justifying the $6.98 equilibrium futures price is to concentrate on the one-year, risk-free interest rate. Suppose that you have $58,000 that you can invest in either a soybean cash and carry transaction, or in a one-year, risk-free bond yielding 10 percent per annum. Choosing the latter strategy will result in the $58,000 growing to a level of $63,800 by the end of the year. If the one-year soybean futures contract price is $6.98 per bushel, then the cash and carry transaction also will result in a year-end balance of $63,800. Thus, you should be indifferent between the two strategies. You will choose one strategy over the other if, without assuming any additional risk, there is an opportunity to end the year with an amount that is greater than $63,800. Any one-year soybean futures contract price that is greater than $6.98 per bushel will offer you this opportunity. Thus, the cash and carry alternative will be pursued in favor of the investment in the risk-free bond. This means that you will bear the same amount of risk as someone who invests in a risk-free bond, but you will achieve a rate of return that is greater than the 10 percent return provided by the risk-free bond. In the above example, the $7.25 per bushel soybean futures contract price resulted in a 14.6 percent return to the cash and carry strategy ($7.25 per bushel sale price minus $.60 per bushel physical carrying costs, minus the $5.80 per bushel spot purchase price, divided by the $5.80 purchase price) as opposed to a 10 percent return from investing in risk-free bonds. It should be clear from this example how important interest rates are in the carrying cost computations and in the pricing of futures contracts.

The above figures imply a total monthly carrying cost of $.0983 per bushel of soybeans, which is obtained by adding the monthly storage, insurance, and transportation costs with the monthly financing cost. The storage, insurance, and transportation costs are given as $.05 per bushel per month. The 10 percent annual interest rate means that the annual interest cost of borrowing to purchase soybeans in the spot market is $.58 per bushel ($5.80 times 10 percent) for a monthly interest cost of $.0483 per bushel.

The monthly carrying cost is important when examining the prices of futures contracts. Theoretically, one would expect the spot price to be lower than the futures contract prices since the spot commodity is not carried forward for delivery. Moreover, one would also expect the prices of the longer-term, or deferred, contracts to be higher than the nearby contracts since the longer a commodity is carried, the greater the cost. If the market embeds the full carrying cost in the price of each futures contract, with the deferred contracts trading at higher prices than the nearby contracts by an amount equal to the carrying cost, then the market is said to be at full carry. To illustrate, consider the soybean example above. If the market is at full carry, and there is one month until the November contract expires, then with a spot price of $5.80 per bushel and a monthly carrying charge of $.0983 per bushel, the relative prices of the futures contracts should be:

| November | January | March | May | July |
|----------|---------|-------|-----|------|
| $5.89 3/4 | $6.09 1/2 | $6.29 1/4 | $6.48 3/4 | $6.68 |

If the market does not embed the full carrying cost in each contract, but still prices the deferred contracts higher than the nearby contracts, then the market is at less than full carry. Deferred futures contract prices that are lower than nearby futures contract prices characterize an inverted market. Generally, the deferred futures contracts on a physical commodity trade at a premium to the nearby futures contracts, reflecting adequate commodity supplies and storage capacity. But there are occasions when these markets invert. Usually this occurs when there is great immediate demand and the commodity is in short supply. In this situation the market is bidding up the price of the nearby contracts relative to the deferred contracts, so that anyone carrying the commodity is penalized by withholding it from the market. This serves to increase the commodity supply in the short term so that the huge immediate demand is satisfied.

The soybean market during the last two weeks in June of 1988 is an excellent example of an inverted market. The nearby futures contracts were trading at a premium to the deferred futures contracts because of the drought in the western and midwestern United States. By the middle of June, the drought's intensity had caused severe damage to the maturing soybean crop, which resulted in a great deal of uncertainty about the soybean harvest for the 1988 crop year. Since there was a high probability that the harvest would be poor and that supplies would be relatively low, two things happened: soybean prices climbed dramatically and the market inverted to attract all available supply to the market to satisfy immediate demand. Thus, on June 23rd, 1988:

| July | August | September | November |
|------|--------|-----------|----------|
| $10.32 1/2 | $10.25 1/2 | $10.12 1/2 | $9.92 |

The drought continued to intensify through early July, and the market remained inverted. Finally, significant amounts of rain began to fall throughout the Midwest during the end of July. The deferred soybean futures contracts began to trade at a small premium to the nearby futures contracts, and continued to do so through August. By the end of August it was clear that while the soybean crop would be relatively small, supplies would not be as tight as was feared in early July. Thus, on September 1st the closing prices for the Chicago Board of Trade soybean contracts were:

| September | November | January | March |
|-----------|----------|---------|-------|
| $8.69 | $8.81 1/2 | $8.88 | $8.90 1/2 |

Treasury Bond and Stock Index futures contracts are based on financial instruments. They can be arbitraged via a cash and carry, and thus are subject to carrying costs. However, since they are not planted, harvested, and stored like soybeans there are no costs which reflect physically carrying and delivering the commodity. The carrying charges are composed entirely of interest, or the net cost of financing the position in the instrument.

Both Treasury Bonds and an S&P 500 stock portfolio provide cash inflows. This cash flow is in the form of coupon payments for Treasury Bonds, while for the S&P 500 portfolio the cash flow takes the form of dividends. These cash flows have an important effect on the prices of both Treasury Bond and S&P 500 futures contracts. The relation of each instrument's percentage inflows (the coupon yield for the Treasury Bonds and dividend yield for the S&P 500 portfolio) to the financing rate will determine if there is a positive or negative net carrying cost. A positive net carry market for financial futures contracts will occur if the financing rate is less than the underlying instrument's inflow yield. Conversely, a negative net carry market for financial futures contracts will occur if the financing rate is greater than the underlying instrument's inflow yield.

The basic pricing relationship can be represented in the following equation.

$$F = C\,(1 + rt - it)$$

In this equation F represents the futures contract price; C is the spot price; r is the financing, or borrowing, rate; i is the inflow yield; and t is the futures contract maturity expressed as a yearly percentage. Notice that if the financing rate equals the inflow yield, then the terms within the parentheses equal 1, and the left-hand side of the equation, the futures price, equals the right-hand side of the equation, the spot price. If the financing rate is greater than the inflow yield, then the terms within the parentheses become greater than 1, and the futures price exceeds the spot price. Finally, if the financing rate is less than the inflow yield, then the terms within the parentheses become less than 1, and the futures price is smaller than the spot price.

Many people consider it normal for Treasury Bond futures contract prices to be less than the Treasury Bond spot prices, reflecting a positive net carry market and a financing rate which is less than the bond's coupon yield. For example, if the annual financing rate is 7 percent , and the coupon rate on a long-term Treasury Bond selling at par is 8 percent , then, using the above equation:

$$\$99{,}500 = \$100{,}000\,(1 + (.07)(180/365) - (.08)(180/365))$$

The theoretical price of a 180-day, $100,000 Treasury Bond futures contract should be $99,500, which is 99–16 or 99 and 16/32. This positive carry example makes it easy to show why the spot bond is at a premium over the futures contract.

In a positive carry market it is better to be long the cash market bond rather the futures contract because of the positive net cash flow generated by the coupon payment. In this case the monthly financing cost for a long position in the cash bond is $583.33 ($100,000 times 7 percent divided by 12 months) while the monthly coupon accrual is $666.67 ($100,000 times 8 percent divided by 12 months) for a net monthly inflow of $83.34, $666.67 − $583.33. Thus, there will be a greater demand for the cash bond and the market will price it at a premium to the futures contract.

Suppose that the 180-day futures contract is trading for 100, the same price as the cash bond. In this situation investors will borrow $100,000 at 7 percent per annum to buy the cash bond and simultaneously sell the futures contract for 100. Since the long bond position was funded by borrowing, and the bond's sale price was guaranteed in 180 days by the short futures position, it means that during the next 180 days the investor gets to keep the net inflows of $83.34 per month without putting any existing funds at risk. This cash and carry bond strategy is a pure arbitrage and will continue to be undertaken until the futures contract trades at a discount to the cash bond. This discount must be sufficiently deep so that there is no incentive to perform the cash and carry transaction. The above figures indicate that the discount should be 16/32, or 1/2 point, which results in a futures contract price of 99–16.

If the financing rate increases to a level greater than the bond's yield, then the market will be in a negative carry situation and the futures contracts will be priced higher than the cash market bonds. Continuing with the above example, suppose that the financing rate increases to 9 percent. With this higher financing rate the equation becomes:

$$\$100,500 = \$100,000\ (1 + (.09)(180/365) - (.08)(180/365))$$

The futures contract price now rises to $100,500, which is 100 16/32 or 100–16. In this market the monthly financing cost for a long position in the cash bond is $750 ($100,000 times 9 percent divided by 12 months) the monthly coupon accrual is unchanged at $666.67

($100,000 times 8 percent divided by 12 months) but now there is a net monthly outflow of $83.34, $750 – $666.67. Investors will avoid this cost associated with holding the cash bond by holding fewer of them; demand for the cash bonds will drop, and the market will price the futures contracts at a premium to the cash market bonds.

Negative carry situations occur when long-term bond yields are less than the short-term financing rates. This situation is quite rare since it means that long-term Treasury Bonds have yields below the Federal Funds rate, i.e., the interest rate that banks charge one another for short-term loans. Usually, the yields on long-term Treasury Bonds are well above the Federal Funds rate, meaning that the market is in positive carry, and that Treasury Bond futures contracts are priced lower than the cash market bonds. It also means that the deferred Treasury Bond futures contracts trade at a discount to the nearby contracts.

A negative carry market is normal for the S&P 500 futures contracts since the dividend yield on the S&P 500 portfolio is lower than the financing rate. The futures contract prices in this market will be at a premium to the cash portfolio, and the deferred contracts will be priced higher than the nearby contracts. For example, if the annual financing rate is 7 percent, the dividend yield on the S&P 500 portfolio is 3 percent, and the cash value of the S&P 500 portfolio is 300, then applying the above equation yields an S&P 500 180-day futures contract quote of

$$305.92 = 300\ (1 + (.07)(180/365) - (.03)(180/365)).$$

Given this quote, the theoretical price of a 180-day, S&P 500 futures contract, traded on the Chicago Mercantile Exchange, should be $152,960. This reflects the fact that the Chicago Mercantile Exchange assigns a $500 value to each S&P Index point.

If the S&P 500 cash portfolio is purchased with borrowed funds, then the monthly net cost of carrying the portfolio in this market is $500. The 7 percent annual financing rate will result in $875 per month in interest charges, $150,000 times 7 percent divided by 12 months. However, the 3 percent annual dividend yield will provide a $375 per month inflow, $150,000 times 3 percent divided by 12 months. The difference between the $875 interest charge and the $500 dividend inflow is the $500 monthly net cost of carry.

If the 180-day S&P 500 futures contract is trading at a higher level, say 310, then arbitragers will undertake a cash and carry strategy to capture the profits embedded in the mispriced futures contract. In this situation arbitragers will borrow the $150,000 cash value of the S&P 500 portfolio—300 points times $500 per point, at 7 percent per annum—to buy the cash portfolio, and then simultaneously sell the futures contract for 310, which translates to a dollar amount of $155,000. Although the long stock position was funded by borrowing at 7 percent per annum, the actual annual interest cost is only 4 percent since the long stock position receives a positive 3 percent annual dividend yield. Therefore, during the next 180 days the arbitrager pays only $500 per month without putting any existing funds at risk. Since the S&P portfolio's sale price was guaranteed in 180 days by the short futures position, it means that this cash and carry bond strategy is a pure arbitrage and will continue to be undertaken until the S&P futures contract premium to the cash portfolio drops to a level of 5.92. At this point there will be no incentive to perform the cash and carry transaction.

It is important to understand that a successful S&P 500 cash and carry is a bit more complex than a soybean or Treasury Bond cash and carry because the S&P cash instrument is more difficult to purchase than the cash instruments for soybeans and Treasury Bonds. The cash position in soybeans is constructed by simply purchasing 5,000 bushels of soybeans in the spot market, while purchasing $100,000 of long-term Treasury Bonds in the spot market results in a long Treasury Bond position. A long S&P 500 cash position is constructed by purchasing the S&P component stocks in the same proportion as their inclusion in the index. This makes it necessary for an arbitrager to purchase many odd lots, i.e., orders which do not equal 100 share blocks, very quickly, at share prices that will result in the cash value of the portfolio being consistent with the cash and carry arbitrage. It is virtually impossible for a small investor to accomplish this feat—only the most sophisticated institutional customers can do so. However, since there are enough institutions that have the means to do this arbitrage, the S&P 500 index futures contracts should trade at their no arbitrage, equilibrium values.

## BASIS

The difference between the spot price of a commodity and the price of the commodity's nearest futures contract is defined as the basis. The basis can be expressed mathematically as

$$B = C - F$$

where B denotes the basis, C specifies the spot price, and F represents the futures price. If C is greater than F, then the basis is positive, the futures contracts are priced at a discount to the spot instrument, and the market is inverted. If C is less than F, then the basis is negative, the futures contracts are priced at a premium to the spot instrument, and the market is reflecting the carrying cost.

The basis can be either positive or negative for soybeans. If the soybean futures contact prices reflect the carrying charges, then the deferred contracts should be priced at a premium to the nearby contracts and to the spot soybeans. Under these circumstances the basis will be negative and the market will be considered normal because there is a sufficient supply of soybeans to satisfy immediate demand, and enough soybeans in storage to satisfy the anticipated demand. Recall the earlier full carry soybean example where the soybean spot price was $5.80 per bushel and the monthly carrying charge was $.0983 per bushel, which resulted in the November through May futures contract prices being:

| November | January | March | May | July |
|----------|---------|-------|-----|------|
| $5.89 3/4 | $6.09 1/2 | $6.29 1/4 | $6.48 3/4 | $6.68 |

These numbers imply a soybean basis of − $.09 3/4 per bushel— the $5.80 spot price less the $5.89 3/4 November futures contract price.

If there is either a dramatic increase in the quantity of beans demanded, such as an extremely large foreign purchase, or a dramatic decrease in the quantity of beans supplied, such as a drought, then the spot soybeans will trade at a premium to the soybean futures contracts, the basis will be positive, and the market will invert. These conditions reflect the fact that the current supply of spot soybeans is too low to satisfy current demand and that beans must be removed from storage to remedy the situation. Suppose that in the above example there was a huge increase in the foreign demand for soybeans so that the spot price rose immediately to a value of $8.00 per bushel, and that the futures contract prices realigned as:

| November | January | March | May | July |
|----------|---------|-------|-----|------|
| $7.89 3/4 | $7.75 1/2 | $7.60 1/4 | $7.48 3/4 | $7.40 |

The basis has changed from − $.09 3/4 per bushel, to + $.10 1/4 per bushel.

The basis normally will be positive for Treasury Bonds and negative for the S&P 500 Index. The negative Treasury Bond basis occurs because long-term Treasury Bond yields will be higher than shorter-term financing rates. Conversely, the positive S&P 500 Index basis is caused by the S&P 500 dividend yield being lower than the short-term financing rate. It is unlikely that either the Treasury Bond basis or the S&P 500 basis will change signs like the soybean basis since long-term bond yields probably will remain greater than the short-term financing rate and the S&P 500 dividend yield will probably stay lower than the short-term financing rate.

It should be clear from the previous cash and carry discussion and examples that futures market price equilibrium depends on the relationship between a commodity's spot price and futures price, or the basis. Arbitragers recognize that the basis for both physical commodities and financial instruments exhibits two desirable properties. First, the basis experiences lower volatility than either the spot price or the futures price. This allows arbitragers to assume positions that are relatively stable, and which will not require as much readjustment in individual positions in either cash or futures market positions. Secondly, as the maturity of the futures contract approaches, the basis approaches zero. This permits arbitragers to trade on price discrepancies prior to maturity knowing that at maturity the discrepancy will have vanished since there will not be any difference between the spot price and futures price. These properties are extremely important to arbitragers since the arbitrage process requires simultaneous spot and futures positions in a commodity.

The explanation of the basis' relatively low volatility is twofold. First, both the spot and futures prices are influenced by the same underlying supply and demand factors. Thus, one should expect the spot price and futures price to change in a similar fashion and exhibit a large positive correlation. Second, since the basis is defined as the spot price minus the futures price, it is equivalent to saying that one has a long position in the cash instrument and a short position in the futures contract. Having opposing positions in highly correlated markets serves to mitigate the effects of changing prices, and thus lower the volatility. Specifically, a long position in the cash market will benefit from rising prices, but will suffer from declining prices; while a short position in the futures market will benefit from falling prices but will deteriorate in value if prices increase.

The movement of the basis toward zero as maturity approaches is caused by the convergence of the spot and futures prices. This occurs because there is less time left to carry the spot commodity to delivery to satisfy a short futures position; therefore, the carrying costs for that commodity decline as the delivery date approaches. If the futures contracts are reflecting the carrying costs and trading at a premium to the spot market, then as maturity approaches the futures prices will drop toward the spot price and the basis will become less negative as it approaches zero. In the full carry soybean example, the basis one week before maturity and delivery should only be − $.024 since the weekly carrying cost is $.024 (the $.0975 monthly carrying cost divided by 4). At maturity, the beans are delivered to satisfy the short futures position, the carrying charges will be zero, the spot and futures prices will be equal, and the basis will be zero. On the other hand, if the market is inverted and the futures contracts are trading at a discount to the spot market, then the basis will become less positive as maturity approaches and the futures prices will increase as they move toward the spot price. In the inverted market soybean example, the basis one week before maturity and delivery should only be + $.026 since the weekly penalty, or opportunity cost, for withholding soybeans from the market is $.026 (the $.1025 monthly opportunity cost divided by 4). At maturity, the beans are delivered to satisfy the short futures position, the opportunity cost will be zero, the spot and futures prices will be equal, and the basis will be zero.

## SUMMARY

This chapter focused on the properties of futures contract prices. The chapter began with a discussion of the general underlying logic of price determination where the interaction of the forces of supply and demand in the price determination process was emphasized. After establishing the general logic of the price determination process, the specific factors influencing the spot prices of soybeans, debt instruments, and equities were examined. Then the process of futures price determination for soybeans, Treasury Bonds, and the S&P 500 Index was explored using carrying cost models. The chapter's final section dealt with the basis. The discussion began by defining the basis as the difference between a commodity's spot price and futures price. Then the concepts of normal and inverted markets were reviewed within the context of basis for soybeans, Treasury Bonds, and the S&P 500 Index. The discussion concluded with an examination of the effects of price convergence and zero basis on arbitrage.

# Chapter 3

# FUNDAMENTAL AND TECHNICAL ANALYSIS

This chapter considers two different analytical methods, fundamental analysis and technical analysis. These methods are similar in that they share a common goal: the accurate prediction of price changes for futures contracts, so that profitable trading strategies can be formulated. They are also similar in that neither is an exact science. They both rely heavily on an analyst's subjective interpretation of data to arrive at their respective predictions. However, these methods differ in philosophy and the means used to arrive at their respective predictions. The fundamental analyst believes that market prices are the result of the interaction of the forces of supply and demand, and that these forces are influenced by the interaction of many factors in the economy. Thus, the fundamental approach attempts to predict the economic, social, and political factors that will have an impact on the supply and demand of a given commodity in the future. The technical analyst also believes that market prices are the result of the interaction of supply and demand forces. However, the technical analyst tries to predict the interaction of the forces of supply and demand via the behavior of past prices, past volume, and past open interest. Technical analysis is based on the belief that the market price is a true reflection of all factors that affect the commodity, and that the prices will exhibit persistent trends. Technical analysts believe that these trends are relatively short-term in nature, and thus they have a rather myopic view of the markets. On the other hand, fundamental analysts have a longer-term view of the markets since the interaction of fundamental economic factors can have far-reaching, long-lasting effects on market prices.

Given the differences between fundamental analysis and technical analysis, one might expect that investors will choose one analytical technique over the other. Although each method has its staunch supporters, many investors analyze prices by combining these procedures. These investors will rely on fundamental analysis to provide a long-term perspective and technical analysis to furnish a shorter-term view. Since it is common practice to use both analytical techniques, it is important to have a working knowledge of both. This chapter provides a basic introduction to both methods via the futures contracts that are being emphasized in this book: soybeans, Treasury Bonds, and the S&P 500 Index.

## *FUNDAMENTAL ANALYSIS*

Fundamental analysis as applied to futures contracts may be defined as the study of fundamental market supply and demand factors that will affect the price of a physical commodity's futures contract, or of a financial futures contract. In general, any factor that is construed as increasing the supply of a commodity relative to its demand will be interpreted as having a negative effect on the futures contract price, and a falling price will be forecast. Conversely, any factor that is seen as increasing the demand of a commodity relative to its supply will be interpreted as having a positive effect on the futures contract price, and will result in a forecast of rising prices.

Since both physical commodity futures and financial futures prices depend heavily on interest rates it is extremely important that a fundamental analyst be familiar with the determinants of market interest rates. When analyzing financial futures contracts, such as the U.S. Treasury Bond contract and the S&P 500 Index contract, physical parameters such as weather, storage costs, storage capacity, and transportation costs have no relevance. Interest rates, and how they affect the supply and demand for credit, assume roles of primary importance. This chapter does not focus on interest rate determinants, but defers the discussion to Chapter Five, on Treasury Bonds, because the concepts of Federal Reserve policy, inflation, and recession are easier to grasp when presented within the framework of Treasury securities.

In Chapter Two an equity valuation model known as the constant growth model was presented. It was shown that a stock's share value was equal to the discounted present value of all future cash flows, where the cash flows were expressed as a stream of dividends that was growing at a constant rate and the discount rate was equal to the firm's risk-adjusted required rate of return. This model can be applied quite easily to the S&P 500 Index portfolio. In the index framework, the growth rate is the market's rate of growth, and the required rate of return is equal to the overall market's risk-adjusted required rate of return.

The constant growth model clearly illustrates the interaction between the long-run growth rate and the risk-adjusted required rate of return. This interaction is present, and the model's insights are valid, whether it is used to value a company's shares or the market in general through the S&P 500 Index. The model also clarifies and defines an analytical strategy for the fundamental analyst: determine the impact of the relationship between the firm's long-run growth rate and risk-adjusted required rate of return on the supply and demand for the S&P 500 Index futures contract.

The S&P 500 Index's long-run growth rate is a function of the economy's overall strength. Therefore, the fundamental analyst must determine if the economy is robust, growing, and continuing to expand, or if it is declining and in danger of falling into a recession. Perhaps the most widely used measures for determining the economy's likely future condition, as well as its current condition, are the government's indexes of leading economic indicators, coincident economic indicators, and lagging economic indicators. These indices are compiled by the federal government and are released on a monthly basis. The leading indicators are useful to the fundamental analyst for making predictions about the direction of the overall economy, and therefore the outlook for the market's growth rate. The coincidental indicators serve as a current barometer of the economy and are employed to verify trends and signals that were first illuminated by the leading indicators. The lagging indicators are designed to view the economy from a historical perspective, and are used as final confirmation of the economy's condition.

The fundamental analyst can use these various indices to estimate the long-run growth rate and then determine its effects on the S&P 500 Index's supply and demand. If the growth rate is expected to decline, then it means smaller future dividend payments, and investors will be unwilling to hold these index futures contracts. Furthermore, the lower dividend payments will cause investors to perceive the market as being more risky. To compensate for this greater risk, investors will demand a higher rate of return. Thus, the differential between the firm's required rate of return and the firm's long-run growth rate increases. The combination of smaller future dividends, investor unwillingness to hold these index futures contracts, and a larger differential between the required rate of return and the growth rate combine to increase the supply of S&P 500 Index futures contracts and decrease the demand for them. Thus, the S&P 500 Index price will be forced downward. If long-run growth is expected to increase, then future dividends can be expected to rise, investors will want to hold more index futures contracts, and the differential between the required rate of return and the growth rate will decrease. Now there will be an increase in demand for the index futures contracts relative to their supply, and thus an increase in the price of the S&P 500 Index futures contracts should occur.

The preceding discussion shows that equity prices are quite sensitive to changing growth rates. However, it is also important for the fundamental analyst to examine the effects of changes in the required risk-adjusted rate of return. The growth rate captures only part of the change in the supply and demand factors; the rate of return captures the rest.

Prior to any fundamental analysis of an equity's required rate of return, the analyst must understand its composition. The required risk-adjusted rate of return is composed of the risk-free rate of interest, i.e., the Treasury Bill rate, and the expected return on the market portfolio, i.e., the S&P 500 Index, adjusted for the equity's relative market risk. Any change in the general level of interest rates will affect the required rate of return in the same manner. An expected increase in the level of market interest rates will cause the required return to rise and equity prices to drop; while declining interest rates will result in a lower required rate of return and higher equity values.

The effects of changing the required rate of return are not always predictable. It is quite possible that index futures contract prices actually will rise when market interest rates, and therefore the rate of return, are rising because the economy is very robust and growth rates are rising by more than the rate of return increase. Conversely, it is possible that share prices will decline when market interest rates and the rate of return are dropping because the economy is in a recession and the companies that comprise the S&P 500 Index are not expected to grow as rapidly as in the past. Since this relationship between the required rate of return and the long-run growth rate makes it difficult to predict share price movement accurately, the fundamental analyst must always consider the growth rate in relation to the required return when attempting to forecast the effects of changing interest rates on S&P 500 Index prices.

It is important for the fundamental analyst to distinguish between financial futures contracts and physical commodities' futures contracts because the prices of physical commodity futures contracts are more dependent upon factors that reflect physical constraints, such as storage capacity and weather, than are financial futures contracts. Thus, a fundamental price analysis of a physical commodity futures contract is somewhat different than a fundamental analysis of a financial futures contract.

When a physical commodity's futures contract, such as soybeans, is being analyzed, the first step is to specify the separate supply and demand factors. Generally speaking, the supply of soybeans is a function of the new crop, the amount of the previous crop that is being carried forward, and any imports that may occur. The total demand for soybeans is determined by domestic consumption, storage capacity, and foreign consumption. Although these are broad categories, they do capture the critical supply and demand elements. Once the general supply and demand factors have been specified, the analyst's next step is to examine each factor in detail.

The most important determinant of the soybean supply is the new crop; and the most important new crop determinant is the weather. Good growing conditions characterized by adequate rainfall and moderate temperatures throughout the soybean producing regions of the United States will result in an excellent harvest and a large new crop. Large crops that increase the supply of beans relative to their demand will depress the price. However, if the weather is harsh throughout the soybean-producing regions, and the new crop is relatively small in terms of the amount harvested, then the supply will drop and the price will rise. Therefore it is mandatory that the fundamental soybean analyst understand the soybean's climatic requirements and pay close attention to the weather.

Although the new crop of soybeans is the single most important supply factor, the amount of the old crop that is carried forward deserves a substantial amount of attention. This carryover cannot be considered in isolation, but must be considered in conjunction with interest rates and any government surpluses that may exist. Interest rates will affect the soybean supply through the carrying charges, and a relatively low interest rate and low overall carrying cost can result in a large amount of beans being carried into the new crop year. This large carryover will cause an increase in the supply of beans, and lower prices after the new crop is harvested. Relatively high interest rates and high carrying charges should reduce the amount of carryover and lower the supply in the new crop year. This smaller supply will cause the price of beans to rise. Obviously, if the government is carrying a large amount of beans as surplus, then the supply will increase, and the price can be expected to drop. On the other hand, if the surplus is small, or nonexistent, then the price of beans cannot be expected to fall. Indeed, the lack of a surplus can contribute to a price increase if the new crop of beans is relatively small.

The final supply determinant, imports, has relatively little impact on the supply, and therefore the price, of beans. However, this is not true of all physical commodities. Consider the impact on the price of oil futures contracts if the amount of crude oil that is imported into the United States is changed significantly. The fundamental analyst should always be aware of the effects of imports on the supply and price of the physical commodity's futures contract that is being analyzed.

When analyzing soybean demand, domestic consumption must be viewed with regard to products which are close substitutes for soybeans and to products that are complements to soybeans. Soybean meal must compete with corn as a source of protein for fattening livestock, and soybean oil must compete with palm oil and coconut oil as a cooking fat. Since these other commodities provide users with alternatives to soybean products, the demand for beans will be quite sensitive to their price, and to the prices of the close substitutes. More soybeans will be demanded as their price drops relative to their substitutes. If soybean prices increase relative to the substitute goods, then the demand for beans will diminish as users switch to other products. The products that are most complementary to soybeans are poultry, hogs, and cattle. These slaughter animals must be fattened in the most cost-efficient manner. It follows that if soybeans are relatively cheap when compared to corn, then animal feeders will use soybeans. Moreover, if consumers are increasing their meat consumption, then more meat animals will be produced and the demand for all types of animal feed will increase. If demand increases relative to supply, then the price can be expected to increase. On the other hand, both soybean demand and soybean prices will drop if overall meat consumption declines.

Treatment of the carryover when estimating soybean demand is similar to the treatment of the carryover when the soybean supply is estimated. Specifically, the impact of interest rates and government surplus capacity on the demand for soybeans must be dealt with. Interest rates will affect soybean demand via the carrying charges. A relatively low interest rate and low overall carrying charges can result in a large number of beans being carried into the new crop year and relatively little available storage capacity. The result will be a decrease in soybean demand and lower prices after the new crop is harvested. Relatively high interest rates and high carrying charges should reduce the amount of carryover, free up storage capacity, and increase the demand in the new crop year. This greater demand should cause the price of beans to rise. If the government is carrying a large amount of beans as surplus, then the demand for beans should drop, and the price can be expected to decline. On the other hand, if the surplus is small, and the government intends to acquire beans at some support price, then the price of beans cannot be expected to fall below that support price.

The presence of the federal government in the form of price supports and subsidies is extremely important for the fundamental analyst since at some point the government's programs will replace the interaction of supply and demand as the determinants of the commodity's price. Under these conditions the commodity's futures contracts will cease to function as a means of risk transference because the government has assumed that role. Thus, there really is very little need for a fundamental analyst in this situation.

Exports, the final soybean demand factor, have a great deal of relevance for the demand for soybeans. Foreign soybean consumption will be reflected in exports; greater foreign consumption should increase the level of soybean exports, while smaller foreign consumption should depress the number of beans that are exported. Higher foreign consumption levels do not lead automatically to increased exports. U.S. soybeans must compete on the world market with South American and European soybeans. This competition will provide foreign customers with alternative sources and will serve to keep various countries' bean prices in line with one another. The fundamental analyst must be aware of the soybean-producing countries' relative prices when calculating the level of U.S. soybean exports. Moreover, the fundamental analyst must take into account the degree of governmental influence in the international soybean market since the federal government can have a significant impact on the level of soybean exports because of treaties and foreign aid agreements. This impact can be manifested in either higher or lower export levels. Recall that grain export levels plunged when the Carter administration imposed the grain embargo on the Soviet Union as a response to the Afghanistan invasion.

## *TECHNICAL ANALYSIS*

Technical analysis as applied to futures contracts may be defined as the use of market data such as price, volume, and open interest to determine the price of a physical commodity's futures contract or of a financial futures contract. Technical analysis avoids using fundamental economic data to analyze prices.

Technical analysis makes three basic assumptions. First, the market-related data—price, volume, and open interest—capture all the information concerning a given futures contract. Second, market prices exhibit persistent trends. Third, history repeats itself. Therefore, trends in price, volume, and open interest will be repeated. These assumptions are manifested by charts which provide technical analysts with the information they need to formulate profitable trading strategies. The information that will trigger technicians to buy or sell is contained in various chart formations. Since technical analysis is an art and not a science, there are probably as many interpretations of various charts and patterns as there are technical analysts. With this in mind, the following discussion will attempt to present only the rudiments of this analytical technique. Those who wish to pursue the topic should consult some of the many more sophisticated sources that are readily available.

Essentially, the movement of futures prices can be classified as either trends or trading ranges. Trends are categorized as uptrends or downtrends. Trading ranges are distinguished as having support and resistance levels. While it is important for the technical analyst to be able to identify these trends and trading ranges, it is crucial that the technical analyst be able to recognize chart patterns that signal major turning points, or transitions, from one trend to another or from a trading range to a trend.

An uptrend is defined as a series of prices which achieve successively higher highs and higher lows. Conversely, a downtrend is a series of prices which fall to successively lower highs and lower lows. Figures 3-1 through 3-4 provide examples of both uptrends and downtrends and illustrate how to draw trendlines. Since two points

## Figures 3-1 to 3-4
### Uptrends Changing into Downtrends

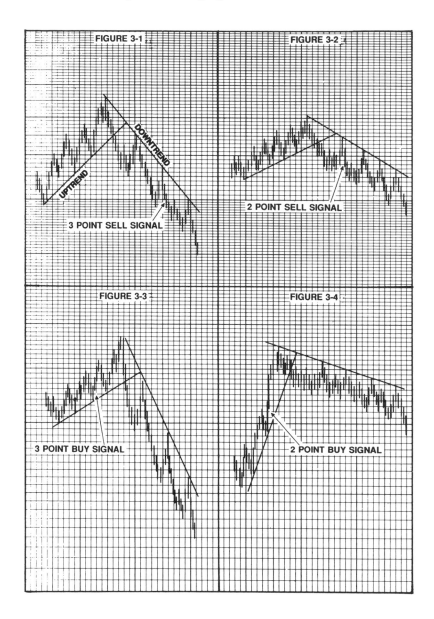

*Source:* Clifford Pistolese, *The Investor's Self-Teaching Seminars: Using Technical Analysis* (Chicago, IL: Probus Publishing Company, 1989).

define a line, a basic requirement for all trendlines is that there be two points that can be connected to establish the trendline. All of the trendlines in Figures 3-1 through 3-4 satisfy this requirement. The uptrends are drawn by connecting successively higher lows, while the downtrends are drawn by connecting successively lower highs.

For many technical analysts, the mere existence of two points that can be used to draw a trendline is not strong enough evidence to confirm the trend's existence. These analysts require three points to confirm the trend and justify the trendline. The trends in Figures 3-1 through 3-3 satisfy this three-point requirement, but the uptrend in Figure 3-4 does not. The uptrend's line in Figure 3-4 was drawn by connecting only two lows. Deciding whether a trend is established from two or three points will affect the trading strategy, since the timing of buy and sell signals will differ. An uptrend will flash a buy signal when the trendline is drawn on the day following the higher low, and the downtrend's sell signal will be flashed on the day that follows the lower high. Obviously the two-point strategy will generate signals much sooner than the three-point strategy. Theoretically, the two-point long position gains should be greater than the three-point long position gains, and the two-point sell signals should result in lower losses than the losses incurred waiting for the three-point sell signals to occur. However, one must realize that the probability of false signals is much higher with the two-point strategy than with the three- point strategy. This has been a painful, and often expensive, lesson for impatient investors who felt they did not need a trend's third confirmation point.

The second general classification of prices is the trading range, also known as a rectangle. It is defined as a series of prices that fluctuate between a clearly established high value and a clearly established low value. The trading range's upper and lower boundaries are known as resistance and support levels, respectively. The resistance level is established when there are more investors who are willing to sell than buy at some level because they think that the security is overpriced, or too rich, at that level. On the other hand, the support level is established at a price where many investors feel that the security is underpriced, or cheap, and are willing to purchase it.

Figures 3-5 and 3-6 show that trading ranges can occur as part of an uptrend or downtrend. Such occurrences are labeled continuations since the general direction of the prices is not changed. Figure 3-7 illustrates a trading range that is part of a transition, or reversal, from an uptrend to a downtrend.

*Figures 3-5 to 3-7*

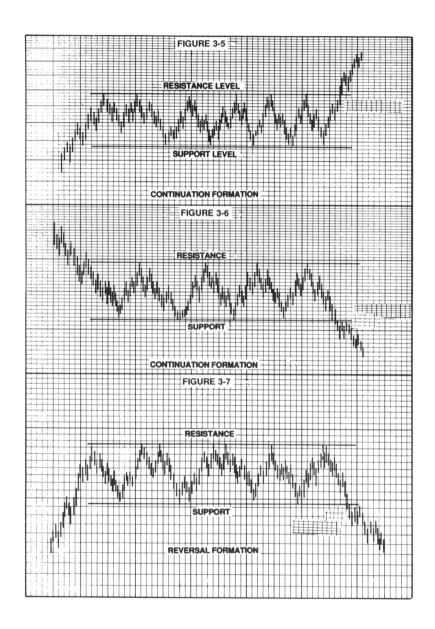

*Source:* Clifford Pistolese, *The Investor's Self-Teaching Seminars: Using Technical Analysis* (Chicago, IL: Probus Publishing Company, 1989).

In Figures 3-1 through 3-4 the changing trends are illustrated by very well-defined, sharp reversals. Unfortunately, the markets do not always behave in such a clear-cut manner. It is more likely that the transition from one market pattern to another will be characterized by a much slower process, such as the trading range shown in Figure 3-7, or by another common formation known as the head and shoulders. A head and shoulders pattern is a formation that has four components: the left shoulder, the head, the right shoulder, and the neckline penetration. A head and shoulders formation cannot be confirmed until the fourth component, the neckline penetration, is observed. The normal head and shoulders formation indicates a reversal from an uptrend to a downtrend, and flashes a sell signal to the prudent investor. When the market experiences a major reversal from a downtrend to an uptrend, an inverted head and shoulders pattern is likely to occur. This formation is a buy signal for the prudent investor. Figures 3-8 and 3-9 provide examples of normal and inverted head and shoulders patterns, respectively.

When performing a technical analysis on futures contracts, it is important to consider both volume and open interest. Open interest indicates how many open positions exist and shows whether a contract has a thin market or a deep market. Increasing open interest levels in a rising market are interpreted as definitely being bullish. Rising open interest in falling markets means that investors are quite bearish. Similarly, the reliability of buy and sell signals can be improved dramatically if these signals are augmented by trading volume. Frequently an increase in volume will confirm the existence of a trend. If prices are moving from a downtrend to an uptrend and volume increases dramatically, then it means that investors are bullish and are willing to commit their funds to the market. An increase in volume when prices are dropping serves to confirm the downtrend and means investors feel that the near-term prospects are not very good. Thus, they start to move to more liquid and less risky cash positions to avoid any further losses. Volume increases along with selling pressure until investors have attained their desired cash positions. Figure 3-10 shows how the huge increase in volume can be used to confirm the two-point buy signal, while Figure 3-11 shows how volume can confirm the two-point sell signal. Figure 3-12 illustrates volume confirmation for the buy signal as the price penetrates the resistance level. Finally, Figure 3-13 shows the volume increase when the neckline penetration occurs in a normal head and shoulders pattern, and verifies the sell signal.

## Figure 3-8
### Normal Head and Shoulders

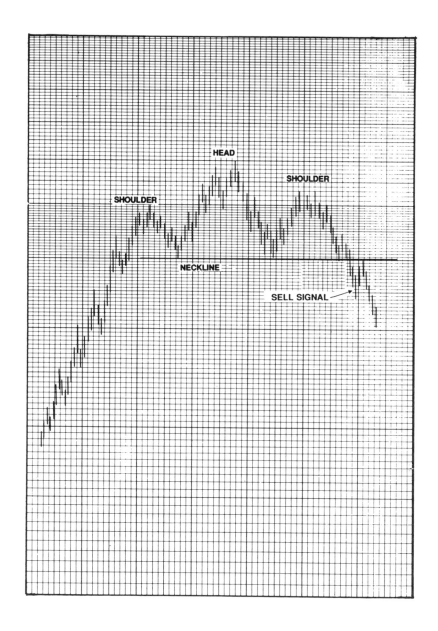

*Source:* Clifford Pistolese, *The Investor's Self-Teaching Seminars: Using Technical Analysis* (Chicago, IL: Probus Publishing Company, 1989).

Figure 3-9
Inverted Head and Shoulders

*Source:* Clifford Pistolese, *The Investor's Self-Teaching Seminars: Using Technical Analysis* (Chicago, IL: Probus Publishing Company, 1989).

While it is important to consider both volume and open interest, the significance of the interaction among price, open interest, and volume can be overstated because of institutional trading activity. This is especially true in the S&P 500 Index markets. Aberrations in volume and open interest may occur because of a few large institutions entering into an index arbitrage to take advantage of a temporary disequilibrium in the relationship between the S&P 500 Index's spot and futures prices. During the time that the disequilibrium exists, institutions will transact in large numbers of S&P 500 futures contracts. Since these situations can occur in any type of market, the institutionally generated increase in volume and open interest may not provide a meaningful indication of market sentiment.

## SUMMARY

This chapter has provided a basic explanation of fundamental and technical analysis. The discussion highlighted the techniques' similarities and differences, and provided a general description of how both methods can be applied to futures contracts. It was shown that these analytical techniques are similar in that they both rely on the

*Figure 3-10*
*Downtrend Changes to Uptrend*

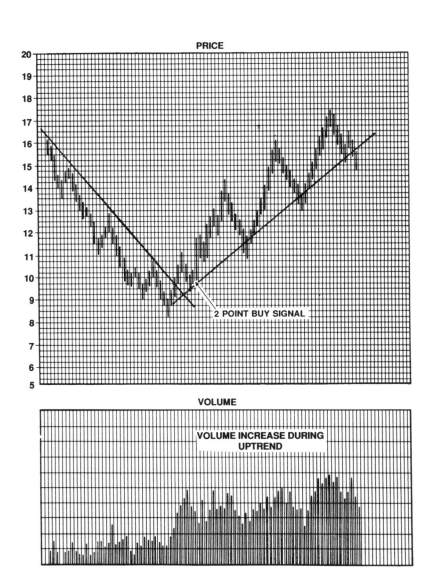

*Figure 3-11*
*Uptrend Changes to Downtrend*

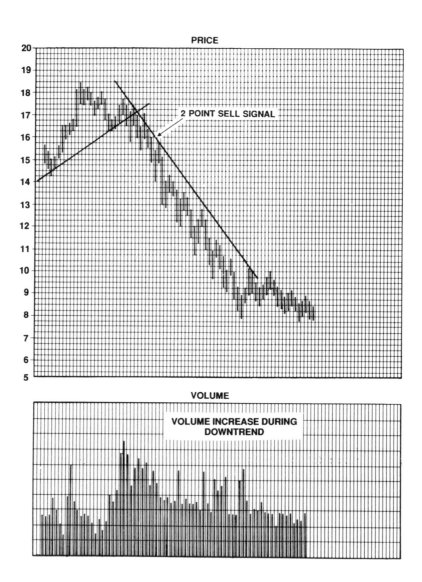

*Source:* Clifford Pistolese, *The Investor's Self-Teaching Seminars: Using Technical Analysis* (Chicago, IL: Probus Publishing Company, 1989).

*Figure 3-12*
*Elongated Trading Range Changes  to Uptrend*

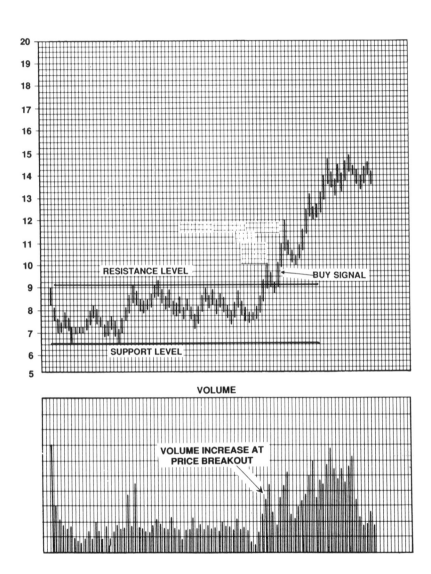

*Source:* Clifford Pistolese, *The Investor's Self-Teaching Seminars: Using Technical Analysis* (Chicago, IL: Probus Publishing Company, 1989).

*Figure 3–13*
*Head and Shoulders Top Changes to Downtrend*

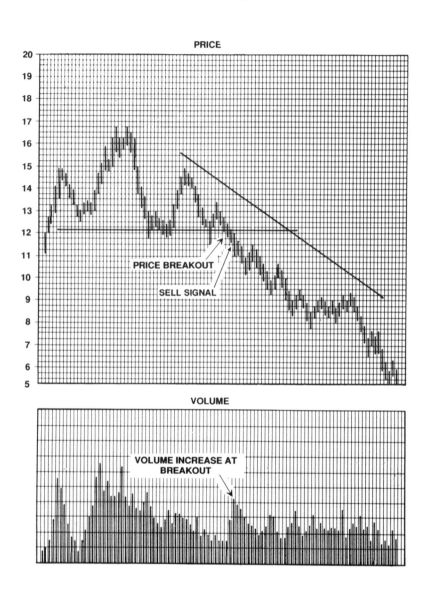

*Source:* Clifford Pistolese, *The Investor's Self-Teaching Seminars: Using Technical Analysis* (Chicago, IL: Probus Publishing Company, 1989).

subjective interpretation of market data to formulate profitable trading strategies. They differ in their analytical philosophies and approaches, however. Fundamental analysis believes that market prices are the result of the interaction of the forces of supply and demand, and that these forces are influenced by the interaction of many factors in the economy. Technical analysis also believes that market prices are the result of the interaction of supply and demand forces, but the technical analyst tries to predict the interaction of the forces of supply and demand via the behavior of past prices, past volume, and past open interest. The fundamental approach attempts to predict the economic, social, and political factors that will have an impact on the supply and demand of a given commodity in the future. The technical approach concentrates on charts that provide data on price movement and changes in volume and open interest to predict the changes of a given futures contract's price.

The next chapter is devoted to soybeans, and pays a great deal of attention to the relationship between the beans and their derivative products, meal and oil. This relationship is known as the crush, and is used as a basic framework for the explanation of how the soybean futures are determined. The fundamental factors are not emphasized explicitly, but the discussion constantly refers to such fundamental factors as weather, storage capacity, and interest rates and how they influence soybean prices.

# Chapter 4

# SOYBEAN TRADING STRATEGIES

## THE SOYBEAN COMPLEX

It is impossible to formulate soybean trading strategies without understanding the soybean's relationship to its derivative products of soybean meal and soybean oil. Cash soybean prices are determined by grain elevator operators who deal in soybeans. These dealers purchase beans from farmers, take delivery, and then resell the beans to processors. It is important to understand that unprocessed soybeans are useful only as seed and dairy cattle feed. However, once processed into meal and oil, soybeans become much more valuable. Soybean meal carries a very high protein content and is quite desirable as livestock feed. However, it is possible to use other sources of protein, such as cottonseed cake and corn, to fatten slaughter animals. Thus, the cash price of soybeans relies in part upon the demand generated by the amount of livestock, i.e., cattle, hogs, and poultry, that are being prepared for slaughter and the supply of protein substitutes. Soybean oil is used widely in edible oil products such as margarines and cooking oils. However, since soybean oil competes with various other animal and vegetable oil products, such as butter and coconut oil, the cash price for soybeans depends upon both the demand for edible oils and the supply of close substitutes.

The relationship of the beans, meal, and oil can be quantified by the gross processing margin. This margin represents the difference between the cost of purchasing a bushel of soybeans and the revenue generated by processing the beans into meal and oil. On average, a 60-pound bushel of soybeans will yield between 47 and 48 pounds of meal and 11 pounds of oil, with the remaining 1 or 2 pounds of beans being lost in processing. After the beans have been processed and converted into meal and oil, the ton becomes the designated trading unit for meal, while oil's trading unit is designated as the pound. Since soybeans are harvested and traded in 60-pound bushels, the meal and oil must be converted to bushel equivalents, using conversion factors of 11 pounds for oil and 48 pounds for meal, before the gross processing margin can be determined.

For example, on April 5, 1994, a gross processing margin of approximately $.89 per bushel can be computed for May 1994 using the May price data from Figure 4-1. The first step is to express the price of oil in bushels rather than in pounds. Since the May '94 oil contract settled at $27.48 per hundredweight, the price of oil per pound is $.2748, implying that the oil's value on a per-bushel basis is $3.0228—the 11-pound conversion factor times the $.2748 price per pound. Although converting the meal price from tons to bushels is a bit more complicated than converting the oil price from pounds to bushels, it is not too difficult. The key to the conversion is expressing the soybean meal as a percentage of a ton. There is .0235 of a ton of soybean meal in a bushel of beans (47/2000) since a 60-pound bushel of soybeans yields 47 pounds of meal. Therefore, if soybean meal is trading at $187.70 per ton, then the per-bushel value of the soybean meal is $4.4110, .0235 times $187.70. Combining the oil's value of $3.0228 with the $4.4110 value of the soybean meal yields $7.4338 in revenue for each bushel of soybeans. If the May soybean futures price is $6.54, then the difference between the $7.4338 revenue and the $6.54 cost is $.8938, or a gross processing margin of approximately $.89. Processors can lock in this margin and hedge their risk in the raw material market (soybeans) and in both finished product markets (meal and oil) by putting on the crush. This is accomplished by purchasing May 1994 soybean futures and selling soybean meal futures and soybean oil futures that also mature in May of 1994.

The soybean spot, or cash, prices that elevator operators are willing to pay will be low when the beans are harvested in the fall if the weather during the growing season has been good, resulting in a large harvest and plentiful supplies relative to demand. However, at this time of the year demand normally increases for high-protein

*Figure 4-1*
*Futures Prices*

Tuesday, April 5, 1994.

**Open Interest Reflects Previous Trading Day.**

| | Open | High | Low | Settle | Change | Lifetime High | Low | Open Interest |
|---|---|---|---|---|---|---|---|---|

## GRAINS AND OILSEEDS

**SOYBEANS (CBT) 5,000 bu.; cents per bu.**

| | Open | High | Low | Settle | Change | Lifetime High | Low | Open Interest |
|---|---|---|---|---|---|---|---|---|
| May | 654 | 657 | 648 | 654 | + 1½ | 751 | 592½ | 50,696 |
| July | 656½ | 658 | 651 | 656¼ | + 2¾ | 750 | 594½ | 50,705 |
| Aug | 650 | 651½ | 645 | 651¼ | + 4¼ | 735 | 628 | 8,273 |
| Sept | 634 | 634½ | 629 | 634 | + 5¼ | 689½ | 617 | 4,626 |
| Nov | 619 | 622 | 615½ | 621 | + 4 | 665¾ | 581½ | 33,168 |
| Ja95 | 626 | 626½ | 621 | 626½ | + 4 | 670 | 618½ | 3,204 |
| Mar | 630½ | 633 | 627 | 632¾ | + 4¾ | 673½ | 627 | 617 |
| July | 636 | 636 | 633 | 636½ | + 5½ | 675 | 631 | 399 |
| Nov | 603 | 604 | 597 | 603 | + 5 | 636 | 597 | 1,095 |

Est vol 70,000; vol Mon 94,016; open int 152,838, +711.

**SOYBEAN MEAL (CBT) 100 tons; $ per ton.**

| | Open | High | Low | Settle | Change | Lifetime High | Low | Open Interest |
|---|---|---|---|---|---|---|---|---|
| May | 187.00 | 188.00 | 186.00 | 187.70 | + 2.00 | 232.00 | 184.70 | 24,045 |
| July | 186.50 | 188.50 | 186.30 | 187.80 | + 2.20 | 230.00 | 185.20 | 30,266 |
| Aug | 185.50 | 187.50 | 185.50 | 187.00 | + 1.80 | 225.00 | 185.00 | 8,667 |
| Sept | 185.00 | 186.50 | 184.50 | 186.00 | + 1.70 | 210.00 | 184.00 | 6,847 |
| Oct | 183.50 | 184.70 | 182.50 | 184.00 | + 1.20 | 206.00 | 182.20 | 3,913 |
| Dec | 181.80 | 183.50 | 181.50 | 182.80 | + 1.00 | 209.00 | 181.00 | 10,674 |
| Ja95 | 182.00 | 183.80 | 182.00 | 183.20 | + 1.40 | 200.00 | 181.50 | 1,017 |
| Mar | 184.00 | 186.00 | 184.00 | 184.50 | + .50 | 194.00 | 183.50 | 258 |

Est vol 28,0000; vol Mon 48,589; open int 85,774, +7,812.

**SOYBEAN OIL (CBT) 60,000 lbs.; cents per lb.**

| | Open | High | Low | Settle | Change | Lifetime High | Low | Open Interest |
|---|---|---|---|---|---|---|---|---|
| May | 27.84 | 27.84 | 27.11 | 27.48 | — .29 | 30.45 | 21.30 | 25,840 |
| July | 27.71 | 27.75 | 27.10 | 27.43 | — .28 | 29.70 | 21.55 | 26,662 |
| Aug | 27.34 | 27.34 | 26.85 | 27.19 | — .19 | 29.20 | 21.65 | 9,717 |
| Sept | 26.85 | 26.85 | 26.55 | 26.78 | — .11 | 28.40 | 22.40 | 8,933 |
| Oct | 25.95 | 25.95 | 25.65 | 25.95 | — .05 | 27.60 | 22.10 | 7,304 |
| Dec | 25.44 | 25.44 | 25.05 | 25.39 | — .05 | 27.05 | 22.00 | 13,706 |
| Ja95 | 25.30 | 25.30 | 25.00 | 25.30 | .... | 26.85 | 22.65 | 1,865 |
| Mar | 25.25 | 25.25 | 25.00 | 25.25 | — .05 | 26.65 | 25.00 | 215 |

Est vol 33,000; vol Mon 33,090; open int 94,349, −5,268.

soybean meal, because with the onset of winter there will be less grazing land available and livestock will need more protein to make it through the cold weather. This increased demand for soybean meal will cause its price to increase when soybean prices are at their lowest, resulting in a favorable processing margin. Favorable margins will make it profitable to produce meal and oil and will stimulate the demand for raw soybeans by processors. After the beans are processed, the increase in the supply of meal and oil should cause their prices to drop, and the gross processing margin to shrink.

A gross processing margin that is less than $.15 per bushel makes it unprofitable to process beans into meal and oil. Such a margin can occur when supplies of raw soybeans are tight due to poor growing conditions or an extremely heavy foreign demand. Low gross processing margins cause processors to reduce the quantity of beans that are purchased and transformed into meal and oil. Furthermore, processors will put on a reverse crush: the soybean futures contracts are sold and the soybean meal and oil futures are purchased. The combined activity of many processors will reduce the demand for beans, and the supply of both meal and oil. Eventually, the relative prices will adjust so that gross processing margins widen to acceptable levels once again.

The late spring and early summer of 1989 provide a good example of how gross processing margins can change over time because of changing market conditions. During this time period many soybean market participants began to get nervous about the lack of snowfall during the winter and the lower than average rainfall during the planting season. It was feared that 1989, like 1988, might be a severely dry year. Furthermore, there was some indication that European demand for soybeans was increasing.

On Tuesday, April 18, 1989, the July soybean futures settled at $7.58 1/2 per bushel, the July soybean meal futures settled at $228.90 per ton, and the July soybean oil futures contract settled at $23.89 per hundredweight. These prices imply a gross processing margin for July of $.4220, computed as follows:

*Per-Bushel Equivalent*

| | |
|---|---|
| July '89 Oil | (11)($.2389) = $2.6279 |
| July '89 Meal | (47/2000)($228.90) = $5.3791 |
| July '89 Beans | $7.5850 |

*Gross Processing Margin*

$$
\begin{array}{r}
\$2.6279 \\
+ \ \$5.3791 \\
\hline
\$8.0070 \\
- \ \$7.5850 \\
\hline
\$ \ .4220
\end{array}
$$

Although the gross processing margin was positive and profitable, the soybean market was inverted. The beans, meal, and oil prices for the July through September contracts were:

| | *Soybeans* | *Soybean Meal* | *Soybean Oil* |
|---|---|---|---|
| *July* | $7.58 1/2 | $228.90 | $23.89 |
| *August* | $7.56 1/2 | $226.70 | $24.16 |
| *September* | $7.44 1/2 | $223.70 | $24.40 |

During the following month soybean prices dropped, but the market remained inverted. On May 17, 1989, the soybean complex was configured as follows:

| | *Soybeans* | *Soybean Meal* | *Soybean Oil* |
|---|---|---|---|
| *July* | $7.12 3/4 | $213.10 | $22.61 |
| *August* | $7.04 | $209.60 | $22.85 |
| *September* | $7.87 1/2 | $205.80 | $23.12 |

With the July soybean futures at $7.12 3/4 per bushel, the July soybean meal futures at $213.10 per ton, and the July soybean oil futures contract at $22.61 per hundredweight the gross processing margin for July dropped to $.37, computed as follows:

*Per-Bushel Equivalent*

| July '89 Oil | $(11)(\$.2261) = \$2.4871$ |
|---|---|
| July '89 Meal | $(47/2000)(\$213.10) = \$5.0079$ |
| July '89 Beans | $7.1275 |

*Gross Processing Margin*

$$\begin{array}{r} \$2.4871 \\ + \ \$5.0079 \\ \hline \$7.4950 \\ - \ \$7.1250 \\ \hline \$ \ .3700 \end{array}$$

The inverted market and the declining processing margin continued throughout May and into June because of a very dry spring in the Midwest. Furthermore, soybean prices began to increase. Thus, on June 16, 1989, the soybean market stood at:

|           | Soybeans   | Soybean Meal | Soybean Oil |
|-----------|------------|--------------|-------------|
| July      | $7.33      | $213.10      | $22.61      |
| August    | $7.05      | $209.60      | $22.85      |
| September | $6.66 3/4  | $205.80      | $23.12      |

This price configuration made it unprofitable to withhold soybeans from the market, and caused the gross processing margin to deteriorate further. The July soybean futures price of $7.33 per bushel, the July soybean meal futures price of $215.20 per ton, and the July soybean oil futures contract price of $20.77 per hundredweight translated to a significantly lower and unprofitable July gross processing margin of $.0119, computed as follows:

*Per-Bushel Equivalent*

| July '89 Oil   | $(11)(\$.2077) = \$2.2847$          |
|----------------|-------------------------------------|
| July '89 Meal  | $(47/2000)(\$215.20) = \$5.0572$    |
| July '89 Beans | $7.1275                             |

*Gross Processing Margin*

$$\begin{array}{r} \$2.2847 \\ + \ \$5.0572 \\ \hline \$7.3419 \\ \$7.3300 \\ \hline \$ \ .0119 \end{array}$$

By mid-July sufficient rain had fallen in the Midwest and there was little danger that yields would suffer. Bean prices fell to approximately $6.00 per bushel in mid-July, and continued to drop to about $5.75 per bushel by the end of the harvest in November. Seven dollars per bushel soybean prices would not be seen again until the summer of 1993, when the Midwest was plagued by severe flooding. The effects of these weather-related events on soybean prices are clearly portrayed in Figure 4-2.

## SPECULATING

In the late spring and early summer of 1993 the Midwest experienced terrible flooding. The heavy spring rains made it impossible for farmers to get into their fields and get the soybean crop planted. Moreover, once they did get the crop in the ground, the ensuing floods swamped the young crop. The outlook was poor for the 1993 soybean crop, and prices rose dramatically.

These weather-related problems provided an opportunity for astute speculators. Long positions in soybean futures contracts seemed to carry an extremely large profit potential. Simply purchasing some August soybean futures contracts was the most straightforward way to capture the expected rise in soybean prices.

Suppose that a retail investor had $50,000 that she wanted to commit to a speculative soybean strategy in June of 1993. If this investor's broker requires speculators to post an initial margin of $1,475 per contract, and then maintain a margin of at least $1,100 per contract, then a trading worksheet like that of Figure 4-3 is a good representation of this speculator's soybean position between June 1 and August 2 of 1993.

Figure 4-3, the Speculative Worksheet, is divided into three sections, with the columns in each section being numbered appropriately. Section I provides a listing of the speculative position's overall activity. Section II gives a detailed account of the margin activity that occurs during the time that the position is open. Finally, the third section provides a record of the amount of cash that was invested and withdrawn from the position.

Columns 1 and 2 in the first section show that the speculator opened her position on June 1st in the August soybean contract. Column 3 shows that the July bean contract was purchased for a price of $5.8775 per bushel. The fourth column shows that 5,000 bushels of soybeans constitute a single futures contract, and the fifth

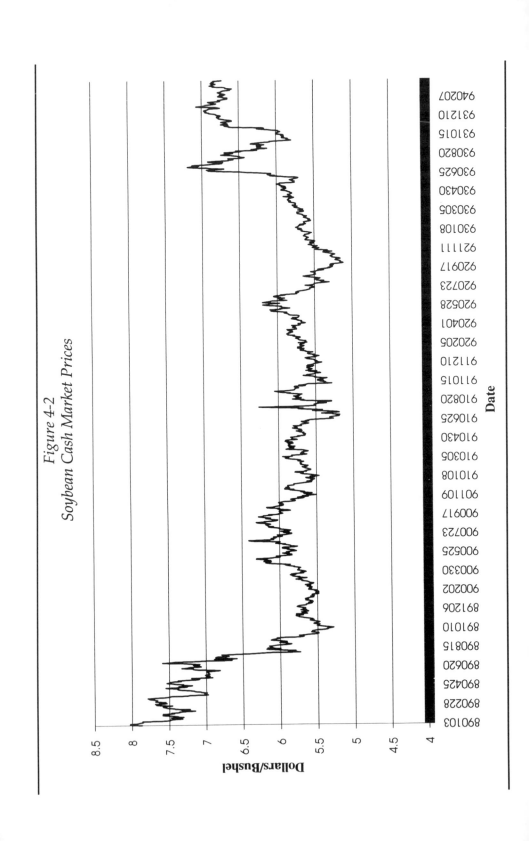

Figure 4-2
Soybean Cash Market Prices

## Figure 4-3
## Long Soybean Speculation Worksheet

### I. Overall Futures Activity

| (1) | (2) | (3) | (4) | (5) | (6) | (7) | (8) | (9) | (10) | (11) |
|---|---|---|---|---|---|---|---|---|---|---|
| Date | Contract | Unit Price | Number of Units per Contract | Number of Contracts +Long/-Short | Position Value | Position +Gain/-Loss | Total Cash+Margin | Invested Cash+Margin | Commission | Cumulative +Gain/-Loss |
| 6/1/93 | August Beans | $5.8775 | 5000 | +20 | $587,750 | $0.00 | $50,000 | $50,000 | | $0 |
| 6/4/93 | August Beans | $5.8600 | 5000 | +20 | $586,000 | ($1,750.00) | $48,250 | $50,000 | | ($1,750) |
| 6/11/93 | August Beans | $5.8650 | 5000 | +20 | $586,500 | $500.00 | $48,750 | $50,000 | | ($1,250) |
| 6/18/93 | August Beans | $6.0550 | 5000 | +20 | $605,500 | $19,000.00 | $67,750 | $50,000 | | $17,750 |
| 6/25/93 | August Beans | $6.2175 | 5000 | +20 | $621,750 | $16,250.00 | $84,000 | $50,000 | | $34,000 |
| 7/2/93 | August Beans | $6.6550 | 5000 | +20 | $665,500 | $43,750.00 | $127,750 | $50,000 | | $77,750 |
| 7/9/93 | August Beans | $7.1150 | 5000 | +20 | $711,500 | $46,000.00 | $173,750 | $50,000 | | $123,750 |
| 7/16/93 | August Beans | $7.2450 | 5000 | +20 | $724,500 | $13,000.00 | $186,750 | $50,000 | | $136,750 |
| 7/23/93 | August Beans | $7.2750 | 5000 | +20 | $727,500 | $3,000.00 | $189,750 | $50,000 | | $139,750 |
| 7/30/93 | August Beans | $6.8550 | 5000 | +20 | $685,500 | ($42,000.00) | $147,750 | $50,000 | | $97,750 |

### II. Margin Activity

Initital Margin Requirement     $1,475   per Contract
Maintenance Margin Requirement     $1,100   per Contract

| (1) | (2) | (3) | (4) | (5) | (6) | (7) | (8) | (9) | (10) |
|---|---|---|---|---|---|---|---|---|---|
| Date | Beginning # of Maintenance Contracts | Margin Account Beginning Balance | Unit Price Change | Position +Gain/-Loss | Interim Margin Balance | Cash Account +From Cash -To Cash | Margin Account Ending Balance | Ending Number of Contracts | Maintenance Requirement |
| 6/1/93 | +20 | $29,500 | 0.0000 | $0 | $29,500 | $0 | $29,500 | +20 | $22,000 |
| 6/4/93 | +20 | $29,500 | (0.0175) | ($1,750) | $27,750 | $0 | $27,750 | +20 | $22,000 |
| 6/11/93 | +20 | $27,750 | 0.0050 | $500 | $28,250 | $0 | $28,250 | +20 | $22,000 |
| 6/18/93 | +20 | $28,250 | 0.1900 | $19,000 | $47,250 | $0 | $47,250 | +20 | $22,000 |
| 6/25/93 | +20 | $47,250 | 0.1625 | $16,250 | $63,500 | $0 | $63,500 | +20 | $22,000 |
| 7/2/93 | +20 | $63,500 | 0.4375 | $43,750 | $107,250 | $0 | $107,250 | +20 | $22,000 |
| 7/9/93 | +20 | $107,250 | 0.4600 | $46,000 | $153,250 | ($100,000) | $53,250 | +20 | $22,000 |
| 7/16/93 | +20 | $53,250 | 0.1300 | $13,000 | $66,250 | $0 | $66,250 | +20 | $22,000 |
| 7/23/93 | +20 | $66,250 | 0.0300 | $3,000 | $69,250 | $0 | $69,250 | +20 | $22,000 |
| 7/30/93 | +20 | $69,250 | (0.4200) | ($42,000) | $27,250 | ($27,250) | $0 | 0 | $0 |

## Figure 4-3
## Long Soybean Speculation Worksheet (continued)

III. Cash Activity

| (1) | (2) | (3) | (4) | (5) |
|-----|-----|-----|-----|-----|
| | Speculative Cash Beginning Balance | Cash Account Flows + Invested -Withdrawn | Margin Account Flows + From Margin -To Margin | Speculative Cash Ending Balance |
| Date | | | | |
| 6/1/93 | $20,500 | $0 | $0 | $20,500 |
| 6/4/93 | $20,500 | $0 | $0 | $20,500 |
| 6/11/93 | $20,500 | $0 | $0 | $20,500 |
| 6/18/93 | $20,500 | $0 | $0 | $20,500 |
| 6/25/93 | $20,500 | $0 | $0 | $20,500 |
| 7/2/93 | $20,500 | $0 | $0 | $20,500 |
| 7/9/93 | $20,500 | $0 | $100,000 | $120,500 |
| 7/16/93 | $120,500 | $0 | $0 | $120,500 |
| 7/23/93 | $120,500 | $0 | $0 | $120,500 |
| 7/30/93 | $120,500 | $0 | $27,250 | $147,750 |

column shows that the speculator purchased 20 contracts initially. The position's value of $587,750 in the sixth column is obtained by first multiplying the unit price, column 3, by the number of units in the contract, column 4, to get the contract value; and then multiplying the result by the number of contracts in the position, column 5. The seventh column simply provides the position's daily gains and losses. The remaining columns cannot be interpreted without referring to the other two sections of the worksheet.

Column 8 in, Section I shows exactly how much money the speculator has left. This balance is composed of the amount that has been posted with the broker as margin, and the amount of cash that can be used to fund the position if the market moves against the speculator. This speculative cash does not have to be put on deposit with the broker, but it should be held in a highly liquid and easily accessible account. The amount in Section I, column 8, must equal the sum of the day's ending margin account balance, Section II, column 8, and the day's ending speculative cash balance, Section III, column 5. The amount of cash plus margin available to the speculator will fluctuate each day as the position gains or loses value. The next column in Section I, column 9, shows the total amount of money that the speculator has invested in the position. This is composed of the initial margin, Section II, column 3, plus the amount of cash that has been held in reserve to fund the position in the event of adverse market movements, Section III, column 2. Column 10 is reserved for commissions. Since commissions can vary widely throughout the industry, I do not even attempt to include them in the various examples. Make sure that you have a thorough understanding of your broker's commission schedule. The final column in Section I, column 11, shows the strategy's cumulative gain or loss. It is computed by subtracting column 9, the amount invested in cash and margin, from column 8, the total cash and margin balance. When appropriate, commissions should also be subtracted from the total cash plus margin amount in column 8. The amount in column 11 of Section I must agree with the position gains and losses and any cash flows reflected in the margin account, Section II, column 8.

The second section of the speculative worksheet provides information about the speculator's margin activity. The section begins with a listing of the margin requirements. In this example the speculator must post an initial margin of $1,475 per soybean contract purchased, and the margin account must have a minimum balance equal to $1,100 per contract at all times. If the margin balance falls below the minimum requirement, then the speculator is required to restore the margin account to a level that is consistent with the initial margin requirement. This can be accomplished in one of two ways: either more cash can be added to the margin account, or enough of the position can be liquidated so that the remaining margin balance is greater than or equal to the initial margin requirement for the remaining contracts.

The remainder of Section II is divided into 10 columns that provide daily data about the margin account. Columns 1 and 2 of Section II are self-explanatory and correspond to columns 1 and 5 of Section I. Column 3 shows the margin account balance at the beginning of each day. The figures in column 4 represent the change in value of the futures contract on a per-unit basis. Column 5, the amount of gain or loss in the futures position, is obtained by multiplying the unit price change, column 4, by the total number of units in the position. The number of units in the position is determined by multiplying the number of units per contract, Section I, column 4, by the number of contracts in the position at the beginning of the day, Section II, column 2. The next column in Section II, column 6, gives the interim margin balance amount. This reflects the gains or losses posted to the margin account as the price changes during the day, and alerts the speculator to the possibility of a margin call. Column 7 provides information about any cash additions to the margin account or withdrawals from the margin account. The figures in the margin account ending balance column, column 8, represent the cumulative effect of the changes in the futures contract price, any cash inflows or outflows that have occurred, and any change in the number of contracts in the position. Column 9 shows the number of futures contracts in the position at the end of the day. This column is particularly important because it reflects any change in the number of contracts that constitute the position. Finally, the position's maintenance requirement is shown in column 10.

Section III is the last section of the speculative worksheet and deals with the speculator's cash activity. As mentioned above, this cash does not have to be put on deposit with the broker, but it should be kept in an account that is extremely liquid and easily accessible. The reason for having such an account is that it will help one withstand the wide price swings in the futures markets.

The futures exchanges attempt to minimize the effects of extremely wide price swings by imposing limits on the daily price change in many futures contracts, and then determining the appropriate margin requirements. The price limits are designed so that the prior day's settlement price is the midpoint of the current day's allowable trading range. For example, if soybeans have a $.30 per bushel daily price limit, and the prior day's settlement price was $7.50 per bushel, it means that the day's trading can occur within a $.60 price range—the price of soybeans on a per-bushel basis can fluctuate between $7.20 and $7.80. If the soybean price violates either limit, then trading ceases since the exchange will not allow the soybean contract to be traded at a price that is outside the range that is defined by the price limits. Both the price limits and margins are subject to change and have been adjusted by the exchange to reflect either more volatile or less volatile markets so that a balance can be maintained between the trading activity, price volatility, and the margin requirements. It is extremely important that a balance be maintained because too low a margin requirement in volatile markets will result in too many contract defaults, since there will not be a sufficient amount of money on deposit to fund the day's profitable positions from the day's losing positions. However, too great a margin requirement in very stable markets will result in relatively fewer contracts being traded since fewer traders will be able to meet it.

The issues of futures price volatility, price limits, and margin are important to the small retail customer since they have an impact on how much cash should be kept in reserve. In Chapter One it was mentioned that a good rule of thumb is for the small retail customer to keep enough in the margin and cash accounts to withstand 5 days worth of limit moves. In Figure 4-3, the $50,000 total cash and margin amount is inadequate for a $.30 per bushel, or $1,500 per contract ($.30 times 5,000 bushels), limit move when there are 20 contracts purchased initially. To be consistent with the 5-day rule of thumb the speculator should have a total of $150,000—20 contracts times $1,500 daily limit move times 5 days—in the cash and margin accounts.

When the retail speculator established her position by purchasing 20 August soybean contracts on Tuesday, June 1, the August beans were selling at $5.8775 per bushel. She deposited $29,500 with her broker to satisfy the initial margin requirement, and kept an additional $20,500 in her reserve account. By Friday, June 4, the price of July beans had fallen by $.0175 per bushel, Section II, column 4, to $5.86, Section I, column 3. Both the speculator's long position and margin account decreased in value by $1,750, Section I, column 7 and Section II, columns 5 and 6. At the end of the day the margin account balance had fallen by $1,750, Section II, column 8, and the total cash and margin amount decreased to $48,250, Section I, column 8. Furthermore, the position showed a cumulative loss of $1,750, Section I, column 11.

At the beginning of trading on Friday, June 11, the speculator was long 20 August soybean contracts, and she had $27,750 in her margin account. During the day August soybeans rose $.005 per bushel for a $500 gain to the speculator, Section II, columns 4 and 5, and Section I, column 7. This $500 gain to the position resulted in the margin account rising to a level of $28,250, Section II, column 6; the $27,750 margin balance at the beginning of the day, plus the $500. The $28,250 balance was $1,250 below the initial balance of $29,500, but well above the $22,000 requirement for a 20-contract position.

Throughout June the floods grew in intensity and the soybean market rose accordingly. Between 6/11/93 and 6/18/93 the August bean contract rose by $.19 per bushel to $6.055 which translated to a $19,000 gain for the long speculator, Section I, column 3, and Section II, columns 4 and 5. When the market closed on Friday, June 18, the long speculator's cumulative gain had reached $17,750 and the margin account had grown to $47,250, Section I, column 11, and Section II, column 8. The following week was also good for the long speculator. The August soybean contract price increased by $.1625 to $6.2175 with a commensurate gain to the margin account of $16,250.

By the end of June the floods were at their worst, with no relief in sight. Vast tracts of midwestern acreage were underwater. Iowa was declared a disaster area, and soybean prices soared during the first two weeks of July. Between 6/25/93 and 7/2/93, August beans went from $6.655 to $7.115, a gain of $.4375 per bushel and a $43,750 increase in the long speculator's account, Section I, column 3, and Section II, columns 4 and 5. August bean prices rose even further during the second week in July. By Friday, July 9, they had posted a $.46 gain per bushel and closed at $7.115. This translated to a $46,000 gain for the speculator—an increase in the margin account's ending balance to $153,250 and a cumulative gain of $136,750, Section II, columns 4, 5, and 8, and Section I, column 11. After the close on Friday, July 9, the long speculator decided to transfer $100,000 from her margin account to her cash reserve account, Section II, column 7, and Section III, column 4. This still left $53,250 in her margin account, more than twice the required maintenance balance, Section II, columns 8 and 10.

The soybean market continued to rise the following week, so that the August contract increased in value by another $.13 per bushel to

$7.245. This resulted in another $13,000 for the long hedger, which brought her margin account balance to $66,250 by week's end. The next week saw the soybean market rise again. By the close of trading on 7/23/93, the August soybean contract had hit $7.275 per bushel, the speculator's margin account stood at $69,250, and the long speculator had accumulated a total gain of $139,750. This was to be the peak for the August soybean contract.

In the final week of July the floodwaters began to recede, and estimates of the crop damage started to emerge. It appeared that although the Iowa and Illinois soybean crop sustained considerable damage, other soybean-producing states would have large enough crops to offset some of the flood damage. Thus, bean prices began to fall. The August bean contract fell by $.42 per bushel for a $42,000 loss to the speculator. This reduced her margin balance to $27,250, and lowered her cumulative gain to $97,750, Section II, column 7 and Section I, column 11.

Given this dramatic drop in prices, the long speculator decided that it would be wise to close out the position. Therefore, after the markets closed on 7/30/93, she liquidated her 20-contract position and withdrew the entire $27,250 balance from her margin account, Section II, column 7, and deposited it in her speculative cash account, Section III, column 4. Since the August bean contract rose by $.9775 between June 1 and July 30, the retailer's strategy provided a $97,750 gain over the eight-week period.

The logic of the short speculative position is not as compelling as the logic for a long position in soybeans. The wet spring and the prediction for greater than normal moisture in the Midwest did not portend of a flood, but the planting delay did nothing to increase the chances that the 1993 crop would be better than average. If anything, it created some concern that the crop might be somewhat smaller than average. Furthermore, spot market soybean prices had been relatively stable, trading between $5.80 and $6.00 per bushel since April, and it did not appear that they would decline by much in the near future.

In spite of this market outlook, suppose that a speculator felt the potential for a drop in soybean prices was much greater than the potential for a continued rise in them. If one wanted to profit from such a decline, then the simplest strategy to take is to sell August soybean futures contracts. Assume that this speculator had $50,000 to commit to such a strategy, and that she decided to sell 10 August soybean futures contracts on 6/01/93. Figure 4-4 examines the outcome of a speculator's strategy.

Although both speculators committed $50,000 to their respective positions, the short speculator, represented by the worksheet in Figure 4-4, differs from the long speculator, represented in Figure 4-3. The most important difference between the two speculators is that the one who was selling 10 bean contracts, the short speculator, had more than enough to withstand 3 day's worth of $.30 per bushel, $1,500 per contract, or $4,500 daily limit moves on a 10-contract position—$45,000—while the one who purchased 20 contracts, the long speculator, had only $50,000 to commit; an amount that would only cover the $30,000 limit move on the 20-contract position for 1 day. If beans moved limit against the long speculator for more than one day, then the long speculator would have a major problem. It is also important to remember that a short position increases in value when the contract price drops and loses value when the price increases, while a long position gains value when the price increases but loses value when the price declines.

The various sections in Figure 4-4, the overall futures activity, the margin activity, and the cash activity, carry the exact same meaning as the sections in Figure 4-3. However, the outcomes are quite a bit different. The short speculator established her position by selling 10 August soybean contracts on 6/01/93, and then maintained this short position. During the following 10 days she managed to gain $625 because of the slight drop in soybean prices. This contrasts to the long speculator's $1,250 loss.

However, by the end of the next week, June 18th, things had changed dramatically for the short speculator. Soybean prices began their spectacular four-week rise because of the severe flooding. When the week ended the short speculator had suffered a $.19 per bushel and $9,500 loss to her position, Section II, columns 4 and 5. Furthermore, her $5,875 interim margin balance was well below the $11,000 maintenance requirement, Section II, column 6, which resulted in a margin call of $8,875 to bring the margin account back up the initial level of $14,750, Section II, columns 7 and 8. This margin call was funded by transferring the cash from the speculative cash account, Section III, column 4.

The following week the speculator sustained another loss to the tune of $8,125, which left her interim margin balance at $6,625 and her speculative cash balance at $26,375, Section II column 6 and Section III column 5. At this time she decided it would be prudent to

# Figure 4-4
## Short Soybean Speculation Worksheet

### I. Overall Futures Activity

| (1) Date | (2) Contract | (3) Unit Price | (4) Number of Units per Contract | (5) Number of Contracts +Long/-Short | (6) Position Value | (7) Position +Gain/-Loss | (8) Total Cash+Margin | (9) Invested Cash+Margin | (10) Commission | (11) Cumulative +Gain/-Loss |
|---|---|---|---|---|---|---|---|---|---|---|
| 6/1/93 | August Beans | $5.8775 | 5000 | -10 | ($293,875) | $0 | $50,000 | $50,000 | | $0 |
| 6/4/93 | August Beans | $5.8600 | 5000 | -10 | ($293,000) | $875 | $50,875 | $50,000 | | $875 |
| 6/11/93 | August Beans | $5.8650 | 5000 | -10 | ($293,250) | ($250) | $50,625 | $50,000 | | $625 |
| 6/18/93 | August Beans | $6.0550 | 5000 | -10 | ($302,750) | ($9,500) | $41,125 | $50,000 | | ($8,875) |
| 6/25/93 | August Beans | $6.2175 | 5000 | -10 | ($310,875) | ($8,125) | $33,000 | $50,000 | | ($17,000) |
| 7/2/93 | August Beans | $6.6550 | 5000 | -4 | ($133,100) | ($8,750) | $24,250 | $50,000 | | ($25,750) |
| 7/9/93 | August Beans | $7.1150 | 5000 | -4 | ($142,300) | ($9,200) | $15,050 | $50,000 | | ($34,950) |
| 7/16/93 | August Beans | $7.2450 | 5000 | -4 | ($144,900) | ($2,600) | $12,450 | $50,000 | | ($37,550) |
| 7/23/93 | August Beans | $7.2750 | 5000 | -4 | ($145,500) | ($600) | $11,850 | $50,000 | | ($38,150) |
| 7/30/93 | August Beans | $6.8550 | 5000 | -4 | ($137,100) | $8,400 | $20,250 | $50,000 | | ($29,750) |

### II. Margin Activity

Initial Margin Requirement $1,475 per Contract
Maintenance Margin Requirement $1,100 per Contract

| (1) Date | (2) Beginning # of Maintenance Contracts | (3) Margin Account Beginning Balance | (4) Unit Price Change | (5) Position +Gain/-Loss | (6) Interim Margin Balance | (7) Cash Account +From Cash -To Cash | (8) Margin Account Ending Balance | (9) Ending Number of Contracts | (10) Maintenance Requirement |
|---|---|---|---|---|---|---|---|---|---|
| 6/1/93 | -10 | $14,750 | $0.0000 | $0 | $14,750 | $0 | $14,750 | -10 | $11,000 |
| 6/4/93 | -10 | $14,750 | ($0.0175) | $875 | $15,625 | $0 | $15,625 | -10 | $11,000 |
| 6/11/93 | -10 | $15,625 | $0.0050 | ($250) | $15,375 | $0 | $15,375 | -10 | $11,000 |
| 6/18/93 | -10 | $15,375 | $0.1900 | ($9,500) | $5,875 | $8,875 | $14,750 | -10 | $11,000 |
| 6/25/93 | -10 | $14,750 | $0.1625 | ($8,125) | $6,625 | $0 | $6,625 | -4 | $4,400 |
| 7/2/93 | -4 | $6,625 | $0.4375 | ($8,750) | ($2,125) | $8,750 | $6,625 | -4 | $4,400 |
| 7/9/93 | -4 | $6,625 | $0.4600 | ($9,200) | ($2,575) | $9,200 | $6,625 | -4 | $4,400 |
| 7/16/93 | -4 | $6,625 | $0.1300 | ($2,600) | $4,025 | $2,600 | $6,625 | -4 | $4,400 |
| 7/23/93 | -4 | $6,625 | $0.0300 | ($600) | $6,025 | $0 | $6,025 | -4 | $4,400 |
| 7/30/93 | -4 | $6,025 | ($0.4200) | $8,400 | $14,425 | ($14,425) | $0 | 0 | $0 |

# Figure 4-4
## Short Soybean Speculation Worksheet (continued)

### III. Cash Activity

| (1) Date | (2) Speculative Cash Beginning Balance | (3) Cash Account Flows + Invested -Withdrawn | (4) Margin Account Flows + From Margin -To Margin | (5) Speculative Cash Ending Balance |
|---|---|---|---|---|
| 6/1/93 | $35,250 | $0 | $0 | $35,250 |
| 6/4/93 | $35,250 | $0 | $0 | $35,250 |
| 6/11/93 | $35,250 | $0 | $0 | $35,250 |
| 6/18/93 | $35,250 | $0 | ($8,875) | $26,375 |
| 6/25/93 | $26,375 | $0 | $0 | $26,375 |
| 7/2/93 | $26,375 | $0 | ($8,750) | $17,625 |
| 7/9/93 | $17,625 | $0 | ($9,200) | $8,425 |
| 7/16/93 | $8,425 | $0 | ($2,600) | $5,825 |
| 7/23/93 | $5,825 | $0 | $0 | $5,825 |
| 7/30/93 | $5,825 | $0 | $14,425 | $20,250 |

liquidate part of her position. Thus, she purchased six August soybean futures contracts which reduced her position to short four August soybean contracts, Section II, column 9. This meant that she would have more than enough in her margin account to satisfy the $5,900 initial margin requirement and $4,400 maintenance margin requirement for four August soybean contracts. Thus, the short speculator ended June and began July with a short position in four August soybean contracts, $6,625 in her margin account, $26,375 in her speculative cash account, and $17,000 in cumulative losses.

The first two weeks in July saw bean prices rise from $6.655 to $7.245, and the short speculator's position lose $8,750, $9,200, and $2,600, respectively. These losses forced the short speculator to transfer more cash into the margin account: $8,750 by July 2nd, $9,200 by July 9th, and $2,600 by July 16th, Section II, column 7 and Section III, column 4. This left her with only $5,825 in her speculative cash account and a cumulative loss of $37,550 on 7/16/93.

The final two weeks in July were not quite so bad for the short speculator. Between 7/16/93 and 7/23/94 she sustained a loss of only $600, while in the last week of July she was rewarded with an $8,400 gain as the August bean prices fell $.42 per bushel from $7.275 to $6.855. At this time the short speculator closed out her position. She bought four August soybean contracts for $6.025 per bushel and transferred her margin account balance, $14,425, to her speculative cash account. This left her with a $20,250 ending balance and a $29,750 cumulative loss, Section III, column 5 and Section I, column 11.

The differences in outcome between Figures 4-3 and 4-4 are to be expected since it follows that when speculators assume price risk there can be only one winner. That is the nature of speculation: there always will be a winner and a loser. Recall that the interaction of speculators and hedgers was discussed in Chapter One, where it was shown that each needed the other because of price risk. Hedgers seek to eliminate price risk while speculators eagerly accept it. The chapter's next section examines the behavior of hedgers, and shows how to transfer price risk effectively in the soybean market.

## HEDGING

One of the most interesting attributes of both Figures 4-5 and 4-6 is in Section IV, column 4, the contract unit price change. It is identical in both worksheets and shows how soybean prices changed during the time between 6/01/93 and 8/2/93. Notice that soybeans generally rose during this time. The price changes were of varying magnitude, and seemed to be rather unpredictable. This unpredictability of the price changes is the essence of price risk and the reason for hedging.

Hedging was explained in Chapter One from two perspectives: that of the commodity producer and that of the commodity user. In this chapter the producer is defined as a farmer, and the user is defined as a soybean processor. In the normal course of business the farmer is exposed to the risk of a price decline in the finished product, soybeans, while within the processor's normal course of business, an increase in the price of the raw input, soybeans, is the risk that must be managed. Since both the farmer and processor are subject to the risk of changing prices in the cash commodity, soybeans, both of them should attempt to minimize this risk via the futures markets.

The farmer's soybean position in the cash market is opposite the processor's cash market position. In this example it is assumed that the time is early June of 1993, and that the processor needs 100,000 bushels of soybeans in August and intends to buy them in the spot market at the lowest available price. It is also assumed that the farmer is located in North Carolina and anticipates harvesting 100,000 bushels of soybeans in early August and selling them in the cash, or spot, market for at least $5.70 per bushel. In this situation the farmer is long the cash commodity, soybeans, and the processor is short the commodity. Thus, to offset their respective cash positions the farmer needs to sell soybean futures contracts and the processor must buy soybean futures contracts. Selling futures contracts to hedge a long cash position makes the farmer a short hedger, and buying futures contracts to hedge a short cash position defines the processor as a long hedger. Figures 4-5 and 4-6 present the outcomes from a short hedger and long hedger, respectively.

Both worksheets have the same construction and are composed of five sections. Section I presents data relating to the activity in the hedger's spot market position. Section II shows the behavior of the basis during the hedge's life. The third section displays the hedger's futures market position, while the fourth and fifth sections show the hedger's margin account and cash account activity. Sections I and II are unique to the hedger's worksheet, and are explained in detail in the following paragraphs. The remaining three sections of the worksheet—Section III, Overall Futures Activity; Section IV, Margin Activ-

## Figure 4-5
### Soybean Short Hedger Worksheet

**I. Overall Spot Activity**

| (1) Date | (2) Spot Commodity | (3) Unit Price | (4) Amount of Spot Commodity | (5) Spot Position Value | (6) Unit Price Change | (7) Spot Position +Gain/-Loss | (8) Commission | (9) Spot Cummulative +Gain/-Loss |
|---|---|---|---|---|---|---|---|---|
| 6/1/93 | Soybeans | $5.7550 | +100000 | $575,500 | $0.0000 | $0 | | $0 |
| 6/4/93 | Soybeans | $5.7550 | +100000 | $575,500 | $0.0000 | $0 | | $0 |
| 6/11/93 | Soybeans | $5.7650 | +100000 | $576,500 | $0.0100 | $1,000 | | $1,000 |
| 6/18/93 | Soybeans | $5.9300 | +100000 | $593,000 | $0.1650 | $16,500 | | $17,500 |
| 6/25/93 | Soybeans | $6.0750 | +100000 | $607,500 | $0.1450 | $14,500 | | $32,000 |
| 7/2/93 | Soybeans | $6.4850 | +100000 | $648,500 | $0.4100 | $41,000 | | $73,000 |
| 7/9/93 | Soybeans | $6.9350 | +100000 | $693,500 | $0.4500 | $45,000 | | $118,000 |
| 7/16/93 | Soybeans | $7.0950 | +100000 | $709,500 | $0.1600 | $16,000 | | $134,000 |
| 7/23/93 | Soybeans | $7.1050 | +100000 | $710,500 | $0.0100 | $1,000 | | $135,000 |
| 7/30/93 | Soybeans | $6.7150 | +100000 | $671,500 | ($0.3900) | ($39,000) | | $96,000 |
| 8/2/93 | Soybeans | $6.9100 | +100000 | $691,000 | $0.1950 | $19,500 | | $115,500 |

**II. Basis Activity**

| (1) Date | (2) Basis Unit Value Spot Futures | (3) Basis Change | (4) Basis Cumulative +Gain/-Loss |
|---|---|---|---|
| 6/1/93 | -0.1225 | 0 | $0 |
| 6/4/93 | -0.1050 | 0.0175 | $1,750 |
| 6/11/93 | -0.1000 | 0.0050 | $2,250 |
| 6/18/93 | -0.1250 | -0.0250 | ($250) |
| 6/25/93 | -0.1425 | -0.0175 | ($2,000) |
| 7/2/93 | -0.1700 | -0.0275 | ($4,750) |
| 7/9/93 | -0.1800 | -0.0100 | ($5,750) |
| 7/16/93 | -0.1500 | 0.0300 | ($2,750) |
| 7/23/93 | -0.1700 | -0.0200 | ($4,750) |
| 7/30/93 | -0.1400 | 0.0300 | ($1,750) |
| 8/2/93 | -0.1350 | 0.0050 | ($1,250) |

## Figure 4-5
### Soybean Short Hedger Worksheet (continued)

**III. Overall Futures Activity**

| (1) Date | (2) Contract | (3) Unit Price | (4) Number of Units per Contract | (5) Number of Contracts +Long/-Short | (6) Futures Position Values | (7) Futures Position +Gain/-Loss | (8) Total Cash + Margin | (9) Invested Cash + Margin | (10) Commission | (11) Futures Cumulative +Gain/-Loss |
|---|---|---|---|---|---|---|---|---|---|---|
| 6/1/93 | Aug Soybeans | $5.8775 | 5000 | -20 | ($587,750) | $0 | $44,500 | $44,500 | | $0 |
| 6/4/93 | Aug Soybeans | $5.8600 | 5000 | -20 | ($586,000) | $1,750 | $46,250 | $44,500 | | $1,750 |
| 6/11/93 | Aug Soybeans | $5.8650 | 5000 | -20 | ($586,500) | ($500) | $45,750 | $44,500 | | $1,250 |
| 6/18/93 | Aug Soybeans | $6.0550 | 5000 | -20 | ($605,500) | ($19,000) | $44,500 | $62,250 | | ($17,750) |
| 6/25/93 | Aug Soybeans | $6.2175 | 5000 | -20 | ($621,750) | ($16,250) | $44,500 | $78,500 | | ($34,000) |
| 7/2/93 | Aug Soybeans | $6.6550 | 5000 | -20 | ($665,500) | ($43,750) | $44,500 | $122,250 | | ($77,750) |
| 7/9/93 | Aug Soybeans | $7.1150 | 5000 | -20 | ($711,500) | ($46,000) | $44,500 | $168,250 | | ($123,750) |
| 7/16/93 | Aug Soybeans | $7.2450 | 5000 | -20 | ($724,500) | ($13,000) | $44,500 | $181,250 | | ($136,750) |
| 7/23/93 | Aug Soybeans | $7.2750 | 5000 | -20 | ($727,500) | ($3,000) | $41,500 | $181,250 | | ($139,750) |
| 7/30/93 | Aug Soybeans | $6.8550 | 5000 | -20 | ($685,500) | $42,000 | $83,500 | $181,250 | | ($97,750) |
| 8/2/93 | Aug Soybeans | $7.0450 | 5000 | -20 | ($704,500) | ($19,000) | $64,500 | $181,250 | | ($116,750) |

**IV. Margin Activity**

Initial Margin Requirement $1,475 per Contract
Maintenance Margin Requirement $1,100 per Contract

| (1) Date | (2) Beginning # of Maintenance Contracts | (3) Margin Account Beginning Balance | (4) Unit Price Change | (5) Position +Gain/-Loss | (6) Interim Margin Balance | (7) Cash Account +From Cash -To Cash | (8) Margin Account Ending Balance | (9) Ending Number of Contracts | (10) Maintenance Requirement |
|---|---|---|---|---|---|---|---|---|---|
| 6/1/93 | -20 | $29,500 | 0 | $0 | $29,500 | $0 | $29,500 | -20 | $22,000 |
| 6/4/93 | -20 | $29,500 | -0.0175 | $1,750 | $31,250 | $0 | $31,250 | -20 | $22,000 |
| 6/11/93 | -20 | $31,250 | 0.0050 | ($500) | $30,750 | $0 | $30,750 | -20 | $22,000 |
| 6/18/93 | -20 | $30,750 | 0.1900 | ($19,000) | $11,750 | $17,750 | $29,500 | -20 | $22,000 |
| 6/25/93 | -20 | $29,500 | 0.1625 | ($16,250) | $13,250 | $16,250 | $29,500 | -20 | $22,000 |
| 7/2/93 | -20 | $29,500 | 0.4375 | ($43,750) | ($14,250) | $43,750 | $29,500 | -20 | $22,000 |
| 7/9/93 | -20 | $29,500 | 0.4600 | ($46,000) | ($16,500) | $46,000 | $29,500 | -20 | $22,000 |
| 7/16/93 | -20 | $29,500 | 0.1300 | ($13,000) | $16,500 | $13,000 | $29,500 | -20 | $22,000 |
| 7/23/93 | -20 | $29,500 | 0.0300 | ($3,000) | $26,500 | $0 | $26,500 | -20 | $22,000 |
| 7/30/93 | -20 | $26,500 | -0.4200 | $42,000 | $68,500 | $0 | $68,500 | -20 | $22,000 |
| 8/2/93 | -20 | $68,500 | 0.1900 | ($19,000) | $49,500 | ($49,500) | $0 | 0 | $0 |

## Figure 4-5
## Soybean Short Hedger Worksheet (continued)

### V. Cash Activity

| (1) Date | (2) Carrying Cash Beginning Balance | (3) Cash Account Flows + Invested -Withdrawn | (4) Margin Account Flows + From Margin -To Margin | (5) Carrying Cash Ending Balance |
|---|---|---|---|---|
| 6/1/93 | $15,000 | $0 | $0 | $15,000 |
| 6/4/93 | $15,000 | $0 | $0 | $15,000 |
| 6/11/93 | $15,000 | $0 | $0 | $15,000 |
| 6/18/93 | $15,000 | $17,750 | ($17,750) | $15,000 |
| 6/25/93 | $15,000 | $16,250 | ($16,250) | $15,000 |
| 7/2/93 | $15,000 | $43,750 | ($43,750) | $15,000 |
| 7/9/93 | $15,000 | $46,000 | ($46,000) | $15,000 |
| 7/16/93 | $15,000 | $13,000 | ($13,000) | $15,000 |
| 7/23/93 | $15,000 | $0 | $0 | $15,000 |
| 7/30/93 | $15,000 | $0 | $0 | $15,000 |
| 8/2/93 | $15,000 | $0 | $49,500 | $64,500 |

## Figure 4-6
## Soybean Long Hedger Worksheet

### I. Overall Spot Activity

| (1) Date | (2) Spot Commodity | (3) Unit Price | (4) Amount of Spot Commodity | (5) Spot Position Value | (6) Unit Price Change | (7) Spot Position +Gain/-Loss | (8) Commission | (9) Spot Cummulative +Gain/-Loss |
|---|---|---|---|---|---|---|---|---|
| 6/1/93 | Soybeans | $5.7550 | -100000 | ($575,500) | $0.0000 | $0 | | $0 |
| 6/4/93 | Soybeans | $5.7550 | -100000 | ($575,500) | $0.0000 | $0 | | $0 |
| 6/11/93 | Soybeans | $5.7650 | -100000 | ($576,500) | $0.0100 | ($1,000) | | ($1,000) |
| 6/18/93 | Soybeans | $5.9300 | -100000 | ($593,000) | $0.1650 | ($16,500) | | ($17,500) |
| 6/25/93 | Soybeans | $6.0750 | -100000 | ($607,500) | $0.1450 | ($14,500) | | ($32,000) |
| 7/2/93 | Soybeans | $6.4850 | -100000 | ($648,500) | $0.4100 | ($41,000) | | ($73,000) |
| 7/9/93 | Soybeans | $6.9350 | -100000 | ($693,500) | $0.4500 | ($45,000) | | ($118,000) |
| 7/16/93 | Soybeans | $7.0950 | -100000 | ($709,500) | $0.1600 | ($16,000) | | ($134,000) |
| 7/23/93 | Soybeans | $7.1050 | -100000 | ($710,500) | $0.0100 | ($1,000) | | ($135,000) |
| 7/30/93 | Soybeans | $6.7150 | -100000 | ($671,500) | ($0.3900) | $39,000 | | ($96,000) |
| 8/2/93 | Soybeans | $6.9100 | -100000 | ($691,000) | $0.1950 | ($19,500) | | ($115,500) |

### II. Basis Activity

| (1) Date | (2) Basis Unit Value Spot Futures | (3) Basis Change | (4) Basis Cumulative +Gain/-Loss |
|---|---|---|---|
| 6/1/93 | -0.1225 | 0 | $0 |
| 6/4/93 | -0.1050 | 0.0175 | ($1,750) |
| 6/11/93 | -0.1000 | 0.0050 | ($2,250) |
| 6/18/93 | -0.1250 | -0.0250 | $250 |
| 6/25/93 | -0.1425 | -0.0175 | $2,000 |
| 7/2/93 | -0.1700 | -0.0275 | $4,750 |
| 7/9/93 | -0.1800 | -0.0100 | $5,750 |
| 7/16/93 | -0.1500 | 0.0300 | $2,750 |
| 7/23/93 | -0.1700 | -0.0200 | $4,750 |
| 7/30/93 | -0.1400 | 0.0300 | $1,750 |
| 8/2/93 | -0.1350 | 0.0050 | $1,250 |

## Figure 4-6
### Soybean Long Hedger Worksheet (continued)

**III. Overall Futures Activity**

| (1) Date | (2) Contract | (3) Unit Price | (4) Number of Units per Contract | (5) Number of Contracts +Long/-Short | (6) Futures Position Values | (7) Futures Position +Gain/-Loss | (8) Total Cash+Margin | (9) Invested Cash+Margin | (10) Commission | (11) Futures Cumulative +Gain/-Loss |
|---|---|---|---|---|---|---|---|---|---|---|
| 6/1/93 | Aug Soybeans | $5.8775 | 5000 | +20 | $587,750 | $0 | $44,500 | $44,500 | | $0 |
| 6/4/93 | Aug Soybeans | $5.8600 | 5000 | +20 | $586,000 | ($1,750) | $42,750 | $44,500 | | ($1,750) |
| 6/11/93 | Aug Soybeans | $5.8650 | 5000 | +20 | $586,500 | $500 | $43,250 | $44,500 | | ($1,250) |
| 6/18/93 | Aug Soybeans | $6.0550 | 5000 | +20 | $605,500 | $19,000 | $62,250 | $44,500 | | $17,750 |
| 6/25/93 | Aug Soybeans | $6.2175 | 5000 | +20 | $621,750 | $16,250 | $78,500 | $44,500 | | $34,000 |
| 7/2/93 | Aug Soybeans | $6.6550 | 5000 | +20 | $665,500 | $43,750 | $122,250 | $44,500 | | $77,750 |
| 7/9/93 | Aug Soybeans | $7.1150 | 5000 | +20 | $711,500 | $46,000 | $168,250 | $44,500 | | $123,750 |
| 7/16/93 | Aug Soybeans | $7.2450 | 5000 | +20 | $724,500 | $13,000 | $181,250 | $44,500 | | $136,750 |
| 7/23/93 | Aug Soybeans | $7.2750 | 5000 | +20 | $727,500 | $3,000 | $184,250 | $44,500 | | $139,750 |
| 7/30/93 | Aug Soybeans | $6.8550 | 5000 | +20 | $685,500 | ($42,000) | $142,250 | $44,500 | | $97,750 |
| 8/2/93 | Aug Soybeans | $7.0450 | 5000 | +20 | $704,500 | $19,000 | $161,250 | $44,500 | | $116,750 |

**IV. Margin Activity**

Initial Margin Requirement $1,475 per Contract
Maintenance Margin Requirement $1,100 per Contract

| (1) Date | (2) Beginning # of Maintenance Contracts | (3) Margin Account Beginning Balance | (4) Unit Price Change | (5) Position +Gain/-Loss | (6) Interim Margin Balance | (7) Cash Account +From Cash -To Cash | (8) Margin Account Ending Balance | (9) Ending Number of Contracts | (10) Maintenance Requirement |
|---|---|---|---|---|---|---|---|---|---|
| 6/1/93 | +20 | $29,500 | 0 | $0 | $29,500 | $0 | $29,500 | +20 | $22,000 |
| 6/4/93 | +20 | $29,500 | -0.0175 | ($1,750) | $27,750 | $0 | $27,750 | +20 | $22,000 |
| 6/11/93 | +20 | $27,750 | 0.0050 | $500 | $28,250 | $0 | $28,250 | +20 | $22,000 |
| 6/18/93 | +20 | $28,250 | 0.1900 | $19,000 | $47,250 | $0 | $47,250 | +20 | $22,000 |
| 6/25/93 | +20 | $47,250 | 0.1625 | $16,250 | $63,500 | $0 | $63,500 | +20 | $22,000 |
| 7/2/93 | +20 | $63,500 | 0.4375 | $43,750 | $107,250 | $0 | $107,250 | +20 | $22,000 |
| 7/9/93 | +20 | $107,250 | 0.4600 | $46,000 | $153,250 | $0 | $153,250 | +20 | $22,000 |
| 7/16/93 | +20 | $153,250 | 0.1300 | $13,000 | $166,250 | $0 | $166,250 | +20 | $22,000 |
| 7/23/93 | +20 | $166,250 | 0.0300 | $3,000 | $169,250 | $0 | $169,250 | +20 | $22,000 |
| 7/30/93 | +20 | $169,250 | -0.4200 | ($42,000) | $127,250 | $0 | $127,250 | +20 | $22,000 |
| 8/2/93 | +20 | $127,250 | 0.1900 | $19,000 | $146,250 | ($146,250) | $0 | 0 | $0 |

*Figure 4-6*
*Soybean Long Hedger Worksheet (continued)*

V. Cash Activity

| (1)<br>Date | (2)<br>Carrying<br>Cash Beginning<br>Balance | (3)<br>Cash Account<br>Flows<br>+ Invested<br>-Withdrawn | (4)<br>Margin<br>Account Flows<br>+ From Margin<br>-To Margin | (5)<br>Carrying<br>Cash Ending<br>Balance |
|---|---|---|---|---|
| 6/1/93 | $15,000 | $0 | $0 | $15,000 |
| 6/4/93 | $15,000 | $0 | $0 | $15,000 |
| 6/11/93 | $15,000 | $0 | $0 | $15,000 |
| 6/18/93 | $15,000 | $0 | $0 | $15,000 |
| 6/25/93 | $15,000 | $0 | $0 | $15,000 |
| 7/2/93 | $15,000 | $0 | $0 | $15,000 |
| 7/9/93 | $15,000 | $0 | $0 | $15,000 |
| 7/16/93 | $15,000 | $0 | $0 | $15,000 |
| 7/23/93 | $15,000 | $0 | $0 | $15,000 |
| 7/30/93 | $15,000 | $0 | $0 | $15,000 |
| 8/2/93 | $15,000 | $0 | $146,250 | $161,250 |

ity; and Section V, Cash Activity—carry the exact same interpretation as in the speculation worksheet, Figures 4-3 and 4-4.

Section II of the hedger's worksheets in, Figures 4-5 and 4-6, depicts the basis, its incremental change and its cumulative change. Since basis trading is the essence of hedging, it is extremely difficult to attain a thorough understanding of hedging without understanding the basis. Recall from the discussion in Chapter Two that the basis can be considered as the equivalent of having a long position in the spot market and a short position in the futures market. Mathematically, this can be expressed as

$$B = (C - F)$$

where B denotes the basis, C specifies the spot price, and F represents the futures price. Remember that the basis has two desirable properties: lower volatility than an open position in either the spot market or the futures market, and the convergence of the spot price and futures price to equality at maturity. The lower volatility of the combined spot and futures position is the whole point of hedging. The hedger is trading the relatively higher price volatility of either the cash or the futures market for the more stable and less volatile combined spot and futures position. The hedger is willing to bear this lower amount of price risk, i.e., the basis volatility, because the effective price of the spot commodity being hedged is much more predictable than if no hedge had been created. The convergence of the spot and futures prices means that the basis becomes zero at maturity. However, prior to maturity the basis can be either positive or negative, thereby creating some opportunities for the hedger to earn a small profit during the life of the hedge as the basis fluctuates.

A fluctuating basis is interpreted as becoming either stronger or weaker. If the basis is becoming more positive, then the commodity's spot, or cash, price is increasing relative to the futures price. On the other hand, if the basis is becoming more negative, then the commodity's spot, or cash, price is decreasing relative to the futures price. A strengthening basis will be profitable if one is long the cash commodity and short the futures contract. A weakening basis will be profitable if one is short the cash commodity and long the futures contract.

These relationships imply certain outcomes for both the short hedger, one who has sold futures contracts to hedge a long spot position, and the long hedger, one who has purchased futures contracts to hedge a short position in the spot market. If the market is normal and the futures contracts are trading at a premium to the spot market, then as the hedge approaches maturity and the basis increases, the short hedger should earn a profit while the long hedger should suffer a loss. Conversely, if the market is inverted and the futures contracts are trading at a discount to the spot market, then as the hedge approaches maturity and the basis decreases, the short hedger should suffer a loss while the long hedger should reap a gain.

In Figure 4-5 the short hedger's, or farmer's, spot market position in soybeans is shown as of 6/01/93, Section I, columns 1, 2, and 4. The cash, or spot, price of beans on that day was $5.755 per bushel, which translates to a position value of $575,500, columns 3 and 5. Column 6 lists the commodity's unit price change in the cash market, and column 7 expresses the price change as either a gain or loss to the spot position. Column 8 is reserved for any commissions that might be incurred as a result of cash market activity. Column 9 accumulates the gains and losses that accrue to the spot position.

The basis, Section II, column 1, is computed by subtracting the futures price, Section II, column 3, from the spot price, Section I, column 3. The negative basis of –$.1225 for 6/01/93 is consistent with a $5.755 per bushel spot price, which is less than the $5.8775 per bushel futures price. On Friday, June 4, the spot price of beans was unchanged, but the August futures contract price fell by –$.0175 to $5.86, Section III, column 3 and Section IV, column 4. This caused the basis to strengthen by $.0175 per bushel and rise to –$.1050 for a position gain of $1,750. At the end of the following week June 11, the spot price of beans had risen by $.01 per bushel to $5.765, Section I, columns 3 and 6; while the August futures contract price rose by $.005 to a level $5.865, Section III, column 3 and Section IV, column 4. This caused the basis to strengthen by $.005 per bushel and rise to –$.1000 for a position gain of $2,250. However, recall that the next five weeks would be characterized by severe flooding in the Midwest and rapidly rising soybean prices.

The next week, 6/18/93, both the soybean spot price and futures price rose by about $.16 per bushel, Section I, column 6 and Section IV, column 4. This price increase caused the basis to weaken by another $.025 per bushel and increased the short hedger's position loss to $250, Section II, columns 3 and 4. Furthermore, the short futures position sustained a $19,000 loss, Section IV, column 5. This caused the interim margin balance to fall to $11,750, well below the $22,000 maintenance requirement, and meant that cash would have to be transferred into the margin account. The short hedger had to deposit $17,750 with the clearing firm to bring the margin account up to the $29,500 required for the 20-contract position. This was the only alternative available. The futures position could not be adjusted since this would destroy the hedge.

Observe that as of 6/18/93, there was only $15,000 available in the speculator's cash account, Section V, column 5; not enough to meet the $17,750 margin call. Thus, the short hedger had to go out and borrow the funds. This is common practice and is encouraged by many banks who deal with customers that use the futures markets to hedge their spot market positions. Usually, a bank will provide the hedger with a line of credit which guarantees that the hedger will have sufficient liquidity to keep the hedge intact.

Over the next four weeks, from 6/18/93 to 7/16/93, the August soybean futures contract continued to rise dramatically, which forced the short hedger to borrow funds each week to meet the margin calls, Section III, columns 3 and 4 and Section IV, column 7. However, during this time the basis weakened and then strengthened so that on July 16th it was –$.15, which meant that the short hedger's overall position had suffered only a $2,750 loss.

The next week saw the August futures price increase by $.03 per bushel, the spot price increase by only $.01, Section IV, column 4 and Section I, column 6, and the basis weaken by $.02, Section II, column 3. For the first time in a month the margin account was able to absorb the loss in the futures position and the hedger did not have to borrow any funds.

During the final two weeks of the hedge, 7/23/93 through 8/02/93, the basis strengthened by $.035 to –$.1350. This $.035 increase in the basis improved the short hedger's position so that when the futures position was closed out on August 2nd, the short hedger's combined loss in the spot and futures market amounted to only $1,250, Section I, column 9, Section III, column 11, and Section II, column 4.

This $1,250 loss was inferior to the $115,500 gain that the farmer would have enjoyed if the soybean crop had not been hedged. However, the goal of hedging is to eliminate as much price risk as possible. Since the crop was not ready for harvest, it was impossible for the farmer to deliver the beans and capture the favorable cash market prices. There always was the threat of a price decline. Indeed, during the last week of July, just before the beans were ready for harvest, the price did drop by $.39 per bushel. When the beans were sold in August the farmer delivered them in the spot market for $6.91 per bushel, or $691,000 for the 100,000 bushels. But the effective price was much lower since the futures market losses had to considered. Thus, the $691,000 spot market revenue had to be reduced by the $116,750 futures market loss for a net cash flow to the farmer of $574,250, or $5.7425 per bushel. Finally, note that the difference between the $116,750 futures market loss and the $115,500 spot market gain equals $1,250, the exact amount of the cumulative loss in the farmer's basis. There can be no other result since the basis is equivalent to having offsetting positions in the cash and futures markets.

Figure 4-6, the long hedger's worksheet, is the mirror image of the short hedger's worksheet, Figure 4-5; however, there are some differences. The basic difference between the two worksheets is that the short hedger is long the cash commodity (soybeans) and is short the futures contract, while the long hedger is short the cash commodity and long the futures contract. This can be seen quite clearly by comparing the signs that precede the spot market positions and futures market positions, Section I, column 4, and Section III, column 5. A more significant difference between the two worksheets is shown in, Section II, column 4, the cumulative gain or loss to the basis. Notice that most of the signs are positive in Figure 4-6, but negative in Figure 4-5. In this example, the processor is benefitting from being a long hedger when the basis weakens. This is exactly opposite the short hedger's outcome portrayed in Figure 4-5.

The most interesting difference between the worksheets is in Sections IV and V, the margin activity and cash activity sections, respectively. The long hedger's margin activity section is straightforward and easy to follow. The margin balance never fell below the maintenance requirement and did not need any cash inflows from the cash account. The same was not true of the short hedger, however. Recall that the short hedger, the farmer, had to borrow funds in order to meet the margin requirements. Moreover, the long hedger's performance was superior to that of the short hedger because of the weakening basis. Note that the short cash position decreased by $115,500, while the long futures position gained $116,750. Although the processor had to purchase the soybeans in the cash market for only $6.91 per bushel, or $691,000, the $116,750 futures market gain reduced the effective cost to $574,250, or $5.7425 per bushel, a much better price than the earlier $6.91 spot price.

## SPREADING

In the chapter's previous two sections, the discussion considered those market participants who were willing to assume large amounts of price risk, speculators, from those market participants who wanted to transfer this risk, hedgers. This section is devoted to a third type of trader: one who is willing to provide liquidity and bear moderate amounts of risk in return for the opportunity to profit from changing price relationships of futures contracts. This person is called a spreader, and follows a very simple trading strategy of simultaneously buying and selling similar futures contracts. The spreader will sell contracts that appear to be overvalued, or rich, relative to other contracts, and will purchase futures contracts that appear to be undervalued, or cheap, relative to other futures contracts.

The spreader does not need the physical commodity in the normal course of business like the hedger, and is not interested in assuming large amounts of price risk via long or short open futures positions like the speculator. The spreader's trading strategy differs from the hedger's in that the spreader never assumes a position in the underlying commodity. Moreover, the spreader's strategy is unlike the speculator's in that the spreader never takes an outright long or short position in any contract, but always combines a long futures position with a short futures position. Clearly, this futures position is much less risky than the speculator's position. It is also less risky than the hedger's futures market position, but more risky than the hedger's overall position. Because the spreader's position is less risky than the futures position of both the speculator and hedger, the spreader's margin requirements are lower.

All commodity spreads fall into one of four basic categories: intramarket spreads, intermarket spreads, intercommodity spreads, and commodity product spreads. Intramarket spreads are the simultaneous purchase and sale of futures contracts that have different maturities, but have the same underlying commodity, and are traded on the same futures exchange. A November-March soybean spread that is created on the Chicago Board of Trade is such a spread. Intermarket spreads are the simultaneous purchase and sale of futures contracts that have the same maturity, have the same underlying commodity, but are traded on different futures exchanges. The purchase of a July wheat futures on the Kansas City Board of Trade and sale of a July wheat futures on the Chicago Board of Trade illustrates this type of spread. Intercommodity spreads are the simultaneous purchase and sale of futures contracts that have the same maturity, but have different yet related underlying commodities. These spreads may be constructed on the same futures exchange or on different exchanges. The TED spread between Treasury Bills and Eurodollars traded on the Chicago Mercantile Exchange is one of the most popular intercommodity spreads. Finally, a commodity product spread is the purchase of a futures contract on a basic commodity with a specific maturity, and the simultaneous sale of a futures contract with the same maturity, whose underlying commodity is derived from the basic commodity. Soybean processors construct such spreads in beans, oil, and meal to lock in favorable gross processing margins.

The only type of spread that is considered in this book is the intramarket spread, which is the simplest to execute and the easiest to understand. This spread can be utilized in both bull and bear markets. The underlying logic of the intramarket bull spread is simple: the nearby futures contract is purchased because it is expected to experience a larger increase in value than the deferred contract, which is sold. The logic for the intramarket bear spread is opposite that of the bull spread, but equally simple; the nearby futures contract is sold because it is expected to decline in value more rapidly than the deferred contract, which is purchased.

One should be careful when trading agricultural commodity spreads because not all of a given commodity's futures contracts have the same crop as the underlying instrument. The USDA has designated that the official crop year for soybeans runs from September 1 to August 31. Thus, the soybean futures contracts that mature between September and the following August are priced according to spot prices for soybeans that are brought to market during this time.

Margin requirements for spreads that are constructed using agriculture futures contracts from the same crop year will be relatively low because of the high correlation among these futures contracts' price changes. However, spreads that span consecutive crop years may not be eligible for spread margins, and will require the investor to post speculative margins for both the long and short positions. These speculative margins require much higher initial and maintenance balances than the initial and maintenance balances for spread margins. The reason for these higher margins is that the factors affecting the underlying crop may be quite different from one year to the next. Thus, the price changes of the futures contracts over the two crop years probably will not be as highly correlated as the price changes of the futures contracts from the same crop year. The July-November soybean spread is a good example of a spread that spans consecutive crop years and requires speculative margins on both the long and short positions. This spread can be extremely volatile and must be watched very closely.

The logic of purchasing the relatively cheap (or undervalued) contract and selling the relatively rich (or overvalued) contract can be illustrated using the Summer 1993 soybean market. Earlier in the chapter the uncertainty about the growing conditions was discussed. The effects of the midwestern flood on the 1993 bean crop served to push the soybean spot price up, invert the market for the soybean futures contracts covering the 1992 crop year, and cause the 1993 soybean futures contracts to trade at less than full carry. During April, May, and June the monthly carrying cost for soybeans was approximately $.12 per bushel. This meant that if the market was normal and trading at full carry, then the price of the September '93 soybean futures contract should have been approximately $.24 less than the November '93 contract, and that the November '93 contract should have been approximately $.24 less than the January '94 contract. Moreover, the September '93 contract should have been about $.48 less than the January '94 contract. In fact, in April and May, the September '93 contract was trading at about a $.025 per bushel discount to the November '93 contract, far below the cost of carry.

One certainly could have argued that the September '93 contract was overvalued relative to the November '93 contract, and that the September contract should be sold and the November contract purchased. But the extreme uncertainty about the flooding during the growing season seemed to make the September '93–November '93 spread too risky. However, on Friday, June 25th, 1993, a golden opportunity presented itself. On this day the price of the September '93 contract exceeded the price of the November '93 contract. This inversion between the two contracts' prices meant that the September '93–November '93 spread could be established for a $.025 per bushel credit. Figure 4-7 provides the details.

There are four sections in Figure 4-7, the Spreader Worksheet, that denote the daily outcomes of the September–November spread. Section I provides the details of the price changes of both the long and short futures positions that constitute the spread. Section II considers the spread activity in conjunction with the cash and margin positions. Section III, the margin activity, and Section IV, the cash activ-

# Figure 4-7
## Soybean Spreader Worksheet

### I. Detailed Futures Activity

| (1) Date | (2) Long Position | (3) Unit Price | (4) Long Units Price Change | (5) Number of Contracts Bought | (6) Short Position | (7) Unit Price | (8) Short Units Price Change | (9) Number of Contracts Sold | (10) Spread Unit Value | (11) Spread Unit Change | (12) Number of Units per Contract | (13) Spread Value |
|---|---|---|---|---|---|---|---|---|---|---|---|---|
| 6/25/93 | Nov Beans | $6.2325 | $0.0000 | +10 | Sep Beans | $6.2350 | $0.0000 | -10 | ($0.0025) | 0 | 5000 | ($125) |
| 6/28/93 | Nov Beans | $6.2425 | $0.0100 | +10 | Sep Beans | $6.2325 | ($0.0025) | -10 | $0.0100 | $0.0125 | 5000 | $500 |
| 6/29/93 | Nov Beans | $6.3700 | $0.1275 | +10 | Sep Beans | $6.3475 | $0.1150 | -10 | $0.0225 | $0.0125 | 5000 | $1,125 |
| 6/30/93 | Nov Beans | $6.5850 | $0.2150 | +10 | Sep Beans | $6.5625 | $0.2150 | -10 | $0.0225 | $0.0000 | 5000 | $1,125 |
| 7/1/93 | Nov Beans | $6.6400 | $0.0550 | +10 | Sep Beans | $6.6100 | $0.0475 | -10 | $0.0300 | $0.0075 | 5000 | $1,500 |
| 7/2/93 | Nov Beans | $6.6775 | $0.0375 | +10 | Sep Beans | $6.6550 | $0.0450 | -10 | $0.0225 | ($0.0075) | 5000 | $1,125 |

### II. Over All Spread Activity

| (1) Date | (2) Spread | (3) Spread Unit Value | (4) Number of Units Per Lot | (5) Number of Lots | (6) Spread Value | (7) Spread + Gain / -Loss | (8) Total Cash + Margins | (9) Invested Cash + Margins | (10) Spread Commission | (11) Cummulative + Gain / -Loss |
|---|---|---|---|---|---|---|---|---|---|---|
| 6/25/93 | -Sep + Nov | ($0.0025) | 5000 | 10 | ($125) | $0 | $7,000 | $7,000 | | $0 |
| 6/28/93 | -Sep + Nov | $0.0100 | 5000 | 10 | $500 | $625 | $7,625 | $7,000 | | $625 |
| 6/29/93 | -Sep + Nov | $0.0225 | 5000 | 10 | $1,125 | $625 | $8,250 | $7,000 | | $1,250 |
| 6/30/93 | -Sep + Nov | $0.0225 | 5000 | 10 | $1,125 | $0 | $8,250 | $7,000 | | $1,250 |
| 7/1/93 | -Sep + Nov | $0.0300 | 5000 | 10 | $1,500 | $375 | $8,625 | $7,000 | | $1,625 |
| 7/2/93 | -Sep + Nov | $0.0225 | 5000 | 10 | $1,125 | ($375) | $8,250 | $7,000 | | $1,250 |

# Figure 4-7
## Soybean Spreader Worksheet (continued)

Initial Margin Requirement:   $400 per Spread
Maintenance Margin Requirement:   $300 per Spread

| (1) Date | (2) Beginning Number of Lots | (3) Margin Account Beginning Balance | (4) Spread Unit Price Change | (5) Position + Gain / -Loss | (6) Interim Margin Balance | (7) Ending Number of Lots | (8) Cash Account + From Cash / -To Cash | (9) Margin Account Ending Balance | (10) Maintenance Requirement |
|---|---|---|---|---|---|---|---|---|---|
| 6/25/93 | +10 | $4,000 | $0.0000 | $0 | $4,000 | 10 | $0 | $4,000 | $3,000 |
| 6/28/93 | +10 | $4,000 | $0.0125 | $625 | $4,625 | 10 | $0 | $4,625 | $3,000 |
| 6/29/93 | +10 | $4,625 | $0.0125 | $625 | $5,250 | 10 | $0 | $5,250 | $3,000 |
| 6/30/93 | +10 | $5,250 | $0.0000 | $0 | $5,250 | 10 | $0 | $5,250 | $3,000 |
| 7/1/93 | +10 | $5,250 | $0.0075 | $375 | $5,625 | 10 | $0 | $5,625 | $3,000 |
| 7/2/93 | +10 | $5,625 | ($0.0075) | ($375) | $5,250 | 0 | ($5,250) | $0 | $0 |

IV. Cash Activity

| (1) Date | (2) Reserve Cash Beginning Balance | (3) Cash Account Flows + Invested / -Withdrawn | (4) Margin Account Flows + From Margin / -To Margin | (5) Reserve Ending Balance |
|---|---|---|---|---|
| 6/25/93 | $3,000 | $0 | $0 | $3,000 |
| 6/28/93 | $3,000 | $0 | $0 | $3,000 |
| 6/29/93 | $3,000 | $0 | $0 | $3,000 |
| 6/30/93 | $3,000 | $0 | $0 | $3,000 |
| 7/1/93 | $3,000 | $0 | $0 | $3,000 |
| 7/2/93 | $3,000 | $0 | $5,250 | $8,250 |

ity, are identical to the margin activity and cash activity sections in the speculator and hedger worksheets, and thus carry the same interpretation.

A close examination of Section I reveals the inner workings of the spread; how it is constructed, how each component changes value, and how the spread's overall value changes. Column 1 provides the date of each transaction, and in this worksheet it shows that the spread was created on 6/25/93 and was liquidated on 7/2/93. Columns 2, 3, and 5 show the number of futures contracts purchased and their price. In this case, the spreader bought 10 November soybean contracts for $6.2325 per bushel. The values in column 4 track the price changes of the long futures contract, and show that the price of the November soybean contract rose during this spread's life. Columns 6 through 9 are the obverse of columns 2 through 5, and provide information about the short side of the spread. In this case the spreader took advantage of the price inversion between the September '93 and November '93 soybean contracts by selling 10 September contracts at $6.235 to offset the long position in the 10 November contracts. Note that the September contract's price behaved in much the same way, column 8, as the November contract, column 4. Column 10 shows the actual value of the spread. This value is obtained by subtracting the short position's price, column 7, from the long position's price. column 4. The values in column 11 depict the change in the spread's value on a per unit basis, while the values in column 13 show the spread's total value. The values in column 13 are computed by multiplying the spread's unit value, column 10, by the total number of units in the spread, the number of contracts in the spread, column 5, multiplied by the number of units per contract, column 12. In this example the spread's value, –$125, as of 6/25/93, is found by multiplying the spread's unit value, –$.0025, by 50,000 units. The remaining values in column 13 show that the spread went from –$125 to $1,125 once the November contract's price rose above the September contract's price.

Section II shows the spread's price behavior in conjunction with the margin and cash accounts, Sections III and IV, respectively. Column 1 of Section II is the date, while column 2 shows the spread components. The spread is presented with the nearby contract first and the deferred contract second, because this is how the spread is quoted. The minus sign that precedes the abbreviation Sep denotes that the spreader has sold the September soybean contract, while the plus sign that precedes the abbreviation Nov indicates that the spreader has purchased the November soybean contract. The next column, column 3, is identical to column 10 of Section I, and shows the spread's unit value. Column 4 provides the number of units per lot, where the term "lot" is used instead of "contract" to denote the size of the position. In this case the spreader's position consists of 10 lots, column 5, since 10 September contracts were sold and 10 November contracts were purchased. Column 6 in Section II is obtained by multiplying columns 3, 4, and 5 together. This number should be equal to the value for the corresponding date in column 13 in Section I, since both have the same meaning. The next column, column 7, tracks the daily gain or loss for the spread. The gains and losses are computed by taking the current value of the spread in column 6 and subtracting the prior day's value. For example, the +$625 is found by subtracting the 6/25/93 value, –$125, from the 6/28/93 value, $500; $500 – (–$125) = $625. Column 8 provides the total cash and margin available to the spreader. This amount will change from day to day as the spread experiences gains and losses. Column 9 shows how much money the spreader has allocated for this strategy. In this case the spreader made a commitment of $7,000. Column 10 provides for commissions, and column 11 shows the spread's cumulative gain or loss. The values in column 11 are computed by subtracting the amount of cash and margin invested in the strategy, column 9, from the current value of the total cash plus margin balance, column 8. For example, the spread's cumulative gain on 6/28/93 of $625 was computed by subtracting the amount of invested cash plus margin, $7,000, from the total cash plus margin amount of $7,625.

The worksheet's final two sections, III and IV, must be considered jointly. Observe that the spreader's margin requirements, $400 initial margin and $300 maintenance margin, are much lower than the margin requirements of both the speculator and the hedger. Recall that the initial margin for either a long or short position in the soybean futures market was $1,475 per contract, and that the maintenance requirement was $1,100 per contract. Since the spreader has a 10-lot position, column 2, the initial balance is $4,000, column 3, and the maintenance requirement is $3,000 column 10. This $4,000 initial margin balance is only a portion of the $7,000 that the spreader has allocated for this strategy. The remaining $3,000 is being held in reserve in a highly liquid account, such as a checking account. Section IV documents the activity for this cash reserve account.

Section III records the effects of the changing futures contract prices on the spreader's margin account. The values in columns 4 and 5 track the spread's unit price change and daily gain or loss. The information in column 4, the spread unit price change, corresponds to Section I, column 11; while the data shown in column 5 of Section III, the position gain or loss, matches the data in Section II, column 7. The values in column 6 show the margin balance prior to marking to market, and alert the spreader to the possibility of having to either post more cash or liquidate part of· the position. During the week between 6/25/93 and 7/2/93, the spread widened to $.03 per bushel by 7/1/93, Section I, column 10, and increased in value to $1,500, Section I, column 13. Thus, on 7/01/93 the margin balance had grown to $5,625, Section III, column 6. However, the next day, 7/2/93 the spread declined in value and the position posted a $375 loss. At this time the spreader decided to liquidate the position and take the $1,250 profit, Section II, column 11. Thus, all the positions were closed out and the margin balance was transferred to the cash account, Section IV, column 4, which resulted in an ending balance of $8,250, Section IV, column 5, and Section II, column 8.

## SUMMARY

This chapter has examined various soybean trading strategies via the relationships that link the soybean cash and futures markets. The chapter began with a discussion of the soybean complex, which encompasses raw soybeans, soybean meal, and soybean oil. Their price relationship, known as the gross processing margin, was explained and discussed within the context of both the cash and futures markets.

The gross processing margin explanation laid the foundation for the discussion of speculators, hedgers, and spreaders. The chapter considered long and short speculative positions, long and short hedged positions, and the intramarket, or time spread. Worksheets were developed for each type of strategy, and were used to explain and illustrate clearly how profits are made and losses incurred in the soybean futures market.

# Chapter 5

# TREASURY BOND
# TRADING STRATEGIES

## PRICE QUOTES

Chapter One discussed the price quotes for a variety of commodity futures contracts. Examples of futures contract price quotes in both *The Wall Street Journal* and *Barron's* were explained. All of the price quotations discussed in Chapter One dealt with agricultural, or physical, commodities; none of the previous examples dealt with financial futures contracts. In this and the following two chapters, the emphasis shifts from futures contracts on physical commodities to futures contracts on financial instruments. This chapter explores the behavior of the Treasury Bond futures contract. Thus, it is important that one be familiar with its price quotations.

Figure 5-1 shows futures price quotes for a variety of financial instruments traded on various futures exchanges as of the close of trading on Wednesday, March 9, 1994. Information regarding the futures contracts of each commodity is presented in a standardized format. This format conveys such information as the trading location of the futures contracts; the size and unit value of the financial futures contracts; the contracts' price changes; and the quantity of contracts traded and held by market participants.

For example, the Treasury Bond quotes show that T-Bond futures contracts are traded on the Chicago Board of Trade (CBT), where each contract controls $100,000 in face value of United States Treasury Bonds, and where the maturities follow a quarterly cycle of De-

*Figure 5-1*
*Futures Prices*

## INTEREST RATE

**TREASURY BONDS (CBT)—$100,000; pts. 32nds of 100%**

|  | Open | High | Low | Settle | Change | Lifetime High | Low | Open Interest |
|---|---|---|---|---|---|---|---|---|
| Mar | 110-12 | 110-23 | 109-31 | 110-20 | + 4 | 120-31 | 94-26 | 73,889 |
| June | 109-09 | 109-22 | 108-31 | 109-19 | + 5 | 119-29 | 94-26 | 298,538 |
| Sept | 108-15 | 108-25 | 108-03 | 108-23 | + 5 | 118-26 | 90-12 | 36,220 |
| Dec | 107-30 | 108-06 | 107-20 | 108-04 | + 4 | 118-08 | 91-19 | 23,057 |
| Mr95 | 107-13 | 107-13 | 107-09 | 107-13 | + 4 | 116-20 | 106-28 | 1,113 |

Est vol 500,000; vol Tues 419,216; op int 432,921, −6,963.

**TREASURY BONDS (MCE)—$50,000; pts. 32nds of 100%**

| Mar | 110-13 | 110-21 | 110-02 | 110-24 | + 12 | 120-30 | 107-26 | 987 |
|---|---|---|---|---|---|---|---|---|
| June | 109-12 | 109-24 | 108-31 | 109-23 | + 12 | 118-31 | 103-16 | 9,457 |

Est vol 7,000; vol Tues 6,732; open int 10,450, +784.

**TREASURY NOTES (CBT)—$100,000; pts. 32nds of 100%**

| Mar | 109-25 | 109-31 | 109-16 | 109-29 | + 11 | 116-09 | 108-00 | 71,748 |
|---|---|---|---|---|---|---|---|---|
| June | 108-26 | 109-00 | 108-16 | 108-30 | + 11 | 115-21 | 108-00 | 215,826 |
| Sept | 108-04 | 108-05 | 107-26 | 108-05 | .... | 115-01 | 107-26 | 2,749 |

Est vol 114,114; vol Tues 107,163; open int 290,399, +108.

**5 YR TREAS NOTES (CBT)—$100,000; pts. 32nds of 100%**

| Mar | 08-245 | 108-26 | 108-15 | 08-245 | − 1 | 13055 | 108-15 | 53,354 |
|---|---|---|---|---|---|---|---|---|
| June | 07-305 | 08-025 | 107-23 | 08-005 | − 1 | 1205 | 107-23 | 148,316 |
| Sept | .... | .... | .... | 07-085 | − 1 | 10195 | 07085 | 439 |

Est vol 75,000; vol Tues 61,879; open int 202,109, −7,927.

**2 YR TREAS NOTES (CBT)—$200,000; pts. 32nds of 100%**

| Mar | 105-08 | 05-082 | 05-045 | 05-075 | .... | 06215 | 05045 | 6,527 |
|---|---|---|---|---|---|---|---|---|
| June | 104-15 | 04-162 | 104-12 | 04-152 | − ½ | 106-00 | 04-12 | 32,854 |

Est vol 6,000; vol Tues 3,320; open int 39,383, −160.

cember, March, June, and September. Trading is active in five T-Bond futures contracts maturing between March of 1994 and March of 1995. These T-Bond futures prices are quoted in points, with 1 point equal to $1,000, and each price change increment, or tick, being equal to 1/32nd of a $1,000 point, or $31.25 per contract. The "Open" column shows that the March 1994 contract began the trading day at a price of 110-12, or 110 and 12/32 points, which equals $110,375 per contract. During the day, the highest price for March 1994 T-Bonds was 110-23, or $110,718.75, while the lowest price was 109 and 31/32, or $109,968.75 per $100,000 bond contract. These levels are indicated by the "High" and "Low" columns, respectively. The "Settle" column denotes that the March '94 T-Bond futures contract closed, or settled, at a price of 110-20, $110,625 per $100,000 bond contract, at the end of the trading day. Notice the plus signs in the "Change" column for all of the T-Bond futures contracts. These signs indicate that all of the bond futures contracts enjoyed a price increase over the settlement price from the prior trading day, Tuesday, March 8, 1994. Specifically, the March '94, June '94, September '94, December '94, and March '95 contracts all increased by 4/32nds over the previous day's settlement price. The last column, "Open Interest," reveals that there are 73,889 long positions in March 1994 Treasury Bond futures contracts which are outstanding. Since every futures contract requires both a buyer and seller, the clearinghouse computes the open interest for a particular contract by summing all the outstanding long positions. "Est vol 210,000" indicates that Friday's estimated trading volume was 210,000 for all Treasury Bond futures contracts, while "vol Tues 76,124" shows that Tuesday's actual volume was 76,124 Treasury Bond futures contracts. Finally, the total open interest for Treasury Bond futures contracts is 433,921, which is 6,963 contracts less than the previous trading day's open interest as indicated by "open int 432,921 – 6,963."

The *Barron's* data, Figure 5-2, are similar to *The Wall Street Journal* data, are grouped by commodity type, and are arranged to show the contracts' "Season," or lifetime, "High" and "Low," followed by the week's: "High" price, "Low" price, closing price, net change in price, and open interest. "Fri. to Thurs. sales" and "Total open interest" provide the total contract volume and sales for the most recent trading week. Notice that the Treasury Bond futures contract data are very similar in both Figures 5-1 and 5-2. Any differences that occur are due to the *Barron's* data encompassing a week's worth of trading, while *The Wall Street Journal* data are reported daily.

## Figure 5-2
### Commodities and Financial Futures

# COMMODITIES AND FINANCIAL FUTURES

Commodities, or futures, contracts originally called for delivery of physical items, such as agricultural products and metals, at a specified price at a specified future date. Increasingly, these contracts have come to apply also to Treasury bills, notes and bonds, certificates of deposit, major market indices and major currencies.

## Interest Rate

| | Season's High | Season's Low | Week's High | Week's Low | Sett | Net Chg | Open Int. |
|---|---|---|---|---|---|---|---|
| **US T. BILLS** | | | | | | | |
| $1 million; pts. of 100 pct. | | | | | | | |
| 96.76 | 96.04 | Jun | 96.29 | 96.04 | 96.07 | −.18 | 27,209 |
| 96.48 | 95.71 | Sep | 95.99 | 95.71 | 95.74 | −.21 | 5,715 |
| 96.10 | 95.34 | Dec | 95.46 | 95.34 | 95.36 | −.25 | 2,871 |
| Fri. to Thurs. sales | | 41,433 | | | | | |
| Total open interest | | 35,745 | | | | | |
| **10 YR. TREASURY** | | | | | | | |
| $100,000 prin; pts & 32nds of 100 pct. | | | | | | | |
| 116-09 | 108 | Mar | 111-08 | 109-14 | 109-27 | −28 | 104,558 |
| 115-21 | 108-10 | Jun | 110-11 | 108-10 | 108-29 | −30 | 179,922 |
| 114-26 | 107-27 | Sep | 109-17 | 108-04 | 108-04 | −31 | 2,691 |
| 114-21 | 107-18 | Dec | 108-26 | 107-18 | 107-16 | −31 | 75 |
| 1-07 | 108-09 | Mar | 111-07 | | 107 | −31 | 2 |
| Fri. to Thurs. sales | | 1,742,847 | | | | | |
| Total open interest | | 287,258 | | | | | |
| **5 YR. TREASURY** | | | | | | | |
| $100,000 prin; pts & 32nds of 100 pct. | | | | | | | |
| 113-055 | 108-18 | Mar | 109-29 | 108-18 | 108-085 | −0-21 | 74,548 |
| 112-051 | 107-245 | Jun | 109-06 | 107-245 | 108-04 | −0-11½ | 138,651 |
| 110-195 | 107-085 | Sep | 108-09 | 107-085 | 107-10 | −0-22 | 435 |
| Fri. to Thurs. sales | | 484,043 | | | | | |
| Total open interest | | 213,634 | | | | | |
| **2 YR. TREASURY** | | | | | | | |
| $200,000; pts. & 128ths of 100 pct. | | | | | | | |
| 106-88 | 105-22 | Mar | 105-68 | 105-22 | 105-36 | −34 | 19,102 |
| 106 | 104-59 | Jun | 105-06 | 104-59 | 104-70 | −46 | 21,794 |
| 104-124 | 104-24 | Sep | 104-68 | | 104-03 | −63 | 2 |
| Fri. to Thurs. sales | | 57,938 | | | | | |
| Total open interest | | 40,396 | | | | | |
| **US TREASURY BONDS** | | | | | | | |
| ($ pct=$100,000;pts & 32nds of 100 pct) | | | | | | | |
| 120-31 | 90 | Mar | 112-20 | 109-31 | 110-24 | −28 | 104,989 |
| 119-29 | 91-06 | Jun | 111-17 | 108-26 | 109-21 | −30 | 273,484 |
| 118-26 | 90-12 | Sep | 110-17 | 108-02 | 108-25 | −30 | 34,773 |
| 118-08 | 91-19 | Dec | 110 | 107-16 | 108-06 | −33 | 23,056 |
| 116-30 | 102-08 | Mar | 109-07 | 106-28 | 107-15 | −33 | 1,045 |
| 113-19 | 98-13 | Jun | 107-24 | | 106-25 | −34 | 64 |
| 112-15 | 108-08 | Sep | | | 106-06 | −34 | 11 |
| 113-14 | 106-25 | Dec | | | 105-21 | −34 | 8 |
| 114-06 | 99-04 | Mar | 106-05 | | 105-06 | −34 | 23 |
| Fri. to Thurs. sales | | 2,627,867 | | | | | |
| Total open interest | | 437,453 | | | | | |
| **MUNICIPAL BONDS** | | | | | | | |
| $1000x index;pts & 32nds of 100 pct | | | | | | | |
| 105-22 | 95-28 | Mar | 99-28 | 95-28 | 96-14 | −85 | 15,245 |
| 104-07 | 95 | Jun | 98-26 | 95 | 95-18 | −83 | 15,953 |
| Last index | | 96-11 | | | | | |
| Fri. to Thurs. sales | | 61,888 | | | | | |
| Total open interest | | 31,198 | | | | | |
| **30 DAY INTEREST RATE** | | | | | | | |
| $5 million; points of 100 pct. | | | | | | | |
| 96.91 | 96.51 | Mar | 96.62 | 96.51 | 94.58 | +.02 | 4,873 |
| 96.87 | 96.34 | Apr | 96.49 | 96.34 | 96.38 | −.06 | 1,648 |
| 96.80 | 96.22 | May | 96.40 | 96.25 | 96.25 | −.09 | 1,273 |
| 96.67 | 96.02 | Jul | 96.02 | | 96.02 | −.12 | 269 |
| 96.58 | 95.90 | Aug | 95.98 | | 95.92 | −.12 | 169 |
| 96.44 | 95.93 | Sep | 95.96 | | 95.76 | −.14 | 269 |
| 96.60 | 95.00 | Dec | 95.84 | | 95.28 | −.10 | |
| 96.72 | 96.10 | Jun | | 96.27 | 96.10 | 96.12 | −.10 | 1,581 |
| Last index | | 3.26, up | 0.01 | | | | |
| Fri. to Thurs. sales | | 9,634 | | | | | |
| Total open interest | | 10,082 | | | | | |

## SPECULATING

In Chapter Two the behavior of both spot prices and futures prices was discussed for agricultural commodities, debt instruments, and equity instruments. It was shown theoretically that the price of debt instruments, or bonds, should move inversely to interest rates. The fact that changing bond prices make it possible to profit from changing interest rates explains why people speculate via futures contracts based on debt instruments. If interest rates are expected to rise, then bond prices can be expected to fall, and speculators will establish short positions, or sell, bond futures contracts. Conversely, if interest rates are expected to fall, then speculators will purchase bond futures contracts in anticipation of rising bond prices. Thus, the key to speculating successfully with bond futures contracts is the ability to accurately predict the direction of interest rate movement. Interest rates cannot be predicted with any precision if one does not understand that the Federal Reserve's response to changing economic conditions exerts an enormous amount of influence on the direction of interest rates.

The Federal Reserve is the central bank of the United States. It is also the agency that is charged with implementing economic policy. As the nation's central banker, the fundamental economic goal of the Federal Reserve is to maintain steady, moderate economic growth in the country's output of goods and services, or Gross National Product. There are two threats to the stable growth in Gross National Product, or GNP; inflation and recession. Inflation is defined as an increase in the economy's price level. When price levels rise faster than income levels it costs more to purchase the same amount of real goods and services. This erosion in purchasing power means that the country's standard of living is declining as well. The drop in the dollar's value also results in rising interest rates since market participants will demand a return on financial assets that exceeds the inflation rate. Recession, defined as the decline in the economy's GNP, causes income levels to drop. Since there is less disposable income, there will be less demand for goods and services. This leads to falling production and lower price levels. Inflation will abate, but unemployment will rise. Market participants will be satisfied with earning a lower rate of interest on financial assets since these assets will maintain their purchasing power as inflation diminishes.

The Federal Reserve's response to these two forces which threaten the economy's stability will dictate the direction of interest rates. If inflation is cause for concern, then the Federal Reserve can be expected to follow a restrictive monetary policy. Such a policy will combat inflation by having less money in circulation in the economy. Less money in circulation will cause interest rates to rise, dampen demand for loanable funds, and cause the economy to slow down at some point. When the economy shows signs of slowing, the concern shifts from inflation to recession. Too little money circulating within the economy means that there is not enough capital to fund moderate growth and expansion in the GNP. Therefore, the Federal Reserve can be expected to increase the money supply when the economy appears headed for a recession. An increase in the money supply will cause interest rates to drop, increase the demand for loanable funds, and stimulate the economy's production of goods and services. Thus, when the Federal Reserve follows a restrictive (or tight money) policy, the higher interest rates will translate to lower bond prices. On the other hand, when the Federal Reserve pursues a freer (or easy money) policy, the lower interest rates will result in rising bond prices.

From the spring of 1992 through the autumn of 1993, the Federal Reserve was concerned about getting the economy out of recession and promoting real growth. Since inflation did not appear to be a problem, the Federal Reserve allowed interest rates to fall, with both short-term rates and long-term rates declining by about 100 basis points. Short-term rates fell from 4.35% to 3.36% while long-term yields dropped from 7.90% to 6.9%. Figure 5-3 graphically portrays the behavior of Treasury Bond prices during this time. Notice the prolonged rise in price and commensurate decline in yields during the first half of 1989, the first quarter of 1990, the second half of 1991, and the first three quarters of 1993, with the longest decline in rates occurring for the 15 months between April of 1991 and July of 1992. However, toward the end of 1993, demand for credit increased and rates on 30-year bonds started to rise after hitting a low of 5.89% in mid-October. As the economy continued its expansion inflationary expectations began to rise, and the market appeared to be expecting the Federal Reserve to respond by tightening credit in early 1994.

Given this environment, it appeared that bond prices were headed downward, and that one would be able to reap some speculative profits by selling, or going short, Treasury Bond futures contracts early in 1994. On Monday, January 31st, the chairman of the Federal Reserve Board, Alan Greenspan, told the Congressional Joint Economic Committee that short-term interest rates were abnormally low in real terms and that rates would have to be increased. This was a clear signal that rates were probably as low as they were going to get, and that in the near future the Federal Reserve would permit rates to rise and bond prices to fall.

Suppose that a small retail investor had $15,000 that she wanted to commit to a speculative Treasury Bond strategy in January of 1994. If this investor's broker requires speculators to post an initial margin of $2025 per contract, and maintain a margin of at least $1,500 per contract, then a trading worksheet like that of Figure 5-4 is a good representation of this speculator's Treasury Bond position between January 31st and February 8th of 1994.

Figure 5-4, the Speculative Worksheet, is divided into three sections, with the columns in each section being numbered appropriately. Section I provides a listing of the speculative position's overall activity. Section II gives a detailed account of the margin activity that occurs during the time that the position is open. Finally, the third section provides a record of the amount of cash that was invested and withdrawn from the position.

Columns 1 and 2 in the first section show that the speculator opened her position on January 31st in the March T-Bond contract. Column 3 shows that the March T-Bond contract was purchased for a price of 117-5/32. The fourth column shows that 100 U.S. Treasury Bonds, each with a $1,000 face value, comprise a single futures contract. The fifth column shows that the speculator's initial purchase was one contract. The position's value of $117,156 in the sixth column is obtained by first multiplying the unit price, column 3, by the number of units in the contract, column 4, to get the contract value, and then multiplying the result by the number of contracts in the position, column 5. The seventh column simply provides the position's daily gains and losses. The remaining columns must be interpreted in reference to the other two sections of the worksheet.

Column 8 in Section I shows exactly how much of the speculator's money remains. This balance is composed of the amount that has been posted with the broker as margin, and the amount of cash that can be used to fund the position if the market moves against the speculator. As stated previously, this speculative cash does not have to be put on deposit with the broker, but should be held in a highly liquid, easily accessible account. The amount in Section I, column 8, must equal the sum of the day's ending margin account balance, Section II, column 8, and the day's ending speculative cash balance, Section III, column 5. The amount of cash plus margin available to

Figure 5-3
U.S. T-Bond Spot Market Price

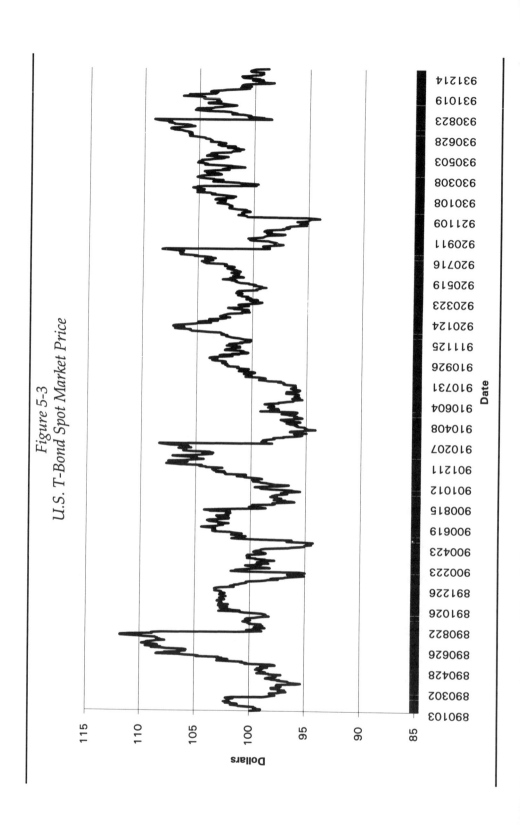

the speculator will fluctuate each day as the position gains or loses value. The next column in Section I, column 9, shows the total amount of money that the speculator has invested in the position. This is composed of the initial margin, Section II, column 3, plus the amount of cash that has been held in reserve to fund the position in the event of adverse market movements, Section III, column 2. Column 10 is reserved for commissions. Since commissions can vary widely throughout the industry, I do not even attempt to include them in the various examples. Make sure that you have a thorough understanding of your broker's commission schedule. The final column in Section I, column 11, shows the strategy's cumulative gain or loss. It is computed by subtracting column 9, the amount invested in cash and margin, from column 8, the total cash and margin balance. When appropriate, commissions should also be subtracted from the total cash plus margin amount in column 8. The amount in column 11 of Section I must agree with the position gains and losses and any cash flows reflected in the margin account, Section II, column 8.

The second section of the speculative worksheet provides information about the speculator's margin activity, and begins with a listing of the margin requirements. In this example the speculator must post an initial margin of $2,025 per T-Bond contract purchased, and the margin account must have a minimum balance equal to $1,500 per contract at all times. If the margin balance falls below the minimum requirement, then the speculator is required to restore the margin account to a level that is consistent with the initial margin requirement. This can be accomplished in one of two ways: either more cash can be added to the margin account or enough of the position can be liquidated so that the remaining margin balance is greater than or equal to the initial margin requirement for the remaining contracts.

The remainder of Section II is divided into 10 columns that provide daily data about the margin account. Columns 1 and 2 of Section II are self-explanatory and correspond to columns 1 and 5 of Section I. Column 3 shows the margin account balance at the beginning of each day. The figures in column 4 represent the change in value of the futures contract on a per-unit basis. Column 5, the amount of gain or loss in the futures position, is obtained by multiplying the unit price change, column 4, by the total number of units in the position. The number of units in the position is determined by multiplying the number of units per contract, Section I, column 4, by the number of contracts in the position at the beginning of the day, Section II, column 2. The next column in Section II, column 6, gives the

## Figure 5-4
## Long U.S. T-Bond Speculative Short Worksheet

I. Overall Futures Activity

| (1) Date | (2) Contract | (3) Unit Price Per $1000 Bond | (4) Number of Units per Contract | (5) Number of Contracts +Long/-Short | (6) Position Value | (7) Position +Gain/-Loss | (8) Total Cash+Margin | (9) Invested Cash+Margin | (10) Commission | (11) Cumulative +Gain/-Loss |
|---|---|---|---|---|---|---|---|---|---|---|
| 1/31/94 | March T-Bonds | $1,171.5625 | 100 | +1 | $117,156 | $0.00 | $15,000 | $15,000 | | $0.00 |
| 2/1/94 | March T-Bonds | $1,161.8750 | 100 | +1 | $116,188 | ($968.75) | $14,031 | $15,000 | | ($968.75) |
| 2/2/94 | March T-Bonds | $1,164.3750 | 100 | +1 | $116,438 | $250.00 | $14,281 | $15,000 | | ($718.75) |
| 2/3/94 | March T-Bonds | $1,159.6875 | 100 | +1 | $115,969 | ($468.75) | $13,813 | $15,000 | | ($1,187.50) |
| 2/4/94 | March T-Bonds | $1,148.7500 | 100 | +1 | $114,875 | ($1,093.75) | $12,719 | $15,000 | | ($2,281.25) |
| 2/7/94 | March T-Bonds | $1,148.1250 | 100 | +1 | $114,813 | ($62.50) | $12,656 | $15,000 | | ($2,343.75) |
| 2/8/94 | March T-Bonds | $1,142.8125 | 100 | +1 | $114,281 | ($531.25) | $12,125 | $15,000 | | ($2,875.00) |

II. Margin Activity

Intitial Margin Requirement $2,025 per Contract
Maintenance Margin Requirement $1,500 per Contract

| (1) Date | (2) Beginning # of Maintenance Contracts | (3) Margin Account Beginning Balance | (4) Unit Price Change | (5) Position +Gain/-Loss | (6) Interim Margin Balance | (7) Cash Account +From Cash -To Cash | (8) Margin Account Ending Balance | (9) Ending Number of Contracts | (10) Maintenance Requirement |
|---|---|---|---|---|---|---|---|---|---|
| 1/31/94 | +1 | $2,025 | 0.0000 | $0.00 | $2,025 | $0 | $2,025 | +1 | ($1,500) |
| 2/1/94 | +1 | $2,025 | (9.6875) | ($968.75) | $1,056 | $969 | $2,025 | +1 | ($1,500) |
| 2/2/94 | +1 | $2,025 | 2.5000 | $250.00 | $2,275 | $0 | $2,275 | +1 | ($1,500) |
| 2/3/94 | +1 | $2,275 | (4.6875) | ($468.75) | $1,807 | $0 | $1,807 | +1 | ($1,500) |
| 2/4/94 | +1 | $1,807 | (10.9375) | ($1,093.75) | $713 | $1,312 | $2,025 | +1 | ($1,500) |
| 2/7/94 | +1 | $2,025 | (0.6250) | ($62.50) | $1,962 | $0 | $1,962 | +1 | ($1,500) |
| 2/8/94 | +1 | $1,962 | (5.3125) | ($531.25) | $1,431 | ($1,431) | $0 | +1 | ($1,500) |

*Figure 5-4*

*Long U.S. T-Bond Speculative Short Worksheet (continued)*

III. Cash Activity

| (1)<br>Date | (2)<br>Speculative<br>Cash Beginning<br>Balance | (3)<br>Cash Account<br>Flows<br>+Invested<br>-Withdrawn | (4)<br>Margin<br>Account Flows<br>+From Margin<br>-To Margin | (5)<br>Speculative<br>Cash Ending<br>Balance |
|---|---|---|---|---|
| 1/31/94 | $12,975 | $0 | $0 | $12,975 |
| 2/1/94 | $12,975 | $0 | ($969) | $12,006 |
| 2/2/94 | $12,006 | $0 | $0 | $12,006 |
| 2/3/94 | $12,006 | $0 | $0 | $12,006 |
| 2/4/94 | $12,006 | $0 | ($1,312) | $10,694 |
| 2/7/94 | $10,694 | $0 | $0 | $10,694 |
| 2/8/94 | $10,694 | $0 | $1,431 | $12,125 |

interim margin balance amount. This reflects the gains or losses posted to the margin account as the price changes during the day, and alerts the speculator to the possibility of a margin call. Column 7 provides information about any cash additions to or withdrawals from the margin account. The figures in the margin account ending balance column, column 8, represent the cumulative effect of the changes in the futures contract price, any cash inflows or outflows that have occurred, and any change in the number of contracts in the position. Column 9 shows the number of futures contracts in the position at the end of the day. This column is particularly important because it reflects any change in the number of contracts that consti- tute the position. Finally, the position's maintenance requirement is shown in column 10.

Section III, the last section of the speculative worksheet, deals with the speculator's cash activity. As mentioned above, this cash does not have to be put on deposit with the broker, but it should be kept in an account that is extremely liquid and easily accessible so that the wide price swings in the financial futures markets can be withstood. Finan- cial futures contracts are no different from their physical commodity counterparts in terms of price volatility, price limits, and margin. It is extremely important that the small retail customer be aware of these attributes since they have an impact on how much cash should be kept in reserve. The rule of thumb that the small investor should keep enough in the margin and cash accounts to withstand five days worth of limit moves still applies. In Figure 5-3, the $15,000 total cash and margin amount is adequate for a $3,000 daily limit move per contract for a one-lot, or one-contract position. This amount is consis- tent with the five-day rule of thumb: $3,000 times five days, times one contract.

When the small retail speculator established her position by selling one March T-Bond contract on 1/31/94, the March bonds were sell- ing at 117 and 5/32. She deposited $2,025 with her broker to satisfy the initial margin requirement, and kept an additional $12,975 in her reserve account. The next trading day, 2/1/94, the price of March bonds fell by 31/32 per contract, or $968.75, Section II, columns 4 and 5, to 116 and 6/32, Section I, column 3. Both the speculator's short position and margin account increased in value by $968.75, Section I, column 7, and Section II, columns 5 and 6. At the end of the day the margin account balance had risen by $968.75, Section II, column 8, and the total cash and margin amount increased to $15,969, Section I, column 8. Furthermore, the position showed a cumulative gain of $968.75, Section I, column 11.

At the beginning of the next day, 2/2/94, the speculator was short one March bond contract, and she had $2,994 in her margin account. During the day March Treasury Bonds rose 8/32 to 116 and 14/32 for a $250 loss to the speculator, Section II, columns 4 and 5, and Section I, column 7. This $250 loss to the position resulted in the margin account falling to the $2,744 level, Section II, column 6—the $2,025 margin balance at the beginning of the day minus the $250 gain. When trading opened on 2/3/94 the speculator was short one March T-Bond contract, Section II, column 2; had $2,744 in her margin account, Section II, column 3; had a total cash and margin balance of $15,719, Section I, column 8; and had enjoyed a cumulative gain of $718.75 Section I, column 11. During the day's trading interest rates rose and bond prices dropped by 15/32, to 115 and 31/32, which resulted in a $468.75 gain to the position, and an interim margin balance of $3,213, Section II, columns 4, 5, and 6, and Section I, columns 3 and 7. At the end of the day both her margin and total cash and margin accounts had grown to $16,188 and $3,213, Section I, column 8, and Section II, column 8; and the position's cumulative gain had risen to +$1,187.50, Section I, column 11.

The next day, 2/4/94, the Federal Reserve announced that it was raising its target for short-term interest rates from 3% to $3\frac{1}{4}$%, and bond prices plunged. The March T-Bond contract dropped by 35/32 from 115–31 to 114–28, Section I, column 3, which translated to a $1,093.75 gain, Section I column 7, Section II, column 5. This caused the speculator's margin account to rise by another $1,093, and boosted the cumulative gain to $2,281.25, Section II, column 5, and Section I, column 11.

The following Monday and Tuesday, 2/7/94 and 2/8/94, rates continued to rise and bond prices continued to erode. On Monday the March T-Bond contract fell 2/32, while on Tuesday it dropped by another 17/32 to 114–9. This latest surge prompted her to close out her short position and to withdraw all the funds in her margin account, $4,900, and put them into her speculative account, Section II, columns 7 and 8, and Section III, columns 4 and 5. Thus, after purchasing her contract, she had no open position at the end of the day and there was no margin required, Section II, columns 9 and 10. Finally, this speculator accumulated $2,875 between 1/31/94 and 2/8/94. Apparently, this speculator was rewarded handsomely for her insights into the interest rate market. Unfortunately, the same cannot be said for the person who was on the other side of this trade, the long speculator.

Although the long speculator suffered a loss, a strong argument can be made for the logic of buying T-Bond futures contracts. It was true that the threat of inflation appeared to have subsided at this time and that the economic recovery was continuing at a moderate pace. It also was true that many felt that raising rates would jeopardize the recovery, though there was no guarantee that the Federal Reserve would continue to pursue an easy money policy and push interest rates lower. In the past, the Federal Reserve frequently had adopted a neutral stance characterized by a steady, unchanging monetary policy. Moreover, Chairman Greenspan was vague about the impending rise in short-term rates. Thus, the long speculator decided to buy T-Bond futures contracts in the hope that the Federal Reserve would not take any action in the near term that would result in higher rates. Suppose that this speculator also had enough to withstand five days of limit moves, $15,000, and that he decided to buy one March Treasury Bond futures contract on 1/31/94. Figure 5-5 examines the outcome of this strategy.

The various sections in Figure 5-5, the overall futures activity, the margin activity, and the cash activity, carry the exact same meaning as the sections in Figure 5-4. The speculator represented by the worksheet in Figure 5-5, the short bond speculator, differs dramatically from the long bond speculator represented in Figure 5-4, however. Notice that the outcomes are quite different. The long speculator established his position by buying One March T-Bond contract on 1/31/94, and then maintained this long position. During the following week he experienced some large losses, which resulted in a net loss of $2,281.25 and an ending cash and margin balance of $12,719 because of rising interest rates and the corresponding drop in bond prices. This is the mirror image of the short speculator's $2,281 gain between 1/31/94 and 2/4/94, and contrasts sharply with the short speculator's $17,875 ending cash and margin balance.

When the long speculator established his position by buying one March T-Bond contract on January 31st, the March bonds were selling at 117 and 5/32. He deposited $2,025 with his broker to satisfy the initial margin requirement and kept an additional $12,975 in his reserve account. The next trading day, 2/1/94, the price of March bonds fell by 31/32 per contract, to 116 and 6/32, Section I, column 3. Both the speculator's long position and margin account dropped in value by $968.75, Section I, column 7, and Section II, columns 5 and 6, and the total cash and margin amount had declined to $14,031, Section I, column 8. Furthermore, at the end of the day the margin account balance had fallen by $969, Section II, column 8, to $1,056, well below the $1,500 requirement for a single contract position. Thus, the speculator's broker informed him that he had to bring his margin account into balance with his contract position in one of two ways: either deposit more cash or liquidate the position. If he decided to liquidate, his short position would be covered by selling a March T-Bond contract at 116 and 6/32, the commissions would be subtracted, and he then would be allowed to withdraw all remaining cash from his margin account.

Since he believed that the position would be profitable if he could stay in the bond market, he decided not to liquidate. Thus, he had to deposit $969 in his margin account so that the balance would equal the initial $2,025 initial margin requirement once again, Section II, columns 5 through 8, and Section III, column 4.

At the beginning of trading on 2/2/94 the speculator was long one March T-Bond contract, Section II, column 2; had $2,025 in his margin account, Section II, column 3; had a total cash and margin balance of $14,031, Section I, column 8; and had suffered a cumulative loss of $968.75, Section I, column 11. During the day, March T-Bonds rose by 8/32 for a $250 gain to the speculator, Section II, columns 4 and 5, and Section I, column 7. This $250 gain to the position resulted in the margin account rising to a level of only $2,275, Section II, column 6—the $2,025 margin balance at the beginning of the day, plus the $250.

On the next day, 2/3/94, interest rates continued to fall, and the March T-Bond futures contract fell by 15/32, which meant that the long speculator's position suffered another loss of $468.75. However, this reduced the margin account to only $1,807, well above the $1,500 maintenance requirement. His position at the end of the day on 2/3/94 is given in Section I, columns 8 and 11; Section II, columns 8, and 9; and Section III, column 5.

The next day, 2/4/94, when the Federal Reserve announced that it was raising its target for short-term interest rates from 3% to 3¼ %, the long speculator suffered a huge loss when bond prices plunged. The March T-Bond contract dropped by 35/32, from 115–31 to 114–28, Section I, column 3, which translated to a $1,093.75 loss, Section I, column 7, and Section II, column 5. This caused the speculator's margin account to fall to $713 and increased the cumulative loss to $2,281.25, Section II, column 5, and Section I, column 11.

## Figure 5-5
## Short U.S. T-Bond Speculative Short Worksheet

**I. Overall Futures Activity**

| (1) | (2) | (3) | (4) | (5) | (6) | (7) | (8) | (9) | (10) | (11) |
|---|---|---|---|---|---|---|---|---|---|---|
| Date | Contract | Unit Price Per $1000 Bond | Number of Units per Contract | Number of Contracts +Long/-Short | Position Value | Position +Gain/-Loss | Total Cash+Margin | Invested Cash+Margin | Commission | Cumulative +Gain/-Loss |
| 1/31/94 | March T-Bonds | $1,171.5625 | 100 | -1 | ($117,156) | $0.00 | $15,000 | $15,000 | | $0.00 |
| 2/1/94 | March T-Bonds | $1,161.8750 | 100 | -1 | ($116,188) | $968.75 | $15,969 | $15,000 | | $968.75 |
| 2/2/94 | March T-Bonds | $1,164.3750 | 100 | -1 | ($116,438) | ($250.00) | $15,719 | $15,000 | | $718.75 |
| 2/3/94 | March T-Bonds | $1,159.6875 | 100 | -1 | ($115,969) | $468.75 | $16,188 | $15,000 | | $1,187.50 |
| 2/4/94 | March T-Bonds | $1,148.7500 | 100 | -1 | ($114,875) | $1,093.75 | $17,281 | $15,000 | | $2,281.25 |
| 2/7/94 | March T-Bonds | $1,148.1250 | 100 | -1 | ($114,813) | $62.50 | $17,344 | $15,000 | | $2,343.75 |
| 2/8/94 | March T-Bonds | $1,142.8125 | 100 | -1 | ($114,281) | $531.25 | $17,875 | $15,000 | | $2,875.00 |

**II. Margin Activity**
Initial Margin Requirement   $2,025 per Contract
Maintenance Margin Requirement   $1,500 per Contract

| (1) | (2) | (3) | (4) | (5) | (6) | (7) | (8) | (9) | (10) |
|---|---|---|---|---|---|---|---|---|---|
| Date | Beginning # of Maintenance Contracts | Margin Account Beginning Balance | Unit Price Change | Position +Gain/-Loss | Interim Margin Balance | Cash Account +From Cash -To Cash | Margin Account Ending Balance | Ending Number of Contracts | Maintenance Requirement |
| 1/31/94 | -1 | $2,025 | 0.0000 | $0.00 | $2,025 | $0 | $2,025 | -1 | $1,500 |
| 2/1/94 | -1 | $2,025 | (9.6875) | $968.75 | $2,994 | $0 | $2,994 | -1 | $1,500 |
| 2/2/94 | -1 | $2,994 | 2.5000 | ($250.00) | $2,744 | $0 | $2,744 | -1 | $1,500 |
| 2/3/94 | -1 | $2,744 | (4.6875) | $468.75 | $3,213 | $0 | $3,213 | -1 | $1,500 |
| 2/4/94 | -1 | $3,213 | (10.9375) | $1,093.75 | $4,306 | $0 | $4,306 | -1 | $1,500 |
| 2/7/94 | -1 | $4,306 | (0.6250) | $62.50 | $4,369 | $0 | $4,369 | -1 | $1,500 |
| 2/8/94 | -1 | $4,369 | (5.3125) | $531.25 | $4,900 | ($4,900) | $0 | -1 | $1,500 |

## Figure 5-5
## Short U.S. T-Bond Speculative Short Worksheet (continued)

III. Cash Activity

| (1) Date | (2) Speculative Cash Beginning Balance | (3) Cash Account Flows + Invested -Withdrawn | (4) Margin Account Flows + From Margin -To Margin | (5) Speculative Cash Ending Balance |
|---|---|---|---|---|
| 1/31/94 | $12,975 | $0 | $0 | $12,975 |
| 2/1/94 | $12,975 | $0 | $0 | $12,975 |
| 2/2/94 | $12,975 | $0 | $0 | $12,975 |
| 2/3/94 | $12,975 | $0 | $0 | $12,975 |
| 2/4/94 | $12,975 | $0 | $0 | $12,975 |
| 2/7/94 | $12,975 | $0 | $0 | $12,975 |
| 2/8/94 | $12,975 | $0 | $4,900 | $17,875 |

This latest loss prompted him to close out his long position, withdraw all remaining funds in his margin account, $713, and deposit them into the speculative account, Section II, columns 7 and 8, and Section III, columns 4 and 5. Thus, after selling a March T-Bond contract, none remained at the end of the day and there was no margin required, Section II, columns 9 and 10. Finally, this speculator suffered a cumulative loss of $2,281.25 in the week between 1/31/94 and 2/4/94.

The differences in outcome for the long speculator and short speculator are to be expected: when speculators assume price risk, there can be only one winner. That is the nature of speculation, and it holds for both physical commodities and financial commodities. Furthermore, speculators and hedgers need each other just as much in the financial commodities markets as in the physical commodities markets. Recall that hedgers seek to eliminate price risk while speculators eagerly accept it. The chapter's next section examines the behavior of hedgers and shows how to transfer interest rate risk effectively in the Treasury Bond market.

## HEDGING

In previous chapters, hedging was explained from two perspectives: that of the commodity producer and that of the commodity user, where the producer was defined as a farmer and the user was defined as a processor. In the normal course of business the farmer was exposed to the risk of a price decline in the finished product, while within the processor's normal course of business an increase in the price of the raw input was the risk that had to be managed. Since both the farmer and processor were subject to the risk of changing prices in the cash commodity, both of them attempted to minimize this risk via the futures markets. The logic is identical for those who use Treasury Bonds in the normal course of their business. In this chapter we will consider two hedgers who want to protect themselves from dramatic changes in interest rates: a bond mutual fund portfolio manager and a securities dealer.

In this example it is assumed that the time is mid-January of 1994 and that the bond mutual fund manager wants to buy $1,000,000 worth of Treasury Bonds at the end of February; the bond manager is short the Treasury Bonds. Since the objective is to buy the bonds at the lowest possible price, the mutual fund manager wants to hedge the effects of falling interest rates and rising bond prices until February 28th. At the same time, the security dealer wants to hedge a long position of $1,000,000 worth of Treasury Bonds, which will be held in inventory until February 28th, against rising interest rates and falling bond prices. To offset their respective cash positions, the securities dealer needs to sell T-Bond futures contracts and the bond mutual fund manager must buy Treasury Bond futures contracts. Selling futures contracts to hedge a long cash position makes the securities dealer a short hedger, and buying futures contracts to hedge a short cash position defines the mutual fund manager as a long hedger. Figures 5-6 and 5-7 present the outcomes from a short hedger and long hedger, respectively.

Both worksheets have the same construction and are composed of five sections. Section I presents data relating to the activity in the hedger's spot market position. Section II shows the behavior of the basis during the hedge's life. The third section displays the hedger's futures market position, while the fourth and fifth sections show the hedger's margin account and cash account activity. Sections I and II are unique to the hedger's worksheet and are explained in detail in the following paragraphs. The remaining three sections of the worksheet—Section III, "Overall Futures Activity; Section IV, "Margin Activity"; and Section V, "Cash Activity"—carry the exact same interpretation as in the speculator's worksheets (Figures 5-4 and 5-5).

Section II of the hedger's worksheet depicts the basis, its incremental change, and its cumulative change. Recall from the discussion in Chapters Two and Four that the basis is the equivalent of having a long position in the spot market and a short position in the futures market, and that the basis has two desirable properties: lower volatility than an open position in either the spot market or the futures market and the convergence of the spot price and futures price to equality at maturity. The financial commodity hedger is trading the relatively higher price volatility of either the cash or the futures market for the more stable and less volatile combined spot and futures position. This behavior is identical to that of the physical commodity hedger. In both cases, the hedger is willing to bear this lower amount of price risk, i.e., the basis volatility, because the effective price of the spot commodity being hedged is much more predictable than if no hedge had been created. The convergence of the spot and futures prices means that the basis becomes zero at maturity. However, prior to maturity the basis can be either positive or negative, thereby creating some opportunities for the hedger to earn a small profit during the life of the hedge as the basis fluctuates. If the basis is becoming more positive, then the commodity's spot, or cash, price is increasing relative to the futures price. On the other hand, if the basis is becoming more negative, then the commodity's spot, or cash, price is decreasing relative to the futures price. A strengthening basis will be profitable if one is long the cash commodity and short the futures contract. A weakening basis will be profitable if one is short the cash commodity and long the futures contract.

These relationships imply certain outcomes for both the short hedger, one who has sold futures contracts to hedge a long spot position, and the long hedger, one who has purchased futures contracts to hedge a short position in the spot market. If the futures contracts are trading at a premium to the spot market, then as the hedge approaches maturity and the basis increases, the short hedger should earn a profit while the long hedger should suffer a loss. Conversely, if the futures contracts are trading at a discount to the spot market, then as the hedge approaches maturity and the basis decreases, the short hedger should suffer a loss while the long hedger should reap a gain.

In Figure 5-6 the short hedger's (or securities dealer's) spot market position in Treasury Bonds is shown as of 1/14/94, in Section I, columns 1, 2, and 4. The cash, or spot, price of 8% equivalent Treasury Bonds that satisfy the terms of the T-Bond futures contract on that day was 99 and 14/32, which translates to a position value of $994,375, columns 3 and 5. Column 6 lists the commodity's unit price change in the cash market, and column 7 expresses the price change as either a gain or loss to the spot position. Column 8 is reserved for any commissions that might be incurred as a result of cash market activity. Column 9 accumulates the gains and losses that accrue to the spot position.

The basis, column 2 of Section II, is computed by subtracting the futures price, Section III, column 3, from the spot price, Section I, column 3. The negative basis of –160.000 for 1/21/94 is consistent with a 99 and 14/32 spot price and a 115 and 14/32 futures price. One week later, 1/21/94, the spot price of bonds rose by 5/32 to 99 and 19/32, Section I, columns 3 and 6; while the March T-Bond futures contract price rose by 25/32 to 116 and 7/32, Section III, column 3, and Section IV, column 4. This caused the basis to weaken and fall to 166.250 for a position loss of $4063.

The short hedger's 25/32 futures position loss—$7,812.5—during the week drove the margin balance below the $15,000 maintenance requirement to $12,438, Section III, column 7, and Section IV, columns 5, and 6, and forced the short hedger to transfer funds from the cash account to the margin account, Section V, column 4. The short hedger had to transfer $7,812.50 to bring the margin account back to $20,250.

By the end of the following week, 1/28/94, bond prices had risen again and the basis had weakened by another $4,062.50 to –$170,312, a $10,313 cumulative loss, Section II, columns 2 and 4. The short hedger's futures position experienced another loss of $12,187.5, which required another funds transfer from the cash account to the margin account, Section IV, columns 5 and 7, and Section V, column 4.

On the day the Federal Reserve announced that it was permitting rates to rise, 2/4/94, the short hedger recouped a large portion of his basis losses. T-Bond spot prices fell by one point and 25/32 from the previous Friday's level of 100–13 to 98–20, while March futures prices dropped by two points and 18/32 to 114–28 from the prior Friday's 117–14. The basis strengthened by $7,812.50, which reduced the short hedger's total loss to $2,500, Section II, columns 3 and 4. The drop in the March bond futures price resulted in a $25,625 gain for the futures position and an increase in the margin account to $45,875.

Over the next week the basis weakened again because the spot prices fell while the March futures prices rose, and the cumulative loss on the basis grew to $11,563, Section I, column 6; Section II, columns 3 and 4; and Section IV, column 4. However, the following week, 2/18/94, saw another large rise in interest rates and a commensurate drop in bond prices. The basis continued to weaken, falling to –$175,312.5, which increased the short hedger's cumulative loss to $15,313. The increase in the short hedger's cumulative loss was due to the spot position losing $28,125, Section I, column 7, while the futures position gained only $24,375.50, Section IV, column 5. This latest bond price decline also caused the short hedger's margin account to increase to $68,063 by the end of trading on 2/18/94, Section IV, column 6.

Finally, by the time the dealer was ready to liquidate his inventory and close out the hedge on 2/28/94, interest rates had risen again. Spot market prices for U.S. T-Bonds stood at 94 and 21/32 and the March T-Bond price settled at 112 and 13/32. The spot position suffered a $47,813 loss, the futures position enjoyed a $30,313 gain, and the basis had weakened to –$177,500 for a cumulative loss of $17,500, Section II, columns 2 and 4.

## Figure 5-6
### U.S. Treasury Bond Short Hedger Worksheet

**I. Overall Spot Activity**

| (1) Date | (2) Spot Commodity | (3) Unit Price Per $1000 Bond | (4) Amount of Spot Commodity | (5) Spot Position Value | (6) Unit Price Change | (7) Spot Position +Gain/-Loss | (8) Commission | (9) Spot Cummulative +Gain/-Loss |
|---|---|---|---|---|---|---|---|---|
| 1/14/94 | US T-Bond | 994.3750 | +10.05 | $999,347 | $0.0000 | $0 | | $0 |
| 1/21/94 | US T-Bond | 995.9375 | +10.05 | $1,000,917 | $1.5625 | $1,570 | | $1,570 |
| 1/28/94 | US T-Bond | 1,004.0625 | +10.05 | $1,009,083 | $8.1250 | $8,166 | | $9,736 |
| 2/4/94 | US T-Bond | 986.2500 | +10.05 | $991,181 | ($17.8125) | ($17,902) | | ($8,166) |
| 2/11/94 | US T-Bond | 979.3750 | +10.05 | $984,272 | ($6.8750) | ($6,909) | | ($15,075) |
| 2/18/94 | US T-Bond | 951.2500 | +10.05 | $956,006 | ($28.1250) | ($28,266) | | ($43,341) |
| 2/28/94 | US T-Bond | 946.5625 | +10.05 | $951,295 | ($4.6875) | ($4,711) | | ($48,052) |

**II. Basis Activity**

| (1) Date | (2) Basis Unit Value Spot Futures | (3) Basis Change | (4) Basis Cumulative +Gain/-Loss |
|---|---|---|---|
| 1/14/94 | -160.0000 | 0 | $0 |
| 1/21/94 | -166.2500 | -6.2500 | ($6,242) |
| 1/28/94 | -170.3125 | -4.0625 | ($10,264) |
| 2/4/94 | -162.5000 | 7.8125 | ($2,541) |
| 2/11/94 | -171.5630 | -9.0630 | ($11,638) |
| 2/18/94 | -175.3125 | -3.7495 | ($15,528) |
| 2/28/94 | -177.5000 | -2.1875 | ($17,739) |

Figure 5-6

## U.S. Treasury Bond Short Hedger Worksheet (continued)

### III. Overall Futures Activity

| (1) Date | (2) Contract | (3) Unit Price Per $1000 Bond | (4) Number of Units per Contract | (5) Number of Contracts +Long/-Short | (6) Futures Position Values | (7) Futures Position +Gain/-Loss | (8) Total Cash+Margin | (9) Invested Cash+Margin | (10) Commission | (11) Futures Cumulative +Gain/-Loss |
|---|---|---|---|---|---|---|---|---|---|---|
| 1/14/94 | US T-Bond | 1,154.3750 | 100 | -10 | ($1,154,375) | $0.00 | $120,250 | $120,250 | | $0 |
| 1/21/94 | US T-Bond | 1,162.1875 | 100 | -10 | ($1,162,188) | ($7,812.50) | $112,438 | $120,250 | | ($7,813) |
| 1/28/94 | US T-Bond | 1,174.3750 | 100 | -10 | ($1,174,375) | ($12,187.50) | $100,250 | $120,250 | | ($20,000) |
| 2/4/94 | US T-Bond | 1,148.7500 | 100 | -10 | ($1,148,750) | $25,625.00 | $125,875 | $120,250 | | $5,625 |
| 2/11/94 | US T-Bond | 1,150.9380 | 100 | -10 | ($1,150,938) | ($2,188.00) | $123,687 | $120,250 | | $3,437 |
| 2/18/94 | US T-Bond | 1,126.5625 | 100 | -10 | ($1,126,563) | $24,375.50 | $148,063 | $120,250 | | $27,813 |
| 2/28/94 | US T-Bond | 1,124.0625 | 100 | -10 | ($1,124,063) | $2,500.00 | $150,563 | $120,250 | | $30,313 |

### IV. Margin Activity

Intitial Margin Requirement $2,025 per Contract
Maintenance Margin Requirement $1,500 per Contract

| (1) Date | (2) Beginning # of Maintenance Contracts | (3) Margin Account Beginning Balance | (4) Unit Price Change | (5) Position +Gain/-Loss | (6) Interim Margin Balance | (7) Cash Account +From Cash -To Cash | (8) Margin Account Ending Balance | (9) Ending Number of Contracts | (10) Maintenance Requirement |
|---|---|---|---|---|---|---|---|---|---|
| 1/14/94 | -10 | $20,250 | 0.0000 | $0.00 | $20,250 | $0 | $20,250 | 10 | $15,000 |
| 1/21/94 | -10 | $20,250 | 7.8125 | ($7,812.50) | $12,438 | $7,812 | $20,250 | 10 | $15,000 |
| 1/28/94 | -10 | $20,250 | 12.1875 | ($12,187.50) | $8,062 | $12,188 | $20,250 | 10 | $15,000 |
| 2/4/94 | -10 | $20,250 | (25.6250) | $25,625.00 | $45,875 | $0 | $45,875 | 10 | $15,000 |
| 2/11/94 | -10 | $45,875 | 2.1880 | ($2,188.00) | $43,687 | $0 | $43,687 | 10 | $15,000 |
| 2/18/94 | -10 | $43,687 | (24.3755) | $24,375.50 | $68,063 | $0 | $68,063 | 10 | $15,000 |
| 2/28/94 | -10 | $68,063 | (2.5000) | $2,500.00 | $70,563 | ($70,563) | $0 | 10 | $15,000 |

## Figure 5-6
### U.S. Treasury Bond Short Hedger Worksheet (continued)

V. Cash Activity

| (1)<br>Date | (2)<br>Carrying<br>Cash Beginning<br>Balance | (3)<br>Cash Account<br>Flows<br>+ Invested<br>- Withdrawn | (4)<br>Margin<br>Account Flows<br>+ From Margin<br>- To Margin | (5)<br>Carrying<br>Cash Ending<br>Balance |
|---|---|---|---|---|
| 1/14/94 | $100,000 | $0 | $0 | $100,000 |
| 1/21/94 | $100,000 | $0 | ($7,812) | $92,188 |
| 1/28/94 | $92,188 | $0 | ($12,188) | $80,000 |
| 2/4/94 | $80,000 | $0 | $0 | $80,000 |
| 2/11/94 | $80,000 | $0 | $0 | $80,000 |
| 2/18/94 | $80,000 | $0 | $0 | $80,000 |
| 2/28/94 | $80,000 | $0 | $70,563 | $150,563 |

This $17,500 loss was far superior to the $47,813 loss that would have occurred if the long cash position in bonds had not been hedged with the short futures position. This becomes obvious when the behaviors of the Treasury Bond spot and futures prices between 1/14/94 and 2/28/94 are examined individually. During this time interest rates rose dramatically and Treasury Bond spot prices fell by 4 and 25/32. Since the securities dealer was long $1,000,000 worth of bonds, their value depreciated by $47,813 during this time period. The effects of this decline in the spot price were minimized by the short position in the futures market, which earned a cumulative gain that amounted to $30,313 Section III, column 11. This gain was the result of the short futures position increasing in value by 3 and 1/32—the difference between the futures contract sales price of 115 and 14/32 on 1/31/94 and the 112 and 13/32 purchase price on 2/28/94. Finally, note that the difference between the $30,313, futures market gain and the $47,813 spot market loss equals $17,500, the exact amount of the cumulative loss in the securities dealer's basis. There can be no other result since the basis is equivalent to having offsetting positions in the cash and futures markets.

Figure 5-7, the long hedger's worksheet, is quite similar to the short hedger's worksheet, Figure 5-6; however, there are some differences. The basic difference between the two worksheets is that the short hedger is long the cash commodity, Treasury Bonds, and is short the futures contract, while the long hedger is short the cash commodity and long the futures contract. This can be seen quite clearly by comparing the signs that precede the spot market positions and futures market positions, Section I, column 4; Section III, column 5; and Section IV, columns 2 and 9. A more significant difference between the two worksheets is shown in Section II, column 4, the cumulative gain or loss to the basis. Notice that all the signs are positive in Figure 5-7, but negative in Figure 5-6. In this example, the long hedger (the bond mutual fund manager) is experiencing a series of gains as the basis weakens. This is exactly opposite the short hedger's outcome portrayed in Figure 5-6.

The most interesting difference between the worksheets is in Sections IV and V, the margin activity and cash activity sections, respectively. Notice that the transfers from the cash account to the margin account occurred on opposite days for the two hedgers. This was because of their opposing positions in the March T-Bond futures contract and the effects of rising interest rates or falling bond prices.

## Figure 5-7
## U.S. Treasury Bond Long Hedger Worksheet

### I. Overall Spot Activity

| (1) Date | (2) Spot Commodity | (3) Unit Price Per $1000 Bond | (4) Amount of Spot Commodity | (5) Spot Position Value | (6) Unit Price Change | (7) Spot Position +Gain/-Loss | (8) Commission | (9) Spot Cummulative +Gain/-Loss |
|---|---|---|---|---|---|---|---|---|
| 1/14/94 | US T-Bond | 994.3750 | -10.05 | ($999,347) | $0.0000 | $0 | | $0 |
| 1/21/94 | US T-Bond | 995.9375 | -10.05 | ($1,000,917) | $1.5625 | ($1,570) | | ($1,570) |
| 1/28/94 | US T-Bond | 1,004.0625 | -10.05 | ($1,009,083) | $8.1250 | ($8,166) | | ($9,736) |
| 2/4/94 | US T-Bond | 986.2500 | -10.05 | ($991,181) | ($17.8125) | $17,902 | | $8,166 |
| 2/11/94 | US T-Bond | 979.3750 | -10.05 | ($984,272) | ($6.8750) | $6,909 | | $15,075 |
| 2/18/94 | US T-Bond | 951.2500 | -10.05 | ($956,006) | ($28.1250) | $28,266 | | $43,341 |
| 2/28/94 | US T-Bond | 946.5625 | -10.05 | ($951,295) | ($4.6875) | $4,711 | | $48,052 |

### II. Basis Activity

| (1) Date | (2) Basis Unit Value Spot Futures | (3) Basis Change | (4) Basis Cumulative +Gain/-Loss |
|---|---|---|---|
| 1/14/94 | -160.0000 | 0 | $0 |
| 1/21/94 | -166.2500 | -6.2500 | $6,242 |
| 1/28/94 | -170.3125 | -4.0625 | $10,264 |
| 2/4/94 | -162.5000 | 7.8125 | $2,541 |
| 2/11/94 | -171.5630 | -9.0630 | $11,638 |
| 2/18/94 | -175.3125 | -3.7495 | $15,528 |
| 2/28/94 | -177.5000 | -2.1875 | $17,739 |

# Figure 5-7

## U.S. Treasury Bond Long Hedger Worksheet (continued)

### III. Overall Futures Activity

| (1) Date | (2) Contract | (3) Unit Price Per $1000 Bond | (4) Number of Units per Contract | (5) Number of Contracts +Long/-Short | (6) Futures Position Values | (7) Futures Position +Gain/-Loss | (8) Total Cash+Margin | (9) Invested Cash+Margin | (10) Commission | (11) Futures Cumulative +Gain/-Loss |
|---|---|---|---|---|---|---|---|---|---|---|
| 1/14/94 | US T-Bond | 1,154.3750 | 100 | +10 | $1,154,375 | $0.00 | $120,250 | $120,250 | | $0 |
| 1/21/94 | US T-Bond | 1,162.1875 | 100 | +10 | $1,162,188 | $7,812.50 | $128,063 | $120,250 | | $7,813 |
| 1/28/94 | US T-Bond | 1,174.3750 | 100 | +10 | $1,174,375 | $12,187.50 | $140,250 | $120,250 | | $20,000 |
| 2/4/94 | US T-Bond | 1,148.7500 | 100 | +10 | $1,148,750 | ($25,625.00) | $114,625 | $120,250 | | ($5,625) |
| 2/11/94 | US T-Bond | 1,150.9380 | 100 | +10 | $1,150,938 | $2,188.00 | $116,813 | $120,250 | | ($3,437) |
| 2/18/94 | US T-Bond | 1,126.5625 | 100 | +10 | $1,126,563 | ($24,375.50) | $92,438 | $120,250 | | ($27,813) |
| 2/28/94 | US T-Bond | 1,124.0625 | 100 | +10 | $1,124,063 | ($2,500.00) | $89,938 | $120,250 | | ($30,313) |

### IV. Margin Activity

Initial Margin Requirement    $2,025 per Contract
Maintenance Margin Requirement    $1,500 per Contract

| (1) Date | (2) Beginning # of Maintenance Contracts | (3) Margin Account Beginning Balance | (4) Unit Price Change | (5) Position +Gain/-Loss | (6) Interim Margin Balance | (7) Cash Account +From Cash -To Cash | (8) Margin Account Ending Balance | (9) Ending Number of Contracts | (10) Maintenance Requirement |
|---|---|---|---|---|---|---|---|---|---|
| 1/14/94 | +10 | $20,250 | 0.0000 | $0.00 | $20,250 | $0 | $20,250 | 10 | $15,000 |
| 1/21/94 | +10 | $20,250 | 7.8125 | $7,812.50 | $28,063 | $0 | $28,063 | 10 | $15,000 |
| 1/28/94 | +10 | $28,063 | 12.1875 | $12,187.50 | $40,250 | $0 | $40,250 | 10 | $15,000 |
| 2/4/94 | +10 | $40,250 | (25.6250) | ($25,625.00) | $14,625 | $5,625 | $20,250 | 10 | $15,000 |
| 2/11/94 | +10 | $20,250 | 2.1880 | $2,188.00 | $22,438 | $0 | $22,438 | 10 | $15,000 |
| 2/18/94 | +10 | $22,438 | (24.3755) | ($24,375.50) | ($1,938) | $22,188 | $20,251 | 10 | $15,000 |
| 2/28/94 | +10 | $20,251 | (2.5000) | ($2,500.00) | $17,751 | ($17,751) | $0 | 10 | $15,000 |

*Figure 5-7*

*U.S. Treasury Bond Long Hedger Worksheet (continued)*

V. Cash Activity

| (1) | (2) | (3) | (4) | (5) |
|-----|-----|-----|-----|-----|
| | Carrying Cash Beginning Balance | Cash Account Flows +Invested -Withdrawn | Margin Account Flows +From Margin -To Margin | Carrying Cash Ending Balance |
| Date | | | | |
| 1/14/94 | $100,000 | $0 | $0 | $100,000 |
| 1/21/94 | $100,000 | $0 | $0 | $100,000 |
| 1/28/94 | $100,000 | $0 | $0 | $100,000 |
| 2/4/94 | $100,000 | $0 | ($5,625) | $94,375 |
| 2/11/94 | $94,375 | $0 | $0 | $94,375 |
| 2/18/94 | $94,375 | $0 | ($22,188) | $72,187 |
| 2/28/94 | $72,187 | $0 | $17,751 | $89,938 |

On 2/4/94, the day of the Federal Reserve announcement, the long hedger's (or mutual fund manager's) margin account suffered an intraday loss of $25,625, Section IV, column 5, which left the margin account balance at $14,625, Section IV, column 6. Since this was far below the $15,000 maintenance requirement for the long 10-contract position, it was necessary to restore the account to its initial margin level of $20,250. This was accomplished by transferring $5,625, the difference between the required $20,250 and the existing $14,625, from the cash account, Section V, column 4, to the margin account, Section IV, column 7, at the end of the trading day. This transfer reduced the balance in the cash account to $94,375, Section V, column 2, and the total cash plus margin account balance to a level of $114,625, Section III, column 8. Notice that the amount transferred from cash to margin, $5,625, is exactly equal to the difference between the short hedger's $120,250 of invested cash and margin, and the amount of that investment which remains, $114,625, Section III, columns 8, 9, and 11. Essentially the same thing occurred on 2/18/94, when the long futures position suffered a $24,375.50 loss which required a $22,188 transfer to the margin account. Recall that these were the best days for the short hedger.

Although the long hedger (the mutual fund manager) lost $30,313 in the futures market and had to transfer some cash to the margin account, the net result was superior to that of the short hedger (the securities dealer). The reason for the long hedger's superior performance is that he was short the basis while the basis weakened. Specifically, during the hedge's life the short cash position's value increased by $47,813, while the long futures position lost $30,313, and the basis weakened from –$160,000 to –$177,500. This resulted in a $17,500 basis gain to the long hedger. Conversely, the short hedger (the securities dealer) was long the basis as it weakened and suffered a $17,500 basis loss. However, the securities dealer was able to mitigate the effects of the dramatic decrease in the cash market price by selling the T-Bond futures contracts.

## SPREADING

The chapter's previous sections examined speculators and hedgers. This section focuses on T-Bond spreaders and intramarket Treasury Bond spreads. The T-Bond spreaders follow the same logic as the soybean spreaders, and employ the same trading strategy of simultaneously buying and selling similar futures contracts. The T-Bond spreader will sell T-Bond futures contracts that appear to be overvalued, or rich, and will purchase T-Bond futures contracts that appear to be undervalued, or cheap.

Recall that the spreader, unlike the hedger, has no use for the physical commodity in the normal course of business and is not interested in assuming large amounts of price risk via long or short open futures positions like the speculator. Thus, the spreader's trading strategy differs from the hedger's in that the spreader never assumes a position in the underlying commodity; and the spreader's strategy is unlike the speculator's since the spreader never takes an outright long or short position in any contract, but always combines a long futures position with a short futures position. Clearly, this overall futures position is much less risky than either the speculator's futures position or the hedger's futures position. Because the spreader assumes less risk than the futures position of both the speculator and hedger, the spreader's margin requirements are lower.

In the spring of 1993 inflation was not a major concern, the economy appeared to be recovering slowly, and interest rates continued to drop. Thus, the time was ripe for a T-Bond bull spread, where the nearby contract is purchased and the deferred contract is sold. The logic for such a spread is that the long position in the nearby contract will appreciate in value by more than the decline in the short position's value in the deferred contract as interest rates decline.

On Thursday, April 1st, 1993, the September Treasury Bond futures contract was priced at 108 and 1/32, and the December Treasury Bond futures contract was trading at 109 and 7/32. The one point and 6/32 difference between their prices defines the value of the September-December T-Bond bull spread. Suppose that a retail customer had $20,000 and wanted to capitalize on falling interest rates and rising bond prices via a bull spread. The customer would simultaneously purchase the June futures contract and sell the September futures contract for a net cost of 1 and 6/32 (or $11,875), post an initial margin of $950 per spread, and maintain a $700 margin balance per spread. Figure 5-8 provides details of this spread.

There are four sections in Figure 5-8, the Spreader Worksheet, that denote the daily outcomes of the June-September bull spread. Section I provides the details of the price changes of both the long and short futures positions that constitute the spread. Section II considers the spread activity in conjunction with the cash and margin positions. Section III, the margin activity, and Section IV, the cash activity, are identical to the margin activity and cash activity sections in the speculator and hedger worksheets, and thus carry the same interpretation.

A close examination of Section I reveals how the spread is constructed, how each component changes value, and how the spread's overall value changes. Column 1 provides the date of each transaction, and shows that the spread was created on 4/01/93 and liquidated on 4/12/93. Columns 2, 3, and 5 show the number and price of the futures contracts that were purchased. In this case, the spreader bought 10 June T-Bond contracts for 109 and 7/32 each. The values in column 4 track the price changes of the long futures contract, and show that the price of the June T-Bond contract generally rose during this spread's life. Columns 6 through 9 are the obverse of columns 2 through 5, and provide information about the short side of the spread. In this case the spreader sold 10 September contracts at 108 and 1/32 to offset the long position in the 10 June contracts. Column 10 shows the actual value of the spread, and is obtained by subtracting the short position's price, column 7, from the long position's price, column 4. The values in column 11 depict the change in the spread's value on a per-unit basis, while the values in column 13 show the spread's total value. The values in column 13 are computed by multiplying the spread's unit value, column 10, by the total number of units in the spread. The total number of units in the spread is computed by multiplying the number of contracts in the spread, column 5, by the number of units per contract, column 12. In this example the spread's value as of 4/01/93, $11,875, is found by multiplying the spread's unit value, $11.875, by 100 units times 10 contracts. The remaining values in column 13 show that the spread rose in value by 3/32, or $937.50, and finished at $12,812.50 on 4/12/93.

Note the similarity in the price behavior of both the June and September contracts, columns 4 and 8. Both contracts exhibited large positive price changes during the 11 days, but the spread's value remained quite stable. It began at $11,875 for a 10-lot position, column 13, and then rose to $12,187.5 on 4/2/93. The spread remained stable between April 2nd and April 7th before rising once again to $12,500 on 4/8/93 for the 10-lot position, column 13. Finally the spread hit $12,812.50 on 2/12/93, when it was liquidated.

Section II shows the spread's price behavior in conjunction with the margin and cash accounts, Sections III and IV, respectively. Column 1 of Section II is the date, while column 2 shows the spread components. The spread is presented with the nearby contract first

## Figure 5-8
## U.S. Treasury Bond Spreader Worksheet

### I. Detailed Futures Activity

| (1) Date | (2) Long Position | (3) Unit Price Per $1000 Bond | (4) Long Units Price Change | (5) Number of Contracts Bought | (6) Short Position | (7) Unit Price | (8) Short Units Price Change | (9) Number of Contracts Bought | (10) Spread Unit Value | (11) Spread Unit Price Change | (12) Number of Units per Contract | (13) Spread Value |
|---|---|---|---|---|---|---|---|---|---|---|---|---|
| 4/1/93 | June Bonds | $1,092.1875 | 0 | +10 | Sep Bonds | $1,080.3125 | 0 | -10 | $11.8750 | 0.0000 | 100 | $11,875.00 |
| 4/2/93 | June Bonds | $1,081.5625 | ($10.63) | +10 | Sep Bonds | $1,069.3750 | ($10.94) | -10 | $12.1875 | 0.3125 | 100 | $12,187.50 |
| 4/5/93 | June Bonds | $1,085.3125 | $3.75 | +10 | Sep Bonds | $1,073.1250 | $3.75 | -10 | $12.1875 | 0.0000 | 100 | $12,187.50 |
| 4/6/93 | June Bonds | $1,093.7500 | $8.44 | +10 | Sep Bonds | $1,081.5625 | $8.44 | -10 | $12.1875 | 0.0000 | 100 | $12,187.50 |
| 4/7/93 | June Bonds | $1,096.8750 | $3.13 | +10 | Sep Bonds | $1,084.3750 | $2.81 | -10 | $12.5000 | 0.3125 | 100 | $12,500.00 |
| 4/8/93 | June Bonds | $1,110.9375 | $14.06 | +10 | Sep Bonds | $1,098.4375 | $14.06 | -10 | $12.5000 | 0.0000 | 100 | $12,500.00 |
| 4/12/93 | June Bonds | $1,118.4375 | $7.50 | +10 | Sep Bonds | $1,105.6250 | $7.19 | -10 | $12.8125 | 0.3125 | 100 | $12,812.50 |

### II. Over All Spread Activity

| (1) Date | (2) Spread | (3) Spread Unit Value | (4) Number of Units Per Contract | (5) Number of Contracts | (6) Spread Value | (7) Spread + Gain / -Loss | (8) Total Cash + Margins | (9) Invested Cash + Margins | (10) Spread Commission | (11) Cumulative + Gain / -Loss |
|---|---|---|---|---|---|---|---|---|---|---|
| 4/1/93 | + June-Sep Bonds | $11.8750 | 100 | 10 | $11,875.00 | $0.00 | $20,000.00 | $20,000 | | $0.00 |
| 4/2/93 | + June-Sep Bonds | $12.1875 | 100 | 10 | $12,187.50 | $312.50 | $20,312.50 | $20,000 | | $312.50 |
| 4/5/93 | + June-Sep Bonds | $12.1875 | 100 | 10 | $12,187.50 | $0.00 | $20,312.50 | $20,000 | | $312.50 |
| 4/6/93 | + June-Sep Bonds | $12.1875 | 100 | 10 | $12,187.50 | $0.00 | $20,312.50 | $20,000 | | $312.50 |
| 4/7/93 | + June-Sep Bonds | $12.5000 | 100 | 10 | $12,500.00 | $312.50 | $20,625.00 | $20,000 | | $625.00 |
| 4/8/93 | + June-Sep Bonds | $12.5000 | 100 | 10 | $12,500.00 | $0.00 | $20,625.00 | $20,000 | | $625.00 |
| 4/12/93 | + June-Sep Bonds | $12.8125 | 100 | 10 | $12,812.50 | $312.50 | $20,937.50 | $20,000 | | $937.50 |

# Figure 5-8
## U.S. Treasury Bond Spreader Worksheet (continued)

III. Margin Activity
Initial Margin Requirement:  $950 per Spread
Maintenance Margin Requirement:  $700 per Spread

| (1) Date | (2) Beginning Number of Contracts | (3) Margin Account Beginning Balance | (4) Spread Unit Price Change | (5) Position + Gain / -Loss | (6) Interim Margin Balance | (7) Ending Number of Contracts | (8) Cash Account + From Cash / -To Cash | (9) Margin Account Ending Balance | (10) Maintenance Requirement |
|---|---|---|---|---|---|---|---|---|---|
| 4/1/93 | 10 | $9,500.00 | 0.0000 | $0.00 | $9,500.00 | 10 | $0 | $9,500.00 | $7,000 |
| 4/2/93 | 10 | $9,500.00 | 0.3125 | $312.50 | $9,812.50 | 10 | $0 | $9,812.50 | $7,000 |
| 4/5/93 | 10 | $9,812.50 | 0.0000 | $0.00 | $9,812.50 | 10 | $0 | $9,812.50 | $7,000 |
| 4/6/93 | 10 | $9,812.50 | 0.0000 | $0.00 | $9,812.50 | 10 | $0 | $9,812.50 | $7,000 |
| 4/7/93 | 10 | $9,812.50 | 0.3125 | $312.50 | $10,125.00 | 10 | $0 | $10,125.00 | $7,000 |
| 4/8/93 | 10 | $10,125.00 | 0.0000 | $0.00 | $10,125.00 | 10 | $0 | $10,125.00 | $7,000 |
| 4/12/93 | 10 | $10,125.00 | 0.3125 | $312.50 | $10,437.50 | 0 | ($10,437.50) | $0 | $0 |

IV. Cash Activity

| (1) Date | (2) Reserve Cash Beginning Balance | (3) Cash Account Flows + Invested / -Withdrawn | (4) Margin Account Flows + From Margin / -To Margin | (5) Reserve Ending Balance |
|---|---|---|---|---|
| 4/1/93 | $10,500 | $0 | $0 | $10,500.00 |
| 4/2/93 | $10,500 | $0 | $0 | $10,500.00 |
| 4/5/93 | $10,500 | $0 | $0 | $10,500.00 |
| 4/6/93 | $10,500 | $0 | $0 | $10,500.00 |
| 4/7/93 | $10,500 | $0 | $0 | $10,500.00 |
| 4/8/93 | $10,500 | $0 | $0 | $10,500.00 |
| 4/12/93 | $10,500 | $0 | $10,437.50 | $20,937.50 |

and the deferred contract second, because this is how the spread is quoted. The plus sign that precedes the abbreviation Jun denotes that the spreader has bought June T-Bond contracts, while the minus sign that precedes the abbreviation Sep indicates that the spreader has sold September T-Bond contracts. The next column, column 3, is identical to column 10 of Section I, and shows the spread's unit value. Column 4 provides the number of units per contract to denote the size of the position. In this case the spreader's position consists of 10 lots, column 5, since 10 June contracts were bought and 10 September contracts were sold. Column 6 in Section II is obtained by multiplying columns 3, 4, and 5 together. This number should be equal to the value for the corresponding date in column 13 in Section I, since both have the same meaning. The next column, column 7, tracks the daily gain or loss for the spread. The gains and losses are computed by taking the current value of the spread in column 6 and subtracting the prior day's value. For example, the $312.50 is found by subtracting the 4/1/93 value, $11,875, from the 4/2/93 value, $12,187.5: $12,187.5 − $11,875 = $312.50. Column 8 provides the total cash and margin available to the spreader. This amount will change from day to day as the spread experiences gains and losses. Column 9 shows how much money the spreader has allocated for this strategy. In this case the spreader made a commitment of $20,000. Column 10 provides for commissions, and column 11 shows the spread's cumulative gain or loss. The values in column 11 are computed by subtracting the amount of cash and margin invested in the strategy, column 9, from the current value of the total cash plus margin balance, column 8. For example, the spread's cumulative gain on 4/7/93 of $625 was computed by subtracting the amount of invested cash plus margin, $20,000, from the total cash plus margin amount of $20,625.

The worksheet's final two sections, III and IV, must be considered jointly. Observe that the spreader's margin requirements, $950 initial margin and $700 maintenance margin, are much lower than the margin requirements of both the speculator and the hedger. Recall that the initial margin for either a long or short position in the T-Bond futures market was $2,025 per contract, and that the maintenance requirement was $1,500 per contract. Since the spreader has a 10-lot position, column 2, the initial balance is $9,500, column 3, and the maintenance requirement is $7,000, column 10. This $9,500 initial margin balance is only a portion of the $20,000 that the spreader has allocated for this strategy. The remaining $10,500 is being held in reserve in a highly liquid account, such as a checking account. It should be mentioned that the spreader's cash and margin position is sufficient to withstand only four days of maximum margin calls of $250 per spread: $250 times 10 contracts = $2,500 per day; 4 days times 2,500 = $10,000. This violates the five-day rule of thumb, but should be sufficient for a spreader, since having offsetting positions in the futures market via a spread is much less volatile than having a single futures position such as that of a speculator or hedger. Section IV documents the activity for this cash reserve account.

Section III records the effects of the changing futures contract prices on the spreader's margin account. The values in columns 4 and 5 track the spread's unit price change and daily gain or loss. The information in column 4, the spread unit price change, corresponds to Section I, column 11, while the data shown in column 5 of Section III, the position gain or loss, matches the data in Section II, column 7. The values in column 6 show the margin balance prior to marking to market, and alert the spreader to the possibility of having to either post more cash or liquidate part of the position. During the spread's 11-day lifespan it widened and rose in value from $11,875 to $12,812.50, Section I, column 13, so that on 4/12/93 the margin balance had grown to $10,437.50, Section III, column 6. At this time the spreader decided to liquidate the position and take the $937.50 profit, Section II, column 11. Thus, all the positions were closed out and the margin balance was transferred to the cash account, Section IV, column 4, which resulted in an ending balance of $20,937.50, Section IV, column 5, and Section II, column 8.

## SUMMARY

This chapter has examined various Treasury Bond trading strategies via the relationships that link the Treasury Bond cash and futures markets. The chapter began with a discussion of the U.S. Treasury Bond market and an explanation of Treasury Bond price quotes as reported in *The Wall Street Journal* and *Barron's*. Next, the role of the Federal Reserve was analyzed, and its impact on the bond markets in general was explored. The chapter continued with a discussion of speculators, hedgers, and spreaders, and considered long and short speculative positions; long and short hedged positions; and the intramarket, or time spread. Worksheets were developed for each type of strategy, and were used to explain and illustrate clearly how profits are made and losses incurred in the Treasury Bond futures market.

# Chapter 6

# STOCK INDEX TRADING STRATEGIES

## PRICE QUOTES

This chapter continues the analysis of financial futures contracts by focusing on the behavior of the Standard and Poor's 500 Stock Index futures contract. Stock indexes are portfolios which are composed of many companies' shares. Different indexes have different values because of the composite shares' performance, and also because of how the shares are weighted in the index. The S&P 500 Index is a value-weighted combination of 500 different companies, representing approximately 80 percent of the value of all the shares traded on the New York Stock Exchange, where each company's weight in the Index is determined by its relative market importance. The S&P 500 Index values are computed by multiplying each company's number of outstanding shares of common stock by the share's current cash market price. Then, these values are summed and compared to a 1941–1943 base period. Finally, the cash value of the S&P Index is determined by multiplying the Index value by $500.

Figure 6-1 shows futures price quotes from *The Wall Street Journal* as of the close of trading on Wednesday, March 16, 1994. Information regarding the Chicago Mercantile Exchange's S&P 500 futures contract is presented in the familiar standardized format. This format conveys such information as the trading location of the futures contracts; the size and unit value of the financial futures contracts; the

*Figure 6-1*
*Future Prices*

Wednesday, March 16, 1994.
**Open Interest Reflects Previous Trading Day.**

| | | | | | Lifetime | | Open |
|---|---|---|---|---|---|---|---|
| Open | High | Low | Settle | Change | High | Low | Interest |

# INDEX

**S&P 500 INDEX (CME) $500 times index**

| | Open | High | Low | Settle | Chg | High | Low | Open Interest |
|---|---|---|---|---|---|---|---|---|
| Mar | 466.60 | 470.20 | 465.55 | 469.25 | + 2.95 | 483.10 | 434.00 | 71,707 |
| June | 467.60 | 471.45 | 466.75 | 470.65 | + 3.00 | 484.00 | 444.50 | 158,270 |
| Sept | 469.25 | 473.30 | 468.90 | 472.60 | + 3.00 | 485.20 | 452.20 | 4,155 |
| Dec | 472.65 | 475.35 | 471.25 | 475.00 | + 3.10 | 487.10 | 463.20 | 4,011 |

Est vol 103,726; vol Thur 114,304; open int 238,143, +8,644.
Indx prelim High 469.85; Low 465.48; Close 469.42 +2.41

**S&P MIDCAP 400 (CME) $500 times index**

| Mar | 181.90 | 182.95 | 181.80 | 182.85 | + 1.45 | 184.30 | 157.65 | 7,669 |
|---|---|---|---|---|---|---|---|---|
| June | 183.25 | 184.25 | 183.05 | 184.20 | + 1.55 | 184.40 | 165.65 | 7,126 |
| Sept | 184.95 | 185.55 | 184.95 | 185.55 | + 1.55 | 185.55 | 171.60 | 116 |

Est vol 3,338; vol Tues 2,328; open int 14,926, +596.
The index: High 183.08; Low 181.64; Close 183.01 +1.44

**NIKKEI 225 Stock Average (CME) −$5 times Index**

| June | 20900. | 20900. | 20830. | 20845. | + 50.0 | 21700. | 16100. | 19,874 |
|---|---|---|---|---|---|---|---|---|

Est vol 1,166; vol Thur 11,868; open int 19,940, +630.
The index: High 20781.98; Low 20518.05; Close 20677.77 +168.92

**NYSE COMPOSITE INDEX (NYFE) 500 times index**

| Mar | 259.10 | 260.90 | 258.50 | 260.65 | + 1.90 | 267.85 | 246.60 | 3,167 |
|---|---|---|---|---|---|---|---|---|
| June | 259.50 | 261.40 | 258.75 | 261.10 | + 1.90 | 267.90 | 250.25 | 2,748 |

Est vol 4,088; vol Tues 3,264; open int 5,956, +26.
The index: High 260.52; Low 258.39; Close 260.34 +1.35

contracts' price changes; and the quantity of contracts traded and held by market participants.

For example, the price quotes show that S&P 500 futures contracts are traded on the Chicago Mercantile Exchange (CME), where contract maturities follow a quarterly cycle of December, March, June, and September. Trading is active in four S&P 500 futures contracts maturing between March and December of 1994. These S&P 500 futures prices are quoted in points, with one point equal to $500, and each price change increment, or tick, being equal to .05 of a point, or $25 per contract. The "Open" column shows that the March 1994 contract began the trading day at a price of 466.60, or 466.60 points, which equals $233,300 per contract, $500 times 466.60. During the day, the highest price for March 1994 S&P 500 futures was 470.20, or $235,100, while the lowest price was 465.55, or $232,775 per contract. These levels are indicated by the "High" and "Low" columns, respectively. The "Settle" column denotes that the March 1994 S&P 500 futures contract closed, or settled, at a price of 469.25, $234,625 per contract, at the end of the trading day. Notice the plus signs in the "Change" column for all of the S&P 500 futures contracts. These signs indicate that all of the futures contracts enjoyed a price increase over the settlement price from the prior trading day, Tuesday, March 15, 1994. Specifically, the March 94 contract increased by 2.95 points, while the June 94 and September 94 contracts rose by 3.00 points and the December 94 contract increased by 3.10 points over the previous day's settlement price. The next two columns deal with the contracts' lifetime "High" and "Low" and show that the March S&P 500 contract has traded as high as 483.10 and as low as 434, the June 1994 contract has fluctuated between 484 and 444.50, the September 1990 contract has ranged between 485.20 and 452.20, and the December 1994 contract has drifted between 487.10 and 463.20. The last column, "Open Interest," reveals that there are 71,707 long positions in March 1994 S&P 500 futures contracts which are outstanding; 158,270 long positions in the June 1994 contract; 4,155 long positions in the September contract; and 4,011 open long positions in the December 1994 contract. "Est vol 103,726" indicates that Wednesday's estimated trading volume was 103,726 for all S&P futures contracts, while "vol Thur" appears to be a misprint. It should actually be "vol Tues," which shows that Tuesday's actual volume was 114,304 S&P futures contracts. Finally, the total open interest for the S&P 500 futures contracts is 238,143, which is 8,644 contracts more than the previous trading day's open interest as indicated by "open int 238,143 +8,644."

The *Barron's* index futures data, Figure 6-2, are similiar to *The Wall Street Journal* data and are arranged to show the contracts' "Season," or lifetime, "High" and "Low," followed by the week's "High" price, "Low" price, closing price, net change in price, and open interest. "Fri. to Thurs. sales" and "Total open interest" provide the total contract volume and sales for the most recent trading week. Notice that the S&P 500 futures contract data are very similar in both Figures 6-1 and 6-2. However, the *Barron's* data shows an "x" where the information pertaining to the March 1994 S&P futures contract should be. The reason is that the March S&P 500 futures contract expired on the previous Friday, March 18th. Any other differences that occur between Figures 6-1 and 6-2 are due to the *Barron's* data encompassing a week's worth of trading while *The Wall Street Journal* data are reported daily.

## *SPECULATING*

In Chapter Two the behavior of both spot prices and futures prices was discussed for agricultural commodities, debt instruments, and equity instruments. It was shown that equity values depend upon the interaction between the required rate of return (i.e., an interest rate adjusted for risk) and the long-run growth rate in dividends and earnings. Recall that it is easier to predict the effects of changing interest rates on debt instruments, since their prices move inversely to interest rates, than to predict the effects of changing interest rates on equities. It is quite possible that share prices actually will rise when interest rates are rising because the economy is very robust and growth rates are rising by more than the increase in interest rates. Conversely, it is possible that share prices will decline when interest rates are dropping because the economy is in a recession and a company is not expected to grow as rapidly as in the past. Although interest rates and changing equity values cannot be forecast with a great deal of precision, it is still important that one understand the influence of the Federal Reserve Board on interest rates.

In the previous chapter, the Federal Reserve Board's influence on interest rates and bond prices was explained. The explanation concentrated on the Federal Reserve Board's concern for economic stability, and its response to the economic forces of inflation and recession that threaten such stability. It is this response to these forces that will dictate the direction of interest rates. If inflation is cause for concern, then the Federal Reserve can be expected to follow a restrictive

## Figure 6-2
### Commodities and Financial Futures

# BARRON'S • MARKET WEEK

#### March 21, 1994

## INDEX FUTURES

**CRB INDEX X 500**
points and cents
| | | | | | | | |
|---|---|---|---|---|---|---|---|
| 230.65 | 216.50 | May | 230.65 | 228.40 | 229.45 | +1.25 | 1,482 |
| 230.75 | 218.70 | Jul | 230.75 | 228.90 | 229.85 | +1.45 | 754 |
| 231.20 | 224.25 | Sep | 231.20 | 229.10 | 230.25 | +1.65 | |
| 231.70 | 228.10 | Dec | 231.70 | 229.70 | 230.65 | +1.65 | 15 |

Last index 228.57, up 1.23
Fri. to Thurs. sales 1,985.
Total open interest 2,636

**EUROTOP 100**
$100 x index
| | | | | | | | |
|---|---|---|---|---|---|---|---|
| 1336.00 | 1229.90 | Jun | 1279.90 | 1254.00 | 1258.00 | +12.80 | 785 |
| 1286.00 | 1228.00 | Sep | 1286.00 | ...... | 1270.00 | +12.80 | 208 |
| 1300.00 | 1300.00 | Dec | 1300.00 | ...... | 1288.00 | +12.80 | 1 |

Last spot 1244.20, up 14.80
Fri. to Thurs. sales 1,795.
Total open interest 1,076

**GSCI**
$250 x GSCI Nearby Index
| | | | | | | | |
|---|---|---|---|---|---|---|---|
| 173.80 | 168.60 | Apr | 173.10 | 169.20 | 171.40 | +1.40 | 1,675 |
| 172.50 | 169.90 | Jun | 172.50 | ...... | 171.20 | +1.70 | 1,365 |
| 170.70 | 170.70 | Aug | 170.70 | ...... | 170.60 | +2.20 | 2 |

Last spot 171.64, up 2.23
Fri. to Thurs. sales 1,473.
Total open interest 3,042

**MAJ. MKT. INDEX X 500**
mmi+500 x index
| | | | | | | | |
|---|---|---|---|---|---|---|---|
| 399.30 | 374.25 | Mar | 387.50 | 381.50 | 387.50 | +4.35 | 2,739 |
| 389.90 | 378.00 | Jul | 385.90 | 382.30 | 384.00 | +.40 | 1,170 |
| 384.50 | 384.50 | May | 384.50 | ...... | 383.85 | +.50 | 60 |
| 392.00 | 362.35 | Jun | ...... | ...... | 384.00 | +.50 | 28 |
| 379.50 | 379.50 | Sep | ...... | ...... | 385.35 | +.50 | 23 |
| 396.10 | 356.50 | Dec | ...... | ...... | 386.25 | +.50 | 128 |

Last spot 387.46, up 3.83
Fri. to Thurs. sales 3,140.
Total open interest 4,148

**NIKKEI 225 AVGS.**
$5 x nsa
| | | | | | | | | |
|---|---|---|---|---|---|---|---|---|
| 20900 | 20450 | Jun | 20900 | | 20590 | 20590 | +285 | 20,631 |
| 20565 | 18115 | Dec | | | | 20850 | +390 | 14 |
| 20410 | 16240 | Sep | | | | 20950 | | 1 |
| | | Mar | | | | 20810 | +400 | 51 |

Fri. to Thurs. sales 5,867.
Total open interest 20,697

**NYSE COMP. INDEX**
points and cents
| | | | | | | | |
|---|---|---|---|---|---|---|---|
| 267.90 | 247.00 | Jun | 261.60 | 258.70 | 260.65 | +1.60 | 2,922 |
| 267.00 | 256.20 | Sep | 262.10 | 260.05 | 261.50 | +1.75 | |
| 264.50 | 237.15 | Dec | 262.60 | 260.70 | 262.25 | +1.80 | 36 |

Last index 261.35, up 2.82
Fri. to Thurs. sales 15,996.
Total open interest 5,894

| Season's | | STOCK | 2000 | Week's | | | PRICE | Net | INDEX | Open |
|---|---|---|---|---|---|---|---|---|---|---|
| High | Low | | | High | Low | Sett | | Chg | | Int. |

**RUSSELL 2000**
$500 x Russell
| | | | | | | | | |
|---|---|---|---|---|---|---|---|---|
| 272.80 | 266.20 | Jun | 272.80 | 267.50 | 272.30 | +5.50 | 1,108 |
| 270.00 | 269.45 | Sep | 270.00 | 269.45 | 273.10 | +3.60 | 12 |
| 275.75 | 271.90 | Dec | 275.75 | ...... | 274.00 | +3.45 | 40 |

Last spot 271.07, up 5.58
Fri. to Thurs. sales 925.
Total open interest 3,876

**S&P COMP. INDEX**
500 x index
| | | | | | | | | |
|---|---|---|---|---|---|---|---|---|
| 484.00 | 448.00 | Jun | 472.00 | 466.50 | 470.15 | +2.75 | 176,771 |
| 485.20 | 460.00 | Sep | 474.10 | 468.60 | 472.25 | +2.80 | 4,306 |
| 487.10 | 429.70 | Dec | 475.90 | 471.25 | 474.15 | +2.40 | 4,040 |

Last spot 471.06, up 4.62
Fri. to Thurs. sales 519,572.
Total open interest 246,679

**S&P MIDCAP INDEX**
$500 x index
| | | | | | | | | |
|---|---|---|---|---|---|---|---|---|
| 184.30 | 160.70 | Mar | 183.75 | 181.25 | 183.70 | +2.40 | 7,057 |
| 185.45 | 173.00 | Jun | 185.45 | 182.30 | 184.65 | +2.30 | 10,760 |
| 186.70 | 171.60 | Sep | 186.70 | 183.90 | 185.00 | +1.55 | 118 |
| 187.05 | 165.25 | Dec | 187.05 | ...... | 186.80 | +2.20 | 15 |

Last spot 184.79, up 3.81
Fri. to Thurs. sales 16,853.
Total open interest 17,950

**US DOLLAR INDEX**
points and cents
| | | | | | | | | |
|---|---|---|---|---|---|---|---|---|
| 99.04 | 54.70 | Jun | 95.35 | 94.30 | 95.20 | +.75 | 4,793 |
| 98.55 | 95.05 | Sep | ...... | ...... | 95.65 | +.70 | |
| 99.00 | 0.04 | Dec | ...... | ...... | 96.00 | +.65 | |
| | | Mar | ...... | ...... | 96.35 | ..... | |

Last spot 94.57, up 0.66
Fri. to Thurs. sales 8,600.
Total open interest 4,817

**VALUE LINE**
points and cents
| | | | | | | | | |
|---|---|---|---|---|---|---|---|---|
| 476.75 | 415.40 | Mar | 476.75 | 467.10 | 476.75 | +9.15 | 1,150 |
| 476.70 | 434.25 | Jun | 476.70 | 469.30 | 476.00 | +6.20 | 625 |
| 472.50 | 469.00 | Sep | ...... | ...... | 477.70 | +5.70 | 3 |

Last spot 476.75, up 8.97
Fri. to Thurs. sales 1,827.
Total open interest 1,778

monetary policy, resulting in rising interest rates. On the other hand, the Federal Reserve can be expected to increase the money supply when the economy appears headed for a recession, which will result in falling interest rates. In general, falling interest rates will result in higher debt and equity prices; while rising interest rates will cause debt and equity prices to decline.

The earlier chapters on soybeans and Treasury Bonds explored commodity price behavior from the autumn of 1992 through the spring of 1994, when there was a dramatic change in interest rates. The behavior of the S&P 500 Index also will be analyzed in this environment to maintain consistency with the earlier chapters. Recall that in the fall of 1992 inflation appeared to be less threatening than recession. Market interest rates dropped steadily throughout the fourth quarter of 1992, and continued to drop in the first quarter of 1993. The Federal Reserve was being pressured to ease credit, and responded by allowing short-term rates to drop below $3\frac{1}{2}\%$ by November of 1992. It appeared that the central bank was less concerned about inflation and was determined to keep the economic recovery on track.

Figure 6-3 presents the behavior of the S&P 500 index between January of 1989 and March of 1994. Notice that the stock market responded positively to the lower interest rates and the subsequent economic recovery. The index rose steadily from November of 1992, when the Federal Reserve let it be known that the target for short-term rates was 3%, until February of 1994 when the target was increased to $3\frac{1}{4}\%$.

Given the economic environment in early 1993, it appeared that one would be able to reap some speculative profits by purchasing, or going long, S&P 500 futures contracts. This is not as easy as it sounds for a small retail investor because of the extremely high speculative margin requirements associated with the S&P 500 futures contract. For example, prior to the October 1987 crash the initial speculative margin was $10,000 per contract, while the maintenance margin was $5,000 per contract. On November 1st, 1987—approximately two weeks after the crash—the initial margin had been increased to $20,000, and the maintenance margin had been raised to $12,500. These actions had been taken by the Clearing Corporation to insure that there was sufficient cash on deposit in an extremely volatile stock market. However, by the spring of 1988 the stock market volatility had declined from the much higher November levels so that the initial margin had been reduced to $17,500, and the maintenance

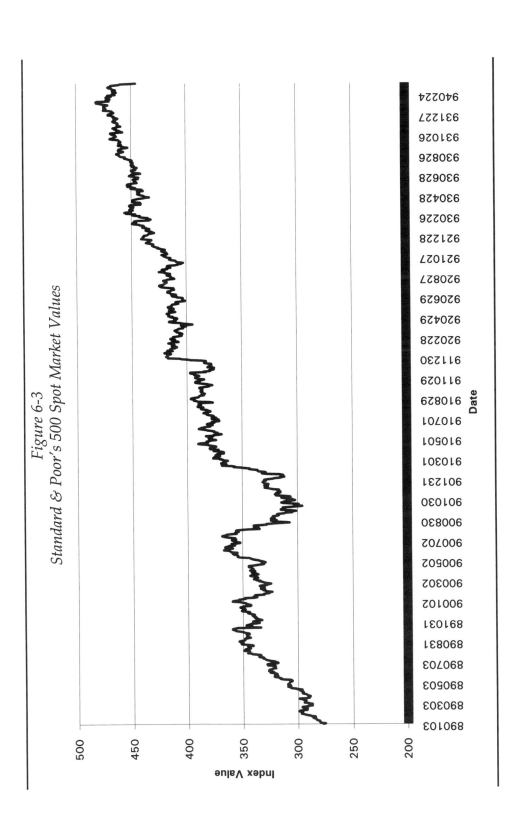

Figure 6-3
Standard & Poor's 500 Spot Market Values

margin had been dropped to $6,000. By January 1993 the initial speculative margin for an S&P 500 futures contract was $11,250 per contract, and the maintenance margin per contract was $10,000.

These much higher, post-crash margin levels reflected both higher market volatility and the imposition of "circuit breakers" by the federal government. These "circuit breakers" effectively established a 35-point daily trading limit for the S&P 500 futures contracts: trading would be halted and the S&P 500 futures would be "locked" after a 35-point move in either direction from the previous day's closing S&P 500 value. Note that the $17,500 initial margin is exactly equal in value to 35 S&P 500 Index points at $500 per point. This 35 S&P 500 Index point move is approximately equal to a 250 Dow-Jones Industrial Average point move. Prior to the federal "circuit breakers" there had not been a daily limit on the S&P 500 futures contracts.

These high speculative margins make it quite difficult for most small investors to take a position in S&P 500 futures contracts. Adhering to the 5-day limit move rule of thumb requires $87,500 per contract: $500 times 35 points times 5 days for each contract. Suppose that a small retail investor had only a small fraction of the recommended $87,500, $20,000, and that he wanted to speculate on the anticipated increase in the stock market in January of 1993. If this investor's broker requires speculators to post an initial margin of $11,250 per contract, and then maintain a margin of at least $10,000 per contract, then a trading worksheet like that of Figure 6-4 is a good representation of this speculator's long position in S&P 500 futures contracts between January 8th and January 25th of 1993.

Figure 6-4, the long S&P speculator's worksheet, is divided into three sections, with the columns in each section being numbered appropriately. Section I provides a listing of the speculative position's overall activity. Section II gives a detailed account of the margin activity that occurs during the time that the position is open. Finally, the third section provides a record of the amount of cash that was invested and withdrawn from the position.

Columns 1 and 2 in the first section show that the speculator opened the position on January 8th in the March S&P 500 futures contract. Column 3 shows that the March S&P contract had an index value of 429.70. The fourth column shows that each point of the S&P 500 futures contract is worth $500, and the fifth column shows that the speculator's initial purchase was one contract. The position's value of $214,850 in the sixth column is obtained by first multiplying the index point value, column 3, by the contract's value per point,

## Figure 6-4
### Standard & Poor's 500 Long Speculation Worksheet

**I. Overall Futures Activity**

| (1) Date | (2) Contract | (3) Unit Price | (4) Number of Units per Contract | (5) Number of Contracts +Long/-Short | (6) Position Value | (7) Position +Gain/-Loss | (8) Total Cash+Margin | (9) Invested Cash+Margin | (10) Commission | (11) Cumulative +Gain/-Loss |
|---|---|---|---|---|---|---|---|---|---|---|
| 1/8/93 | March S&P 500 | 429.70 | $500 | +1 | $214,850 | $0.00 | $20,000 | $20,000 | | $0 |
| 1/11/93 | March S&P 500 | 431.00 | $500 | +1 | $215,500 | $650.00 | $20,650 | $20,000 | | $650 |
| 1/12/93 | March S&P 500 | 431.45 | $500 | +1 | $215,725 | $225.00 | $20,875 | $20,000 | | $875 |
| 1/13/93 | March S&P 500 | 433.35 | $500 | +1 | $216,675 | $950.00 | $21,825 | $20,000 | | $1,825 |
| 1/14/93 | March S&P 500 | 436.30 | $500 | +1 | $218,150 | $1,475.00 | $23,300 | $20,000 | | $3,300 |
| 1/15/93 | March S&P 500 | 436.45 | $500 | +1 | $218,225 | $75.00 | $23,375 | $20,000 | | $3,375 |
| 1/18/93 | March S&P 500 | 437.30 | $500 | +1 | $218,650 | $425.00 | $23,800 | $20,000 | | $3,800 |
| 1/19/93 | March S&P 500 | 435.55 | $500 | +1 | $217,775 | ($875.00) | $22,925 | $20,000 | | $2,925 |
| 1/20/93 | March S&P 500 | 433.15 | $500 | +1 | $216,575 | ($1,200.00) | $21,725 | $20,000 | | $1,725 |
| 1/21/93 | March S&P 500 | 436.30 | $500 | +1 | $218,150 | $1,575.00 | $23,300 | $20,000 | | $3,300 |
| 1/22/93 | March S&P 500 | 436.65 | $500 | +1 | $218,325 | $175.00 | $23,475 | $20,000 | | $3,475 |
| 1/25/93 | March S&P 500 | 440.35 | $500 | +1 | $220,175 | $1,850.00 | $25,325 | $20,000 | | $5,325 |

**II. Margin Activity**
Initial Margin Requirement  $11,250 per Contract
Maintenance Margin Requirement  $10,000 per Contract

| (1) Date | (2) Beginning # of Maintenance Contracts | (3) Margin Account Beginning Balance | (4) Unit Price Change | (5) Position +Gain/-Loss | (6) Interim Margin Balance | (7) Cash Account +From Cash -To Cash | (8) Margin Account Ending Balance | (9) Ending Number of Contracts | (10) Maintenance Requirement |
|---|---|---|---|---|---|---|---|---|---|
| 1/8/93 | +1 | $11,250 | 0 | $0 | $11,250 | $0 | $11,250 | +1 | $10,000 |
| 1/11/93 | +1 | $11,250 | 1.3000 | $650 | $11,900 | $0 | $11,900 | +1 | $10,000 |
| 1/12/93 | +1 | $11,900 | 0.4500 | $225 | $12,125 | $0 | $12,125 | +1 | $10,000 |
| 1/13/93 | +1 | $12,125 | 1.9000 | $950 | $13,075 | $0 | $13,075 | +1 | $10,000 |
| 1/14/93 | +1 | $13,075 | 2.9500 | $1,475 | $14,550 | $0 | $14,550 | +1 | $10,000 |
| 1/15/93 | +1 | $14,550 | 0.1500 | $75 | $14,625 | $0 | $14,625 | +1 | $10,000 |
| 1/18/93 | +1 | $14,625 | 0.8500 | $425 | $15,050 | $0 | $15,050 | +1 | $10,000 |
| 1/19/93 | +1 | $15,050 | -1.7500 | ($875) | $14,175 | $0 | $14,175 | +1 | $10,000 |
| 1/20/93 | +1 | $14,175 | -2.4000 | ($1,200) | $12,975 | $0 | $12,975 | +1 | $10,000 |
| 1/21/93 | +1 | $12,975 | 3.1500 | $1,575 | $14,550 | $0 | $14,550 | +1 | $10,000 |
| 1/22/93 | +1 | $14,550 | 0.3500 | $175 | $14,725 | $0 | $14,725 | +1 | $10,000 |
| 1/25/93 | +1 | $14,725 | 3.7000 | $1,350 | $16,575 | ($16,575) | $0 | 0 | $0 |

## Figure 6-4
## Standard & Poor's 500 Long Speculation Worksheet *(continued)*

III. Cash Activity

| (1) Date | (2) Speculative Cash Beginning Balance | (3) Cash Account Flows + Invested - Withdrawn | (4) Margin Account Flows + From Margin - To Margin | (5) Speculative Cash Ending Balance |
|---|---|---|---|---|
| 1/8/93 | $8,750 | $0 | $0 | $8,750 |
| 1/11/93 | $8,750 | $0 | $0 | $8,750 |
| 1/12/93 | $8,750 | $0 | $0 | $8,750 |
| 1/13/93 | $8,750 | $0 | $0 | $8,750 |
| 1/14/93 | $8,750 | $0 | $0 | $8,750 |
| 1/15/93 | $8,750 | $0 | $0 | $8,750 |
| 1/18/93 | $8,750 | $0 | $0 | $8,750 |
| 1/19/93 | $8,750 | $0 | $0 | $8,750 |
| 1/20/93 | $8,750 | $0 | $0 | $8,750 |
| 1/21/93 | $8,750 | $0 | $0 | $8,750 |
| 1/22/93 | $8,750 | $0 | $0 | $8,750 |
| 1/25/93 | $8,750 | $0 | $16,575 | $25,325 |

column 4, to get the contract value, and then multiplying the result by the number of contracts in the position, column 5. The seventh column simply provides the position's daily gains and losses. The remaining columns must be interpreted in reference to the other two sections of the worksheet.

Column 8 in Section I shows exactly how much of the speculator's money remains. This balance is composed of the amount that has been posted with the broker as margin and the amount of cash that can be used to fund the position if the market moves against the speculator. The amount in Section I, column 8, must equal the sum of the day's ending margin account balance, Section II, column 8, and the day's ending speculative cash balance, Section III, column 5. The amount of cash plus margin available to the speculator will fluctuate each day as the position gains or loses value. The next column in Section I, column 9, shows the total amount of money that the speculator has invested in the position. This is composed of the initial margin, Section II, column 3, plus the amount of cash that has been held in reserve to fund the position in the event of adverse market movements, Section III, column 2. Column 10 is reserved for commissions. Once again, commissions can vary widely throughout the industry; thus, they are not included in the various examples. Be certain that you have a thorough understanding of your broker's commission schedule. The final column in Section I, column 11, shows the strategy's cumulative gain or loss. It is computed by subtracting column 9, the amount invested in cash and margin, from column 8, the total cash and margin balance. When appropriate, commissions should also be subtracted from the total cash plus margin amount in column 8. The amount in column 11 of Section I must agree with the position gains and losses and any cash flows reflected in the margin account, Section II, column 8.

The speculative worksheet's second section provides information about the speculator's margin activity, and begins with a listing of the margin requirements. In this example the speculator must post an initial margin of $11,250 per S&P 500 futures contract purchased, and the margin account must have a minimum balance equal to $10,000 per contract at all times. If the margin balance falls below the minimum requirement, then the speculator is required to restore the margin account to a level that is consistent with the initial margin requirement. This can be accomplished in one of two ways: either more cash can be added to the margin account, or enough of the position can be liquidated so that the remaining margin balance is greater than or equal to the initial margin requirement for the remaining contracts.

The remainder of Section II is divided into 10 columns that provide daily data about the margin account. Columns 1 and 2 of Section II are self-explanatory and correspond to columns 1 and 5 of Section I. Column 3 shows the margin account balance at the beginning of each day. The figures in column 4 represent the change in value of the S&P 500 Index for the March futures contract. Column 5, the amount of gain or loss in the futures position, is obtained by multiplying the index point change (column 4) by $500 and then multiplying the result by the number of contracts in the position at the beginning of the day, Section II, column 2. The next column in Section II, column 6, gives the interim margin balance amount. This reflects the gains or losses posted to the margin account as the price changes during the day, and alerts the speculator to the possibility of a margin call. Column 7 provides information about any cash additions to the margin account or withdrawals from the margin account. The figures in the margin account ending balance column, column 8, represent the cumulative effect of the changes in the futures contract price, any cash inflows or outflows that have occurred, and any change in the number of contracts in the position. Column 9 shows the number of futures contracts in the position at the end of the day. This column is particularly important because it reflects any change in the number of contracts that constitute the position. Finally, the position's maintenance requirement is shown in column 10.

Section III, the last section of the speculative worksheet, deals with the speculator's cash activity. As mentioned in previous chapters, this cash does not have to be put on deposit with the broker, but it should be kept in an account that is extremely liquid and easily accessible so that the wide price swings in the financial futures markets can be withstood. In Figure 6-4, the $20,000 total cash and margin amount is inadequate and inconsistent with the 5-day rule of thumb since the S&P 500 futures contract can move by as much as $17,500 per day and $87,500 per week—$500 times 35 points times 5 days. There is a good chance that this speculator will lose the entire $20,000 if the market drops rapidly for a couple of days.

When the small retail speculator established his position by purchasing one March S&P 500 contract on Friday, January 8th, the March S&P contracts were selling at 429.70. He deposited $11,250 with his broker to satisfy the initial margin requirement, and kept an additional $8,750 in the reserve account. The next trading day,

1/11/93, the price of the March S&P contract rose by 1.3 index points, or $650, Section II, columns 4 and 5, to 431, Section I, column 3. Both the speculator's long position and margin account increased in value by $650, Section I, column 7, and Section II, columns 5 and 6. At the end of the day the margin account balance had risen by $650, Section II, column 8, and the total cash and margin amount increased to $20,650, Section I, column 8. Furthermore, the position showed a cumulative gain of $650, Section I, column 11.

At the beginning of the next day, 1/12/93, the speculator was long one March S&P 500 contract, and had $11,900 in his margin account. During the day, March S&P 500 futures rose by .45 index points to 431.45 for a $225 gain to the speculator, Section II, columns 4 and 5, and Section I, column 7. This $1,775 gain to the position resulted in the margin account rising to $12,125, Section II, column 6: the $11,900 margin balance at the beginning of the day plus the $225 gain. When trading opened on 1/13/93 the speculator still was long one March S&P 500 contract, Section II, column 2; had $12,125 in his margin account, Section II, column 3; had a total cash and margin balance of $20,87,5 Section I, column 8; and had enjoyed a cumulative gain of $87,5 Section I, column 11. During the day's trading the S&P Index rose by 1.9 points, to 433.34, which resulted in a $950 gain to the position and an interim margin balance of .$13,075, Section II, columns 4, 5, and 6, and Section I, columns 3 and 7. At the end of the day both his margin and total cash and margin accounts had grown to $21,825 and $13,075, Section I, column 8, and Section II, column 8; and the position's cumulative gain had risen to +$1,825 Section I, column 11. The S&P Index continued to rise the next day, 1/14/93, resulting in a robust 2.95 index point rise in the March S&P contract, for a $1,475 gain to the position, Section II, column 5, and an ending margin balance of $14,550, Section II, column 8.

The next day, 1/15/93, the March S&P contract closed the week with a small .15 point gain, which increased the margin account and total cash account by $75 and boosted the cumulative gains to $3,375 for the week.

The following week was characterized by greater volatility in the S&P Index. On Monday, 1/18/93, the index posted another .85-point gain which added $425 to the margin account and brought the cumulative gains up to $3,800. Tuesday, 1/19/93, saw the index fall by 1.75 points, Section II, column 4, which created an $875 loss for the long speculator, Section II, column 3, and reduced the margin to $14,175, Section II, column 6, and the cumulative gain to $2,925, Section I, column 11. The next day, 1/20/93, the March S&P contract moved lower by 2.4 points to 433.15 from 435.55, Section I, column 3, which translated to a $1,200, loss Section I, column 7, and Section II, column 5. This caused the speculator's margin account to fall by $1,200, and lowered the cumulative gain to $1,725 from the prior day's balance of $2,925, Section II, column 5, and Section I, column 11. The market reversed itself on Thursday and Friday. On Thursday, 1/21/93, the market gained 3.15 index points and recouped $1,575 of the prior days' losses, Section II, columns 4 and 5, and increased the margin account balance to $14,550, Section II, column 8. The Index rose slightly, .35, on Friday, which added $175 to the margin account, Section II, columns 5 and 6, and lifted the cumulative gain to $3,475, Section I, column 11.

The Index continued its upward march on Monday, 1/25/93, and increased by 3.7 points from 436.65 to 440.35, Section I, column 3. This translated to a $1,850 position gain, Section II, column 5, a $16,575 margin account balance, Section II, column 6, a total cash and margin account balance of $25,325, and a $5,325 cumulative gain, Section I, column 11. This latest increase convinced the speculator to close out his long position and to withdraw all the funds in the margin account, $16,575, and put them into his speculative account, Section II, columns 7 and 8, and Section III, columns 4 and 5. Thus, after selling the contract, he had no open position at the end of the day and there was no margin required, Section II, columns 9 and 10. Finally, this speculator enjoyed a $5,325 gain between 1/8/93 and 1/25/93. The outcome was not as pleasant for one who was a short speculator in the S&P 500 futures contract.

Although a short S&P 500 position resulted in a loss, the strategy was not ill-advised in January of 1993. Inflation appeared to have subsided, but there was no guarantee that the Federal Reserve would continue to pursue an easy money policy and push interest rates lower. Furthermore, there was a great deal of pessimism concerning the economic recovery's strength in the fourth quarter, and thus the quality of the quarter's corporate earnings. Given these conditions, the short speculator decided to sell S&P 500 futures contracts in anticipation of a slowing economy and a deteriorating stock market. Suppose that this speculator had $20,000 to commit to such a strategy, and that he decided to sell one March S&P 500 futures contract on 1/8/93. Figure 6-5 examines the outcome of this strategy.

Notice that the short S&P 500 speculator, represented by the worksheet in Figure 6-5, also suffers from inadequate reserves. If the posi-

## Figure 6-5
## Standard & Poor's 500 Short Speculation Worksheet

### I. Overall Futures Activity

| (1) Date | (2) Contract | (3) Unit Price | (4) Number of Units per Contract | (5) Number of Contracts +Long/-Short | (5) Position +Gain/-Loss | (6) Position Value | (7) Position +Gain/-Loss | (8) Total Cash+Margin | (9) Invested Cash+Margin | (10) Commission | (11) Cumulative +Gain/-Loss |
|---|---|---|---|---|---|---|---|---|---|---|---|
| 1/8/93 | March S&P 500 | 429.70 | $500 | -1 | $0 | ($214,850) | $0.00 | $20,000 | $20,000 | | $0 |
| 1/11/93 | March S&P 500 | 431.00 | $500 | -1 | ($650) | ($215,500) | ($650.00) | $19,350 | $20,000 | | ($650) |
| 1/12/93 | March S&P 500 | 431.45 | $500 | -1 | ($225) | ($215,725) | ($225.00) | $19,125 | $20,000 | | ($875) |
| 1/13/93 | March S&P 500 | 433.35 | $500 | -1 | ($950) | ($216,675) | ($950.00) | $18,175 | $20,000 | | ($1,825) |
| 1/14/93 | March S&P 500 | 436.30 | $500 | -1 | ($1,475) | ($218,150) | ($1,475.00) | $16,700 | $20,000 | | ($3,300) |
| 1/15/93 | March S&P 500 | 436.45 | $500 | -1 | ($75) | ($218,225) | ($75.00) | $16,625 | $20,000 | | ($3,375) |
| 1/18/93 | March S&P 500 | 437.30 | $500 | -1 | ($425) | ($218,650) | ($425.00) | $16,200 | $20,000 | | ($3,800) |
| 1/19/93 | March S&P 500 | 435.55 | $500 | -1 | $875 | ($217,775) | $875.00 | $17,075 | $20,000 | | ($2,925) |
| 1/20/93 | March S&P 500 | 433.15 | $500 | -1 | $1,200 | ($216,575) | $1,200.00 | $18,275 | $20,000 | | ($1,725) |
| 1/21/93 | March S&P 500 | 436.30 | $500 | -1 | ($1,575) | ($218,150) | ($1,575.00) | $16,700 | $20,000 | | ($3,300) |
| 1/22/93 | March S&P 500 | 436.65 | $500 | -1 | ($175) | ($218,325) | ($175.00) | $16,525 | $20,000 | | ($3,475) |
| 1/25/93 | March S&P 500 | 440.35 | $500 | -1 | ($1,850) | ($220,175) | ($1,850.00) | $14,675 | $20,000 | | ($5,325) |

### II. Margin Activity

Initial Margin Requirement $11,250 per Contract
Maintenance Margin Requirement $10,000 per Contract

| (1) Date | (2) Beginning # of Maintenance Contracts | (3) Margin Account Beginning Balance | (4) Unit Price Change | (5) Position +Gain/-Loss | (6) Interim Margin Balance | (7) Cash Account +From Cash -To Cash | (8) Margin Account Ending Balance | (9) Ending Number of Contracts | (10) Maintenance Requirement |
|---|---|---|---|---|---|---|---|---|---|
| 1/8/93 | -1 | $11,250 | 0 | $0 | $11,250 | $0 | $11,250 | -1 | $10,000 |
| 1/11/93 | -1 | $11,250 | 1.3000 | ($650) | $10,600 | $0 | $10,600 | -1 | $10,000 |
| 1/12/93 | -1 | $10,600 | 0.4500 | ($225) | $10,375 | $0 | $10,375 | -1 | $10,000 |
| 1/13/93 | -1 | $10,375 | 1.9000 | ($950) | $9,425 | $1,825 | $11,250 | -1 | $10,000 |
| 1/14/93 | -1 | $11,250 | 2.9500 | ($1,475) | $9,775 | $1,475 | $11,250 | -1 | $10,000 |
| 1/15/93 | -1 | $11,250 | 0.1500 | ($75) | $11,175 | $0 | $11,175 | -1 | $10,000 |
| 1/18/93 | -1 | $11,175 | 0.8500 | ($425) | $10,750 | $0 | $10,750 | -1 | $10,000 |
| 1/19/93 | -1 | $10,750 | -1.7500 | $875 | $11,625 | $0 | $11,625 | -1 | $10,000 |
| 1/20/93 | -1 | $11,625 | -2.4000 | $1,200 | $12,825 | $0 | $12,825 | -1 | $10,000 |
| 1/21/93 | -1 | $12,825 | 3.1500 | ($1,575) | $11,250 | $0 | $11,250 | -1 | $10,000 |
| 1/22/93 | -1 | $11,250 | 0.3500 | ($175) | $11,075 | $0 | $11,075 | -1 | $10,000 |
| 1/25/93 | -1 | $11,075 | 3.7000 | ($1,850) | $9,225 | ($9,225) | $0 | 0 | $0 |

Figure 6-5

Standard & Poor's 500 Short Speculation Worksheet (continued)

III. Cash Activity

| (1) Date | (2) Speculative Cash Beginning Balance | (3) Cash Account Flows + Invested - Withdrawn | (4) Margin Account Flows + From Margin - To Margin | (5) Speculative Cash Ending Balance |
|---|---|---|---|---|
| 1/8/93 | $8,750 | $0 | $0 | $8,750 |
| 1/11/93 | $8,750 | $0 | $0 | $8,750 |
| 1/12/93 | $8,750 | $0 | $0 | $8,750 |
| 1/13/93 | $8,750 | $0 | ($1,825) | $6,925 |
| 1/14/93 | $6,925 | $0 | ($1,475) | $5,450 |
| 1/15/93 | $5,450 | $0 | $0 | $5,450 |
| 1/18/93 | $5,450 | $0 | $0 | $5,450 |
| 1/19/93 | $5,450 | $0 | $0 | $5,450 |
| 1/20/93 | $5,450 | $0 | $0 | $5,450 |
| 1/21/93 | $5,450 | $0 | $0 | $5,450 |
| 1/22/93 | $5,450 | $0 | $0 | $5,450 |
| 1/25/93 | $5,450 | $0 | $9,225 | $14,675 |

tion suffers a loss which results in a maintenance margin balance less than the $10,000 required for a one-contract position, then the short speculator's $8,750 cash reserve will not last long if the S&P 500 Index experiences some dramatic gains.

When the small retail speculator established his position by selling one March S&P 500 contract on Friday, January 8th, the March S&P contracts were selling at 429.70. He deposited $11,250 with his broker to satisfy the initial margin requirement, and kept an additional $8,750 in the reserve account. The next trading day, 1/11/93, the price of the March S&P contract rose by 1.3 index points, or $650, Section II, columns 4 and 5, to 431 Section I, column 3. Both the speculator's short position and margin account declined by $650, Section I, column 7, and Section II, columns 5 and 6. At the end of the day the margin account balance had fallen to $10,600, Section II, column 8, and the total cash and margin amount was at $19,350, Section I, column 8. Furthermore, the position showed a cumulative loss of $650, Section I, column 11.

At the beginning of the next day, 1/12/93, the speculator was short one March S&P 500 contract and had $10,600 in his margin account. During the day, March S&P 500 futures rose by .45 index points to 431.45, a $225 loss to the speculator, Section II, columns 4 and 5, and Section I, column 7. This loss to the position resulted in the margin account dropping to $10,375, Section II, column 6: the $10,600 margin balance at the beginning of the day less the $225 loss. When trading opened on 1/13/93 the speculator still was short one March S&P 500, contract Section II, column 2; had $10,375 in his margin account, Section II, column 3; had a total cash and margin balance of $19,125, Section I, column 8; and had suffered a cumulative loss of $875, Section I, column 11. During the day's trading the S&P Index rose by 1.9 points, to 433.34, which resulted in a $950 loss to the position and an interim margin balance of $9,425, $575 less than the required $10,000, Section II, columns 4, 5, 6, and 10, and Section I, columns 3 and 7. This meant that the short speculator had to transfer $1,825 from the cash reserve account to the margin account in order to restore it to the $11,250 initial level, Section II, column 7, and Section III, column 4. The S&P Index continued to rise the next day, 1/14/93, resulting in another large loss for the short speculator. The March S&P contract rose 2.95 points on Thursday, 1/14/93, for a $1,475 position loss, Section II, column 5, and a $1,475 transfer from the cash reserve account to the margin account, Section II, columns 5 and 7, and Section III, column 4. The next day, 1/15/93, the March S&P contract closed the week with a small .15 point gain, which decreased the margin account and total cash account by $75 and boosted the cumulative loss to $3,375 for the week.

The following week was characterized by greater volatility in the S&P Index. On Monday, 1/18/93, the index posted another .85 point gain, which eroded another $425 from the margin account and brought the cumulative losses up to $3,800. Tuesday, 1/19/93, saw the Index fall by 1.75 points, Section II, column 4, which created an $875 gain for the short speculator, Section II, column 3, raised the margin to $11,625, Section II, column 6, and lowered the cumulative loss to $2,925, Section I, column 11. The next day, 1/20/93, the March S&P contract moved lower by another 2.4 points to 433.15 from 435.55, Section I, column 3, which translated to a $1,200 gain, Section I, column 7, and Section II, column 5. This caused the speculator's margin account to increase by $1,200, to $12,825, and lowered the cumulative loss to $1,725 from the prior day's balance of $2,925, Section II, columns 5 and 6, and Section I, column 11.

However, when the market reversed itself on Thursday and Friday, it meant more losses for the short speculator. On Thursday 1/21/93 the market gained 3.15 index points and tacked on another $1,575 in trading losses, Section II columns 4 and 5, and decreased the margin account balance to $11,250, Section II column 8. The index rose slightly, .35, on Friday, which cost the short speculator another $175, and lowered the margin balance to $11,075, Section II, columns 5 and 6, and increased the cumulative loss to $3,475, Section I, column 11.

The index continued its upward march on Monday, 1/25/93, and increased by 3.7 points from 436.65 to 440.35, Section I, column 3. Thus, the short speculator was hit with another $1,850 position loss, Section II, column 5, which brought his margin account balance down to $9,225, Section II, column 6, his total cash and margin account balance to $14,675, for a $5,325 cumulative loss, Section I, column 11. This latest loss convinced the speculator to close out his short position and to withdraw all the funds in the margin account, $9,225, and put them into his speculative account, Section II, columns 7 and 8, and Section III, columns 4 and 5. Thus, after covering his short position by purchasing one March S&P contract, he had no open position at the end of the day and there was no margin required, Section II, columns 9 and 10.

The differences in outcome for the long speculator and short speculator are exactly what is expected: both of them accept the price risk associated with the stock market, yet only one will profit. The chapter's next section examines the behavior of hedgers and shows how to transfer equity market price risk via the S&P 500 futures market.

## HEDGING

In the previous chapter, hedging was discussed from the perspective of a bond mutual fund manager and a securities dealer, where each of them wanted to avoid the effects of changing interest rates. In this chapter we will consider two hedgers who want to use S&P futures contracts to manage their equity positions. The first individual is a private portfolio manager who has been able to achieve a steady gain throughout 1992, and wants to protect his clients' $20,000,000 portfolio from any dramatic declines in the equity market during the next six weeks. Thus, he will hedge his long equity position by becoming a short hedger and selling S&P 500 futures contracts. The second hedger is a woman who is in the process of selling some real estate and expects to receive approximately $1,000,000 on March 1st, 1993. She has decided that she wants to invest 80 percent, or $800,000, in a well-diversified portfolio of stocks, with the remainder going to a mix of Treasury Bills and some high-quality corporate bonds. Since she does not have the cash to invest at this time she has a short position in the equity market; therefore she will follow a long hedging strategy and purchase an appropriate number of S&P 500 futures contracts as a temporary substitute for her cash market transaction. Figures 6-6 and 6-7 present the outcomes for the short hedger and long hedger, respectively.

Both worksheets have the same construction and are composed of five sections. Section I presents data relating to the activity in the hedger's cash market position. Section II shows the behavior of the basis during the hedge's life. The third section displays the hedger's futures market position, while the fourth and fifth sections show the hedger's margin account and cash account activity. Sections I and II are unique to the hedger's worksheet, and are explained in detail in the following paragraphs. The remaining three sections of the worksheet: Section III, "Overall Futures Activity;" Section IV, "Margin Activity;" and Section V, "Cash Activity," carry the exact same interpretation as in the speculator's worksheets in Figures 6-4 and 6-5. These hedges are unique in that there is no difference between the initial margin and maintenance margin. Therefore any losses must be replenished that same day.

Section II of the hedger's worksheet (Figures 6-6 and 6-7) depicts the basis, its incremental change, and its cumulative change. Recall from the discussion in previous chapters that the basis is the equivalent of having a long position in the cash market and a short position in the futures market; and that the basis has two desirable properties: lower volatility than an open position in either the spot market or the futures market, and the convergence of the spot price and futures price to equality at maturity. Again, the financial commodity hedger is trading the relatively higher price volatility of either the cash or the futures market for the more stable and less volatile combined cash and futures position. The convergence of the spot and futures prices means that the basis becomes zero at maturity. However, prior to maturity the basis can be either positive or negative, thereby creating some opportunities for the hedger to earn a small profit during the life of the hedge as the basis fluctuates. A strengthening basis will be profitable for one who is long the cash commodity and short the futures contract, i.e., a short hedger. On the other hand, a weakening basis will be profitable if one is a long hedger since the short position in the cash commodity will be more profitable than the long futures position.

In Figure 6-6 the short hedger's, or portfolio manager's, cash market position in equities is shown as of 1/14/94, in Section I, columns 1 through 5. The cash, or spot, value of the S&P 500 Index on that day was 474.91, and the value of the portfolio manager's equity position was $20,000,000. The cash position can be expressed in terms of S&P 500 Index points by dividing the cash value of the equity position, $20,000,000, by the S&P 500 Index value, 474.91: ($20,000,000/474.91) = $42,113.24 per S&P Index point. However, this amount is meaningless unless it is converted to reflect the cash market position in terms of the S&P 500 futures contract. Thus, the S&P 500 equity cash position must be divided by the S&P 500 futures contract single-point value of $500. In this example, dividing $42,113.24 by $500 yields a value of 84.23 (column 4), which expresses the $20,000,000 equity cash position in terms of the S&P 500 futures contract.

The importance of columns 4 and 5 cannot be overemphasized since they dictate how many S&P 500 futures contracts must be included in the hedge. In this example, the portfolio manager's equity cash position is equivalent to 84.23 S&P 500 futures contracts. Therefore, 84 S&P 500 futures contracts must be sold to hedge this cash

## Figure 6-6
## Standard & Poor's 500 Short Hedger Worksheet

I. Overall Spot Activity

| (1) Date | (2) Spot Commodity | (3) Unit Price | (4) Amount of Spot Commodity | (5) Spot Position Value | (6) Unit Price Change | (7) Spot Position +Gain/-Loss | (8) Commission | (9) Spot Cummulative +Gain/-Loss |
|---|---|---|---|---|---|---|---|---|
| 1/14/94 | S&P 500 | 474.91 | +84.23 | $20,000,835 | 0.0000 | $0 | | $0 |
| 1/21/94 | S&P 500 | 474.73 | +84.23 | $19,993,254 | (0.1800) | ($7,581) | | ($7,581) |
| 1/28/94 | S&P 500 | 478.70 | +84.23 | $20,160,451 | 3.9700 | $167,197 | | $159,616 |
| 2/4/94 | S&P 500 | 469.81 | +84.23 | $19,786,048 | (8.8900) | ($374,402) | | ($214,787) |
| 2/11/94 | S&P 500 | 470.02 | +84.23 | $19,794,892 | 0.2100 | $8,844 | | ($205,942) |
| 2/18/94 | S&P 500 | 467.68 | +84.23 | $19,696,343 | (2.3400) | ($98,549) | | ($304,491) |
| 2/28/94 | S&P 500 | 467.14 | +84.23 | $19,673,601 | (0.5400) | ($22,742) | | ($327,234) |

II. Basis Activity

| (1) Date | (2) Basis Unit Value Spot Futures | (3) Basis Change | (4) Basis Cumulative +Gain/-Loss |
|---|---|---|---|
| 1/14/94 | 0.2600 | 0 | $0 |
| 1/21/94 | 1.1300 | 0.8700 | $36,519 |
| 1/28/94 | 0.0000 | -1.1300 | ($10,484) |
| 2/4/94 | 0.8600 | 0.8600 | $24,614 |
| 2/11/94 | 0.0200 | -0.8400 | ($10,642) |
| 2/18/94 | -0.4700 | -0.4900 | ($31,491) |
| 2/28/94 | 0.9900 | 1.4600 | $29,766 |

## Figure 6-6
### Standard & Poor's 500 Short Hedger Worksheet (continued)

**III. Overall Futures Activity**

| (1) Date | (2) Contract | (3) Unit Price | (4) Number of Units per Contract | (5) Number of Contracts +Long/-Short | (6) Futures Position Values | (7) Futures Position +Gain/-Loss | (8) Total Cash+Margin | (9) Invested Cash+Margin | (10) Commission | (11) Futures Cumulative +Gain/-Loss |
|---|---|---|---|---|---|---|---|---|---|---|
| 1/14/94 | March S&P 500 | 474.65 | 500 | -84 | ($19,935,300) | $0 | $2,840,000 | $2,840,000 | | $0 |
| 1/21/94 | March S&P 500 | 473.60 | 500 | -84 | ($19,891,200) | $44,100 | $2,884,100 | $2,840,000 | | $44,100 |
| 1/28/94 | March S&P 500 | 478.70 | 500 | -84 | ($20,105,400) | ($214,200) | $2,669,900 | $2,840,000 | | ($170,100) |
| 2/4/94 | March S&P 500 | 468.95 | 500 | -84 | ($19,695,900) | $409,500 | $3,079,400 | $2,840,000 | | $239,400 |
| 2/11/94 | March S&P 500 | 470.00 | 500 | -84 | ($19,740,000) | ($44,100) | $3,035,300 | $2,840,000 | | $195,300 |
| 2/18/94 | March S&P 500 | 468.15 | 500 | -84 | ($19,662,300) | $77,700 | $3,113,000 | $2,840,000 | | $273,000 |
| 2/28/94 | March S&P 500 | 466.15 | 500 | -84 | ($19,578,300) | $84,000 | $3,197,000 | $2,840,000 | | $357,000 |

**IV. Margin Activity**

Initial Margin Requirement $10,000 per Contract
Maintenance Margin Requirement $10,000 per Contract

| (1) Date | (2) Beginning # of Maintenance Contracts | (3) Margin Account Beginning Balance | (4) Unit Price Change | (5) Position +Gain/-Loss | (6) Interim Margin Balance | (7) Cash Account +From Cash -To Cash | (8) Margin Account Ending Balance | (9) Ending Number of Contracts | (10) Maintenance Requirement |
|---|---|---|---|---|---|---|---|---|---|
| 1/14/94 | -84 | $840,000 | 0 | $0 | $840,000 | $0 | $840,000 | 84 | $840,000 |
| 1/21/94 | -84 | $840,000 | -1.0500 | $44,100 | $884,100 | $0 | $884,100 | 84 | $840,000 |
| 1/28/94 | -84 | $884,100 | 5.1000 | ($214,200) | $669,900 | $170,100 | $840,000 | 84 | $840,000 |
| 2/4/94 | -84 | $840,000 | -9.7500 | $409,500 | $1,249,500 | $0 | $1,249,500 | 84 | $840,000 |
| 2/11/94 | -84 | $1,249,500 | 1.0500 | ($44,100) | $1,205,400 | $0 | $1,205,400 | 84 | $840,000 |
| 2/18/94 | -84 | $1,205,400 | -1.8500 | $77,700 | $1,283,100 | $0 | $1,283,100 | 84 | $840,000 |
| 2/28/94 | -84 | $1,283,100 | -2.0000 | $84,000 | $1,367,100 | ($1,367,100) | $0 | 84 | $840,000 |

## Figure 6-6
## Standard & Poor's 500 Short Hedger Worksheet (continued)

V. Cash Activity

| (1) | (2) | (3) | (4) | (5) |
|---|---|---|---|---|
| | Carrying | Cash Account Flows | Margin Account Flows | Carrying |
| | Cash Beginning | + Invested | + From Margin | Cash Ending |
| Date | Balance | -Withdrawn | -To Margin | Balance |
| 1/14/94 | $2,000,000 | $0 | $0 | $2,000,000 |
| 1/21/94 | $2,000,000 | $0 | $0 | $2,000,000 |
| 1/28/94 | $2,000,000 | $0 | ($170,100) | $1,829,900 |
| 2/4/94 | $1,829,900 | $0 | $0 | $1,829,900 |
| 2/11/94 | $1,829,900 | $0 | $0 | $1,829,900 |
| 2/18/94 | $1,829,900 | $0 | $0 | $1,829,900 |
| 2/28/94 | $1,829,900 | $0 | $1,367,100 | $3,197,000 |

## Figure 6-7
## Standard & Poor's 500 Long Hedger Worksheet

### I. Overall Spot Activity

| (1) Date | (2) Spot Commodity | (3) Unit Price | (4) Amount of Spot Commodity | (5) Spot Position Value | (6) Unit Price Change | (7) Spot Position +Gain/-Loss | (8) Commission | (9) Spot Cummulative +Gain/-Loss |
|---|---|---|---|---|---|---|---|---|
| 1/14/94 | S&P 500 | 474.91 | -3.37 | ($800,223) | 0.0000 | $0 | | $0 |
| 1/21/94 | S&P 500 | 474.73 | -3.37 | ($799,920) | (0.1800) | $303 | | $303 |
| 1/28/94 | S&P 500 | 478.70 | -3.37 | ($806,610) | 3.9700 | ($6,689) | | ($6,386) |
| 2/4/94 | S&P 500 | 469.81 | -3.37 | ($791,630) | (8.8900) | $14,980 | | $8,594 |
| 2/11/94 | S&P 500 | 470.02 | -3.37 | ($791,984) | 0.2100 | ($354) | | $8,240 |
| 2/18/94 | S&P 500 | 467.68 | -3.37 | ($788,041) | (2.3400) | $3,943 | | $12,183 |
| 2/28/94 | S&P 500 | 467.14 | -3.37 | ($787,131) | (0.5400) | $910 | | $13,092 |

### II. Basis Activity

| (1) Date | (2) Basis Unit Value Spot Futures | (3) Basis Change | (4) Basis Cumulative +Gain/-Loss |
|---|---|---|---|
| 1/14/94 | 0.2600 | 0 | $0 |
| 1/21/94 | 1.1300 | 0.8700 | ($1,272) |
| 1/28/94 | 0.0000 | -1.1300 | ($311) |
| 2/4/94 | 0.8600 | 0.8600 | $44 |
| 2/11/94 | 0.0200 | -0.8400 | $1,265 |
| 2/18/94 | -0.4700 | -0.4900 | $2,433 |
| 2/28/94 | 0.9900 | 1.4600 | $342 |

## Figure 6-7
## Standard & Poor's 500 Long Hedger Worksheet (continued)

**III. Overall Futures Activity**

| (1) Date | (2) Contract | (3) Unit Price | (4) Number of Units per Contract | (5) Number of Contracts +Long/-Short | (6) Futures Position Values | (7) Futures Position +Gain/-Loss | (8) Total Cash+Margin | (9) Invested Cash+Margin | (10) Commission | (11) Futures Cumulative +Gain/-Loss |
|---|---|---|---|---|---|---|---|---|---|---|
| 1/14/94 | March S&P 500 | 474.65 | 500 | +3 | $711,975 | $0 | $150,000 | $150,000 | | $0 |
| 1/21/94 | March S&P 500 | 473.60 | 500 | +3 | $710,400 | ($1,575) | $148,425 | $150,000 | | ($1,575) |
| 1/28/94 | March S&P 500 | 478.70 | 500 | +3 | $718,050 | $7,650 | $156,075 | $150,000 | | $6,075 |
| 2/4/94 | March S&P 500 | 468.95 | 500 | +3 | $703,425 | ($14,625) | $141,450 | $150,000 | | ($8,550) |
| 2/11/94 | March S&P 500 | 470.00 | 500 | +3 | $705,000 | $1,575 | $143,025 | $150,000 | | ($6,975) |
| 2/18/94 | March S&P 500 | 468.15 | 500 | +3 | $702,225 | ($2,775) | $140,250 | $150,000 | | ($9,750) |
| 2/28/94 | March S&P 500 | 466.15 | 500 | +3 | $699,225 | ($3,000) | $137,250 | $150,000 | | ($12,750) |

**IV. Margin Activity**

Initial Margin Requirement     $10,000   per Contract
Maintenance Margin Requirement    $10,000   per Contract

| (1) Date | (2) Beginning # of Maintenance Contracts | (3) Margin Account Beginning Balance | (4) Unit Price Change | (5) Position +Gain/-Loss | (6) Interim Margin Balance | (7) Cash Account +From Cash -To Cash | (8) Margin Account Ending Balance | (9) Ending Number of Contracts | (10) Maintenance Requirement |
|---|---|---|---|---|---|---|---|---|---|
| 1/14/94 | +3 | $30,000 | 0 | $0 | $30,000 | $0 | $30,000 | 3 | $30,000 |
| 1/21/94 | +3 | $30,000 | -1.0500 | ($1,575) | $28,425 | $1,575 | $30,000 | 3 | $30,000 |
| 1/28/94 | +3 | $30,000 | 5.1000 | $7,650 | $37,650 | $0 | $37,650 | 3 | $30,000 |
| 2/4/94 | +3 | $37,650 | -9.7500 | ($14,625) | $23,025 | $6,975 | $30,000 | 3 | $30,000 |
| 2/11/94 | +3 | $30,000 | 1.0500 | $1,575 | $31,575 | $0 | $31,575 | 3 | $30,000 |
| 2/18/94 | +3 | $31,575 | -1.8500 | ($2,775) | $28,800 | $1,200 | $30,000 | 3 | $30,000 |
| 2/28/94 | +3 | $30,000 | -2.0000 | ($3,000) | $27,000 | ($27,000) | $0 | 0 | $30,000 |

## Figure 6-7
### Standard & Poor's 500 Long Hedger Worksheet (continued)

V. Cash Activity

| (1) Date | (2) Carrying Cash Beginning Balance | (3) Cash Account Flows + Invested - Withdrawn | (4) Margin Account Flows + From Margin - To Margin | (5) Carrying Cash Ending Balance |
|---|---|---|---|---|
| 1/14/94 | $120,000 | $0 | $0 | $120,000 |
| 1/21/94 | $120,000 | $0 | ($1,575) | $118,425 |
| 1/28/94 | $118,425 | $0 | $0 | $118,425 |
| 2/4/94 | $118,425 | $0 | ($6,975) | $111,450 |
| 2/11/94 | $111,450 | $0 | $0 | $111,450 |
| 2/18/94 | $111,450 | $0 | ($1,200) | $110,250 |
| 2/28/94 | $110,250 | $0 | $27,000 | $137,250 |

position. This will not be a perfect hedge since the short futures position will be less than the long position by .23 futures contracts. However, this is the best hedge that can be achieved under these circumstances.

The remaining columns in the Spot Activity section of the worksheet document the spot position price changes. Column 6 lists the commodity's unit price change in the cash market, and column 7 expresses the price change as either a gain or loss to the spot position. Column 8 is reserved for any commissions that might be incurred as a result of cash market activity, while column 9 accumulates the gains and losses that accrue to the spot position. The basis, column 1 of Section II, is computed by subtracting the futures price, Section III, column 3, from the spot price, Section I, column 3. The positive basis of .26 for 1/14/94 is consistent with a 474.91 spot price and a 474.65 futures price. One week later, 1/21/94, the S&P 500 spot price had fallen by .18 index points, or $90, to 474.73, Section I, columns 3 and 6, while the March S&P 500 futures contract price fell by 1.05 index points to 473.60, for a gain of $44,100, Section III, column 3, and Section IV, columns 4 and 5. This caused the basis to strengthen and rise to 1.13, for a position gain of $36,519: the change in the basis (1.13 − (.26)) multiplied by $500 per point multiplied by 84 contracts.

Over the next week, the basis weakened by −1.13 and stood at 0.00 at the end of the day on January 28th, which meant that the short hedger's overall position had incurred a loss relative to the prior week. The short futures position suffered a 5.1 index-point change for a $214,200 loss, Section IV, columns 4 and 5, which brought the margin account down to $669,900, $170,100 below the $840,000 maintenance level, Section IV, columns 6 and 8. This meant that $170,100 had to be transferred from the reserve account to the margin account, Section IV, column 7, and Section V, column 4, to restore it to the $840,000 initial margin level.

During the subsequent week the Federal Reserve permitted short-term rates to rise, and the S&P Index responded in dramatic fashion. By Friday's close, 2/4/94, the basis had risen by .86 to .86 index points, Section II, columns 2 and 3. This resulted in an overall gain for the short hedger of $24,614, Section II, column 4. This was due to the −8.89 drop, a $374,402 loss, in the spot position value, Section I, columns 6 and 7, which was more than offset by the −9.75 index point drop, a $409,500 gain, to the short futures position, Section IV, columns 4 and 5. This futures gain served to increase the margin account to $1,249,500.

The next two weeks saw the S&P 500 Index basis decline by –.84 and –.49, respectively, which raised the cumulative loss to the short hedger to –$31,491, Section II, column 4. Thus, the final week of the hedge began with the hedger being short 84 March S&P 500 futures contracts, and the margin account at $1,283,100, Section IV, columns 2 and 3. During the week the spot value of the index rose .54 index points, while the March futures contract fell by 2 index points, which translated to a 1.46-point gain for the basis. This increase in the basis mitigated the short hedger's earlier losses, so that when the futures position was closed out on February 28th, the short hedger's overall gain was $29,766 for the 84-contract position—a better outcome than what would have been achieved if the long cash position in equities had not been hedged with the short futures position.

Figure 6-7, the long hedger's worksheet, is quite similar to the short hedger's worksheet, Figure 6-6; however, there are some differences. The basic difference between the two worksheets is that the short hedger is long the cash commodity, a well-diversified equity portfolio, and is short the futures contract, while the long hedger is short the cash commodity and long the futures contract. This can be seen quite clearly by comparing the signs that precede the spot market positions and futures market positions: Section I, column 4; Section III, column 5; and Section IV, columns 2 and 9. Although the long hedger's short spot position, Section I, columns 1 through 6, is much smaller than the short hedger's spot position, it is determined in precisely the same way. The long hedger's cash position can be expressed in terms of S&P 500 Index points by dividing the cash value of the equity position, $800,000, by the S&P 500 Index value, 474.91: ($800,000/474.91) = $1,684.53 per S&P Index point. This amount is divided by the S&P 500 futures contract single point value of $500 to express the $800,000 equity cash position in terms of the S&P 500 futures contract—($1,684.53/$500) = 3.369—and is used to determine how many S&P 500 futures contracts to include in the hedge. In this situation, the long hedger must purchase three futures contracts to hedge the short cash position. Again, this is not a perfect hedge, but the best that can be done in this situation.

In Figure 6-7, the long hedger's futures activity and margin activity sections show that the long hedger's futures account experienced some rather large losses between January 14th and February 28th. During the hedge's life the total cash plus margin account decreased in value by $12,750, from $150,000 on 1/14/94 to $137,250 on 2/28/94, because of the drop in the S&P 500 Index and the long position in three futures contracts, Section III, columns 5 and 11. These results differ from those in Figure 6-6 where the short hedger's ending margin account balance increased in value by $357,000 because of the gains achieved by the short futures position in a declining market.

The most interesting aspect of the two worksheets is shown in the cumulative gain or loss to the basis, Section II, column 4. Notice that both the short and long hedgers captured a basis gain. The reasoning is straightforward for the short hedger. Because the portfolio manager was long the basis, long the spot market, and short the futures market, the short hedger was able to benefit from the strengthening basis. On the other hand, one would expect the long hedger to suffer a loss since she was short the spot market and long the futures market, or short the basis. This did not occur because in reality the long hedger was carrying a small short position in the cash market, −.37 S&P Index points, as the S&P Index fell. Thus, she captured a small $342 gain.

Closer examination of Figure 6-7 reveals how the long hedger protected herself from the turmoil caused by the changing interest rates at this time. The positive basis of .26 for 1/14/94 is consistent with a 474.91 spot price and a 474.65 futures price. One week later, 1/21/94, the S&P 500 spot price had fallen by .18 index points to 474.73, for a $303 gain to the spot market position, Section I, columns 3 and 6, while the March S&P 500 futures contract price fell by 1.05 index points to 473.60, for a loss of $1,575, Section III, column 3, and Section IV, columns 4 and 5. This caused the basis to strengthen and rise to 1.13, for a position loss of $1,272—the spot position gain minus the futures position loss. Note that the $1,575 futures position loss caused the margin account to fall below the $30,000 maintenance level and required a $1,575 transfer from the reserve account to the margin account, Section IV, column 7, and Section V, column 4, to restore it to the initial margin level.

Over the next week the basis weakened by −1.13 and stood at 0.00 at the end of the day on January 28th, which meant that the long hedger's overall position had improved to where her overall loss was only $311, Section II, column 4. The long futures position benefitted from a 5.1 index point rise for a $7,650 gain, Section IV, columns 4 and5, which brought the margin account up to $37,650.

During the following week the Federal Reserve permitted short-term rates to rise, and the S&P Index dropped significantly. By Friday's close, 2/4/94, the basis had risen by .86 to .86 index points,

Section II, columns 2 and 3. This resulted in an overall gain for the long hedger of $44, Section II, column 4. This was due to the –8.89 drop, $14,980 gain, in the spot position value, Section I, columns 6 and 7, which more than offset the $14,625 loss to the long futures position, Section IV, column 5. This futures loss served to decrease the margin account to $23,025 and made it necessary to transfer another $6,975 to the margin account from the reserve account, Section IV, column 7, and Section V, column 4.

The next two weeks saw the S&P 500 Index basis decline by –.84 and –.49, respectively, which raised the cumulative gain to the long hedger to $2,433, Section II, column 4, but required another $1,200 transfer of cash to the margin account on 2/18/94. Thus, the final week of the hedge began with the hedger being long three March S&P 500 futures contracts, and the margin account at $30,000, Section IV, columns 2 and 3. During the week the spot value of the index rose .54 index points, while the March futures contract fell by two index points, which translated to a 1.46 point gain for the basis. This increase in the basis eroded the long hedger's earlier basis gains, so that when the futures position was closed out on February 28th, the long hedger's overall gain was $342 for the three-contract position—an inferior outcome to what would have been achieved if the short cash position in equities had not been hedged with the long futures position. However, that is what the long hedger was willing to live with.

## SPREADING

The chapter's previous sections examined speculators and hedgers. This section focuses on stock index spreaders and intramarket S&P 500 spreads. Recall that the spreader's trading strategy differs from the hedger's in that the spreader never assumes a position in the underlying commodity, and differs from the speculator's strategy since the spreader never takes an outright long or short position in any contract, but always combines a long futures position with a short futures position. Because the spreader assumes less risk than the futures position of both the speculator and hedger, the spreader's margin requirements are lower. This is especially true for the S&P 500 spreader, where the intramarket spread's initial margin is $400 and the maintenance margin is only $400. These low spread margins indicate that the S&P 500 intramarket spreads are extremely stable, and that it is extremely difficult for a small retail customer to profit via S&P 500 futures contract spreads.

The cause of the S&P 500 intramarket spread's stability can be attributed to the activity of arbitragers, who have the ability to execute purchases and sales of futures contracts almost instantaneously and who can finance these futures contract positions by borrowing at very favorable interest rates. These arbitragers are always willing to purchase the nearby futures contract and sell the deferred contract. If the percentage difference between the long position's, or nearby contract's, purchase price and the short position's, or deferred contract's, sale price is greater than the financing rate, then these arbitragers will have earned a guaranteed profit without assuming any risk. The logic of the arbitrager's action with regard to S&P 500 futures contracts is identical to that of the arbitrager's in the S&P 500 cash and carry process discussed in Chapter Two. In both situations it is the relationship between the arbitrager's financing costs and the rate of return on the S&P 500 position that will determine the relative prices of the S&P 500 futures contracts.

In the early winter of 1993 inflation was not a major concern and interest rates began to drop. The economy was coming out of a recession and the stock market showed signs of strength. Indeed, if the Federal Reserve did permit interest rates to drop further, then it would almost be assured that the stock market would begin to rise steadily.

This environment of declining interest rates and rising stock prices did not necessarily mean that the S&P 500 spreads would change significantly, since all of the S&P 500 futures contracts exhibit almost identical price behavior. On Friday, January 29th, 1993, the annualized 90-day Treasury Bill rate expected to prevail between March and June was 2.96%, the March S&P 500 futures contract was priced at 438.25, and the June S&P 500 futures contract was trading at 438.60. The .35 index point difference between the March and June futures contract prices defines the value of the 90-day March-June S&P 500 spread. This .35 difference translates to an approximate .3% annualized rate of return to a strategy of buying the S&P 500 March futures contract and selling the June S&P 500 futures contract: the percentage difference between the March and June contract prices, 438.6 − 438.25 divided by 438.25 times 4 (since there are approximately four 90-day periods in a year). Note that this is 2.66 percentage points, or 266 basis points, less than the applicable 90-day T-Bill rate. Thus, if one wanted to finance a long position in the March S&P 500 futures contract and a short position in the June S&P 500 futures contract, then the net borrowing cost would be 2.66%. The only way to earn a profit on this position is to have the ability to borrow at the strategy's .3% annualized rate of return. This is extremely difficult for large, sophisticated institutions, and virtually impossible for retail customers.

Figure 6-8, the spreader worksheet, illustrates the March-June S&P 500 spread's stability and the difficulty of reaping large gains. The worksheet assumes that a retail customer had $10,000 and wanted to capitalize on falling interest rates and rising stock prices via an S&P 500 intramarket spread. The customer would simultaneously purchase the March futures contract and sell the June futures contract for a net cost of .35 index points, or $175, post an initial margin of $450 per spread, and maintain a $400 margin balance per spread. Since the long position's value is less than the short position's value, the spread carries a negative sign and will generate a profit if the spread narrows over time. If the spread widens over time, then the spreader will suffer a loss.

There are four sections in Figure 6-8 that denote the daily outcomes of the March-June spread. Section I provides the details of the price changes of both the long and short futures positions that constitute the spread. Section II considers the spread activity in conjunction with the cash and margin positions. Section III, the margin activity, and Section IV, the cash activity, are identical to the margin activity and cash activity sections in the speculator and hedger worksheets, and thus carry the same interpretation.

A close examination of Section I reveals how the spread is constructed, how each component changes value, and how the spread's overall value changes. Column 1 provides the date of each transaction; it shows that the spread was created on 1/29/93 and was liquidated on 2/11/93. Columns 2, 3, and 5 show the number and price of the futures contracts that were purchased. In this case, the spreader bought 10 March S&P 500 futures contracts for 438.25 each. The values in column 4 track the price changes of the long futures contract and show that the price of the March S&P 500 contract generally rose during this spread's life. Columns 6 through 9 are the obverse of columns 2 through 5, providing information about the short side of the spread. In this case the spreader sold 10 June S&P 500 futures contracts at 438.60 to offset the long position in the 10 March contracts. Column 10 shows the actual value of the spread, and is obtained by subtracting the short position's price, column 7, from the long position's price, column 4, and then multiplying the result by $500. The values in column 11 depict the change in the spread's value on a per-unit basis, while the values in column 13 show the spread's

## Figure 6-8
## Standard & Poor's 500 Spreader Worksheet

### I. Detailed Futures Activity

| (1) Date | (2) Long Position | (3) Unit Price | (4) Long Units Price Change | (5) Number of Contracts Bought | (6) Short Position | (7) Unit Price | (8) Short Units Price Change | (9) Number of Contracts Bought | (10) Spread Unit Value | (11) Spread Unit Price Change | (12) Number of Units per Contract | (13) Spread Value |
|---|---|---|---|---|---|---|---|---|---|---|---|---|
| 1/29/93 | March S&P 500 | 438.25 | 0 | +10 | June S&P 500 | 438.60 | 0 | -10 | ($175.00) | $0.00 | $500 | $1,750.00 |
| 2/1/93 | March S&P 500 | 442.50 | $2,125.00 | +10 | June S&P 500 | 442.90 | $2,150.00 | -10 | ($200.00) | $25.00 | $500 | $2,000.00 |
| 2/2/93 | March S&P 500 | 443.05 | $275.00 | +10 | June S&P 500 | 443.50 | $300.00 | -10 | ($225.00) | $25.00 | $500 | $2,250.00 |
| 2/3/93 | March S&P 500 | 447.90 | $2,425.00 | +10 | June S&P 500 | 448.30 | $2,400.00 | -10 | ($200.00) | ($25.00) | $500 | $2,000.00 |
| 2/4/93 | March S&P 500 | 449.55 | $825.00 | +10 | June S&P 500 | 449.95 | $825.00 | -10 | ($200.00) | $0.00 | $500 | $2,000.00 |
| 2/5/93 | March S&P 500 | 449.35 | ($100.00) | +10 | June S&P 500 | 449.75 | ($100.00) | -10 | ($200.00) | $0.00 | $500 | $2,000.00 |
| 2/8/93 | March S&P 500 | 448.45 | ($450.00) | +10 | June S&P 500 | 448.90 | ($425.00) | -10 | ($225.00) | $25.00 | $500 | $2,250.00 |
| 2/9/93 | March S&P 500 | 446.10 | ($1,175.00) | +10 | June S&P 500 | 446.55 | ($1,175.00) | -10 | ($225.00) | $0.00 | $500 | $2,250.00 |
| 2/10/93 | March S&P 500 | 447.10 | $500.00 | +10 | June S&P 500 | 447.55 | $500.00 | -10 | ($225.00) | $0.00 | $500 | $2,250.00 |
| 2/11/93 | March S&P 500 | 448.05 | $475.00 | +10 | June S&P 500 | 448.55 | $500.00 | -10 | ($250.00) | $25.00 | $500 | $2,500.00 |

### II. Over All Spread Activity

| (1) Date | (2) Spread | (3) Spread Unit Value | (4) Number of Units Per Contract | (5) Number of Contracts | (6) Spread Value | (7) Spread +Gain/-Loss | (8) Total Cash + Margins | (9) Invested Cash + Margins | (10) Spread Commission | (11) Cummulative +Gain/-Loss |
|---|---|---|---|---|---|---|---|---|---|---|
| 1/29/93 | +March-Jun S&P 500 | ($175.00) | $500 | 10 | $1,750 | $0.00 | $10,000.00 | $10,000 | | $0.00 |
| 2/1/93 | +March-Jun S&P 500 | ($200.00) | $500 | 10 | $2,000 | $250.00 | $10,250.00 | $10,000 | | $250.00 |
| 2/2/93 | +March-Jun S&P 500 | ($225.00) | $500 | 10 | $2,250 | $250.00 | $10,500.00 | $10,000 | | $500.00 |
| 2/3/93 | +March-Jun S&P 500 | ($200.00) | $500 | 10 | $2,000 | ($250.00) | $10,250.00 | $10,000 | | $250.00 |
| 2/4/93 | +March-Jun S&P 500 | ($200.00) | $500 | 10 | $2,000 | $0.00 | $10,250.00 | $10,000 | | $250.00 |
| 2/5/93 | +March-Jun S&P 500 | ($200.00) | $500 | 10 | $2,000 | $0.00 | $10,250.00 | $10,000 | | $250.00 |
| 2/8/93 | +March-Jun S&P 500 | ($225.00) | $500 | 10 | $2,250 | $250.00 | $10,500.00 | $10,000 | | $500.00 |
| 2/9/93 | +March-Jun S&P 500 | ($225.00) | $500 | 10 | $2,250 | $0.00 | $10,500.00 | $10,000 | | $500.00 |
| 2/10/93 | +March-Jun S&P 500 | ($225.00) | $500 | 10 | $2,250 | $0.00 | $10,500.00 | $10,000 | | $500.00 |
| 2/11/93 | +March-Jun S&P 500 | ($250.00) | $500 | 10 | $2,500 | $250.00 | $10,750.00 | $10,000 | | $750.00 |

## Figure 6-8
### Standard & Poor's 500 Spreader Worksheet (continued)

III. Margin Activity
Initial Margin Requirement: $450 per Spread
Maintenance Margin Requirement: $400 per Spread

| (1) Date | (2) Beginning Number of Contracts | (3) Margin Account Beginning Balance | (4) Spread Unit Price Change | (5) Position + Gain / -Loss | (6) Interim Margin Balance | (7) Ending Number of Contracts | (8) Cash Account + From Cash / -To Cash | (9) Margin Account Ending Balance | (10) Maintenance Requirement |
|---|---|---|---|---|---|---|---|---|---|
| 1/29/93 | 10 | $4,500.00 | 0.00 | $0.00 | $4,500.00 | 10 | $0 | $4,500.00 | $4,000 |
| 2/1/93 | 10 | $4,500.00 | 25.00 | $250.00 | $4,750.00 | 10 | $0 | $4,750.00 | $4,000 |
| 2/2/93 | 10 | $4,750.00 | 25.00 | $250.00 | $5,000.00 | 10 | $0 | $5,000.00 | $4,000 |
| 2/3/93 | 10 | $5,000.00 | (25.00) | ($250.00) | $4,750.00 | 10 | $0 | $4,750.00 | $4,000 |
| 2/4/93 | 10 | $4,750.00 | 0.00 | $0.00 | $4,750.00 | 10 | $0 | $4,750.00 | $4,000 |
| 2/5/93 | 10 | $4,750.00 | 0.00 | $0.00 | $4,750.00 | 10 | $0 | $4,750.00 | $4,000 |
| 2/8/93 | 10 | $4,750.00 | 25.00 | $250.00 | $5,000.00 | 10 | $0 | $5,000 | $4,000 |
| 2/9/93 | 10 | $5,000.00 | 0.00 | $0.00 | $5,000.00 | 10 | $0 | $5,000 | $4,000 |
| 2/10/93 | 10 | $5,000.00 | 0.00 | $0.00 | $5,000.00 | 10 | $0 | $5,000 | $4,000 |
| 2/11/93 | 10 | $5,000.00 | 25.00 | $250.00 | $5,250.00 | 0 | ($5,250) | $0 | $0 |

IV. Cash Activity

| (1) Date | (2) Reserve Cash Beginning Balance | (3) Cash Account Flo + Invested / -Withdrawn | (4) rgin Account Flo + From Margin / -To Margin | (5) Reserve Ending Balance |
|---|---|---|---|---|
| 1/29/93 | $5,500 | $0 | $0 | $5,500.00 |
| 2/1/93 | $5,500 | $0 | $0 | $5,500.00 |
| 2/2/93 | $5,500 | $0 | $0 | $5,500.00 |
| 2/3/93 | $5,500 | $0 | $0 | $5,500.00 |
| 2/4/93 | $5,500 | $0 | $0 | $5,500.00 |
| 2/5/93 | $5,500 | $0 | $0 | $5,500.00 |
| 2/8/93 | $5,500 | $0 | $0 | $5,500.00 |
| 2/9/93 | $5,500 | $0 | $0 | $5,500.00 |
| 2/10/93 | $5,500 | $0 | $0 | $5,500.00 |
| 2/11/93 | $5,500 | $0 | $5,250 | $10,750.00 |

total value. Note the similarity in the price behavior of both the March and June contracts, columns 4 and 8. Both contracts exhibited similar positive and negative price changes during the week, but the spread's value remained quite stable. The values in column 13 are computed by multiplying the spread's unit value, column 10, by the total number of contracts in the spread. In this example the spread's value as of 1/29/93, $1,750, is found by multiplying the spread's unit value, $175, by 10 contracts. The remaining values in column 13 show that the spread remained quite stable and finished at $2,500 on 2/11/93.

Section II shows the spread's price behavior in conjunction with the margin and cash accounts, Sections III and IV, respectively. Column 1 of Section II is the date, while column 2 shows the spread components. The spread is presented with the nearby contract first and the deferred contract second, because this is how the spread is quoted. The plus sign that precedes the abbreviation "Mar" denotes that the spreader has bought March S&P 500 futures contracts, while the minus sign that precedes the abbreviation "Jun" indicates that the spreader has sold June S&P 500 futures contracts. Column 3 is identical to column 10 of Section I, and shows the spread's unit value. Column 4 provides the number of units per lot where the term "lot" is used instead of "contract" to denote the size of the position. In this case the spreader's position consists of 10 lots, column 5, since 10 March contracts were bought and 10 June contracts were sold. Column 6 in Section II is obtained by multiplying columns 3, 4, and 5 together. This number should be equal to the value for the corresponding date in column 13 in Section I, since both have the same meaning. Column 7 tracks the daily gain or loss for the spread. The gains and losses are computed by taking the current value of the spread in column 6 and subtracting the prior day's value. For example, the first +$250 is found by subtracting the 1/29/93 value, $1,750, from the 1/29/93 value, $2,000. Column 8 provides the total cash and margin available to the spreader. This amount will change from day to day as the spread experiences gains and losses. Column 9 shows how much money the spreader has allocated for this strategy. In this case the spreader made a commitment of $10,000. Column 10 provides for commissions, and column 11 shows the spread's cumulative gain or loss. The values in column 11 are computed by subtracting the amount of cash and margin invested in the strategy (column 9) from the current value of the total cash plus margin balance (column 8). For example, the spread's cumulative gain on

2/2/93 of $500 was computed by subtracting the amount of invested cash plus margin, $10,000, from the total cash plus margin amount of $10,500.

The worksheet's final two sections, III and IV, must be considered jointly. Observe that the spreader's margin requirements, $450 initial margin and $400 maintenance margin, are much lower than the margin requirements of both the speculator and the hedger. Recall that the initial margin for either a long or short position in the S&P 500 futures market was $10,000 per contract, and that the maintenance requirement was $10,000 per contract. Since the spreader has a 10-lot position, column 2, the initial balance is $4,500, column 3, and the maintenance requirement is $4,000, column 10. This $4,500 initial margin balance is only a portion of the $10,000 that the spreader has allocated for this strategy. The remaining $5,500 is being held in reserve in a highly liquid account, such as a checking account. It should be mentioned that the spreader's cash and margin position is sufficient to withstand only one day of maximum margin calls of $400 per spread: $400 times 10-contracts = $4,000 per day. This is an egregious violation of the 5-day rule of thumb, and is not recommended. However, the spreader probably is safe since this intramarket spread is quite stable and is unlikely to require a margin call.

Section III records the effects of the changing futures contract prices on the spreader's margin account. The values in columns 4 and 5 track the spread's unit price change and daily gain or loss. Notice that the spread generally increased in value and that no transfers from the cash reserve account to the margin account were required. The information in column 4, the spread unit price change, corresponds to Section I, column 11; while the data shown in column 5 of Section III, the position gain or loss, matches the data in Section II, column 7. The values in column 6 show the margin balance prior to marking to market, and alert the spreader to the possibility of having to either post more cash or liquidate part of the position. During the spread's two-week lifespan it fell from –$175 to –$250, Section I, column 10, so that on 2/11/93 the margin balance had grown to $5,250. Section III, column 6. At this time the spreader decided to liquidate the position and take the $750 profit, Section II, column 11. Thus, all the positions were closed out and the margin balance was transferred to the cash accounts Section IV, column 4, which resulted in an ending balance of $10,750, Section IV, column 5, and Section II, column 8.

## *SUMMARY*

This chapter has examined various S&P 500 Index trading strategies via the relationships that link the S&P 500 cash and futures markets. The chapter began with a discussion of the S&P 500 Index and an explanation of S&P 500 price quotes as reported in *The Wall Street Journal* and *Barron's*. The chapter continued with a discussion of speculators, hedgers, and spreaders, and considered long and short speculative positions, long and short hedged positions, and the intra-market, or time spread. Worksheets were developed for each type of strategy, and were used to explain and illustrate clearly how profits are made and losses incurred in the S&P 500 futures market.

# Chapter 7

# *FOREIGN EXCHANGE TRADING STRATEGIES*

## *FOREIGN EXCHANGE MARKETS*

Foreign exchange is another country's currency. The foreign exchange market is the network of hedgers, speculators, and arbitragers that buy and sell currencies. On a given day, between six hundred billion and one trillion dollars worth of currencies changes hands around the world. Without this market it would be virtually impossible to conduct international trade.

International trade involves the purchase and sale of goods and services by the residents of one country from the residents of another country. When such a transaction occurs, there are usually two currencies involved—the buyer's home currency and the seller's home currency. It may be possible for the goods to be purchased with the buyer's home currency, but ultimately the foreign producer must be able to obtain his home currency as payment. For example, if an American purchases a German automobile and pays for it in U.S. dollars, those dollars will not be of much use to the auto manufacturer when it comes time to pay the employees. The employees need deutsche marks to exist within the German economy. During the time the transaction is pending, fluctuating currency values can have an adverse effect on the wealth of the buyer or seller. These adverse effects are termed currency risk, or foreign exchange risk. Foreign exchange futures contracts can be used to minimize this risk.

Figure 7-1 shows foreign exchange prices, as quoted in *The Wall Street Journal*, for many of the world's currencies as of the close of trading on Monday, April 4, 1994. The first column denotes the country in bold type and the currency in parentheses. The next two columns provide the value of one unit of foreign currency in terms of U.S. dollars for the last two business days. When currencies are quoted in terms of the U.S. dollar they are said to be quoted in American terms. Additionally, 30-, 90-, and 180-day forward price quotes are provided for the major currencies: the British pound, Canadian dollar, French franc, German mark, Japanese yen, and Swiss franc. For example, on Monday the German mark closed at $.5900 in the cash market, and if one wanted to buy or sell the mark in 30 days then the price was $.5890, while the price for marks in 90 days was $.5876 If marks were needed in 180 days the price was $.5864 per mark. On the previous Friday the mark closed at $.5900 in the cash market, $.5890 30 days forward, $.5876 90 days forward, and $.5865 180 days forward. The remaining two columns show the value of the U.S. dollar in terms of the foreign currencies and are deemed European quotes. The German mark example reveals that on Monday the U.S. dollar settled at DM 1.6950 in the cash market, DM 1.6979 30 days forward, DM 1.7019 90 days forward, and DM 1.7053 180 days forward. The previous Friday's closing prices for the dollar were DM 1.6950 in the cash market, DM 1.6978 30 days forward, DM 1.7018 90 days forward, and DM 1.7050 180 days forward.

Notice that there was not much movement in the deutsche mark over the weekend. To get a better idea of the daily changes in the foreign exchange market, examine the differences between the Monday and Friday price quotes for the British pound and the Canadian dollar.

Figure 7-2 is a matrix of exchange rates for 10 of the world's largest economies. When currency values are expressed without using the U.S. dollar, the quote is said to be a "cross rate." If one reads down a given column, then the cross rate values of that specific currency, in terms of each of the other nine countries' currencies, can be found. Conversely, reading across each row supplies the cross rate values of each of the nine currencies in terms of the country represented in that specific row. For example, the value of the British pound in each of the other nine currencies can be determined by reading down the "Pound" column. These quotes show that it took 2.0461 Canadian

*Figure 7-1*
*Currency Trading*

THE WALL STREET JOURNAL TUESDAY, APRIL 5, 1994

# CURRENCY TRADING

## EXCHANGE RATES

Monday, April 4, 1994
The New York foreign exchange selling rates below apply to trading among banks in amounts of $1 million and more, as quoted at 3 p.m. Eastern time by Bankers Trust Co., Dow Jones Telerate Inc. and other sources. Retail transactions provide fewer units of foreign currency per dollar.

| Country | U.S. $ equiv. Mon. | Fri. | Currency per U.S. $ Mon. | Fri. |
|---|---|---|---|---|
| Argentina (Peso) | 1.01 | 1.01 | .99 | .99 |
| Australia (Dollar) | .7043 | .7065 | 1.4198 | 1.4154 |
| Austria (Schilling) | .08386 | .08386 | 11.92 | 11.92 |
| Bahrain (Dinar) | 2.6522 | 2.6522 | .3771 | .3771 |
| Belgium (Franc) | .02863 | .02863 | 34.93 | 34.93 |
| Brazil (Cruzeiro real) | .0010852 | .0011056 | 921.51 | 904.50 |
| Britain (Pound) | 1.4680 | 1.4740 | .6812 | .6784 |
| 30-Day Forward | 1.4661 | 1.4721 | .6821 | .6793 |
| 90-Day Forward | 1.4630 | 1.4691 | .6835 | .6807 |
| 180-Day Forward | 1.4600 | 1.4651 | .6849 | .6825 |
| Canada (Dollar) | .7166 | .7203 | 1.3955 | 1.3883 |
| 30-Day Forward | .7155 | .7193 | 1.3977 | 1.3903 |
| 90-Day Forward | .7124 | .7167 | 1.4038 | 1.3953 |
| 180-Day Forward | .7085 | .7131 | 1.4115 | 1.4023 |
| Czech. Rep. (Koruna) | | | | |
| Commercial rate | .0341309 | .0341309 | 29.2990 | 29.2990 |
| Chile (Peso) | .002415 | .002406 | 414.08 | 415.65 |
| China (Renminbi) | .114986 | .114929 | 8.6967 | 8.7010 |
| Colombia (Peso) | .001218 | .001218 | 820.78 | 821.14 |
| Denmark (Krone) | .1501 | .1501 | 6.6627 | 6.6605 |
| Ecuador (Sucre) | | | | |
| Floating rate | .000478 | .000478 | 2090.04 | 2091.00 |
| Finland (Markka) | .18237 | .18251 | 5.4833 | 5.4791 |
| France (Franc) | .17275 | .17270 | 5.7888 | 5.7905 |
| 30-Day Forward | .17241 | .17236 | 5.8000 | 5.8017 |
| 90-Day Forward | .17184 | .17182 | 5.8193 | 5.8202 |
| 180-Day Forward | .17132 | .17130 | 5.8370 | 5.8378 |
| Germany (Mark) | .5900 | .5900 | 1.6950 | 1.6950 |
| 30-Day Forward | .5890 | .5890 | 1.6979 | 1.6978 |
| 90-Day Forward | .5876 | .5876 | 1.7019 | 1.7018 |
| 180-Day Forward | .5864 | .5865 | 1.7053 | 1.7050 |
| Greece (Drachma) | .004015 | .003997 | 249.05 | 250.17 |
| Hong Kong (Dollar) | .12942 | .12942 | 7.7268 | 7.7268 |
| Hungary (Forint) | .0097456 | .0097456 | 102.6100 | 102.6100 |
| India (Rupee) | .03212 | .03212 | 31.13 | 31.13 |
| Indonesia (Rupiah) | .0004640 | .0004651 | 2155.03 | 2150.00 |
| Ireland (Punt) | 1.4189 | 1.4248 | .7048 | .7019 |
| Israel (Shekel) | .3372 | .3359 | 2.9655 | 2.9770 |
| Italy (Lira) | .0006121 | .0006149 | 1633.77 | 1626.36 |

| Country | U.S. $ equiv. Mon. | Fri. | Currency per U.S. $ Mon. | Fri. |
|---|---|---|---|---|
| Japan (Yen) | .009699 | .009645 | 103.10 | 103.68 |
| 30-Day Forward | .009712 | .009657 | 102.97 | 103.55 |
| 90-Day Forward | .009742 | .009686 | 102.65 | 103.24 |
| 180-Day Forward | .009803 | .009743 | 102.01 | 102.63 |
| Jordan (Dinar) | 1.4535 | 1.4599 | .6880 | .6850 |
| Kuwait (Dinar) | 3.3656 | 3.3639 | .2971 | .2973 |
| Lebanon (Pound) | .000590 | .000590 | 1694.50 | 1695.50 |
| Malaysia (Ringgit) | .3736 | .3736 | 2.6765 | 2.6765 |
| Malta (Lira) | 2.6008 | 2.6042 | .3845 | .3840 |
| Mexico (Peso) | | | | |
| Floating rate | .2982849 | .2978140 | 3.3525 | 3.3578 |
| Netherland (Guilder) | .5252 | .5253 | 1.9042 | 1.9038 |
| New Zealand (Dollar) | .5631 | .5650 | 1.7759 | 1.7699 |
| Norway (Krone) | .1357 | .1358 | 7.3707 | 7.3648 |
| Pakistan (Rupee) | .0329 | .0329 | 30.40 | 30.40 |
| Peru (New Sol) | .4737 | .4718 | 2.11 | 2.12 |
| Philippines (Peso) | .03690 | .03683 | 27.10 | 27.15 |
| Poland (Zloty) | .00004521 | .00004521 | 22119.00 | 22119.00 |
| Portugal (Escudo) | .005750 | .005750 | 173.91 | 173.91 |
| Saudi Arabia (Riyal) | .26665 | .26667 | 3.7503 | 3.7500 |
| Singapore (Dollar) | .6370 | .6370 | 1.5698 | 1.5698 |
| Slovak Rep. (Koruna) | .0306937 | .0306937 | 32.5800 | 32.5800 |
| South Africa (Rand) | | | | |
| Commercial rate | z | z | z | z |
| Financial rate | z | z | z | z |
| South Korea (Won) | .0012378 | .0012389 | 807.90 | 807.20 |
| Spain (Peseta) | .007214 | .007214 | 138.62 | 138.62 |
| Sweden (Krona) | .1265 | .1265 | 7.9072 | 7.9063 |
| Switzerland (Franc) | .7027 | .7013 | 1.4230 | 1.4260 |
| 30-Day Forward | .7023 | .7009 | 1.4238 | 1.4268 |
| 90-Day Forward | .7023 | .7008 | 1.4238 | 1.4270 |
| 180-Day Forward | .7036 | .7017 | 1.4213 | 1.4251 |
| Taiwan (Dollar) | .037929 | .037874 | 26.37 | 26.40 |
| Thailand (Baht) | .03956 | .03960 | 25.28 | 25.25 |
| Turkey (Lira) | .0000434 | .0000442 | 23054.93 | 22639.34 |
| United Arab (Dirham) | .2723 | .2723 | 3.6725 | 3.6725 |
| Uruguay (New Peso) | | | | |
| Financial | .212089 | .218007 | 4.72 | 4.59 |
| Venezuela (Bolivar) | | | | |
| Floating rate | .00874 | .00874 | 114.40 | 114.40 |
| — — — | | | | |
| SDR | 1.40405 | 1.40384 | .71223 | .71233 |
| ECU | 1.13780 | 1.13920 | .... | .... |

Special Drawing Rights (SDR) are based on exchange rates for the U.S., German, British, French and Japanese currencies. Source: International Monetary Fund.
European Currency Unit (ECU) is based on a basket of community currencies.
z-Not quoted.

*Figure 7-2*
*Key Currency Cross Rates*
*(Late New York Trading, April 4, 1994)*

**THE WALL STREET JOURNAL** TUESDAY, APRIL 5, 1994

|              | Dollar | Pound  | SFranc  | Guilder | Peso    | Yen    | Lira   | D-Mark | FFranc | CdnDlr |
|--------------|--------|--------|---------|---------|---------|--------|--------|--------|--------|--------|
| Canada ........ | 1.3955 | 2.0461 | .97895 | .73197 | .41626 | .01352 | .00085 | .82219 | .24067 | .... |
| France ......... | 5.7983 | 8.501 | 4.0676 | 3.0413 | 1.72955 | .05619 | .00354 | 3.4162 | .... | 4.1550 |
| Germany ...... | 1.6973 | 2.4886 | 1.1907 | .89027 | .50628 | .01645 | .00104 | .... | .29272 | 1.2163 |
| Italy ........... | 1638.7 | 2402.7 | 1149.58 | 859.55 | 488.81 | 15.879 | .... | 965.49 | 282.62 | 1174.3 |
| Japan ......... | 103.20 | 151.31 | 72.396 | 54.131 | 30.783 | .... | .06298 | 60.802 | 17.798 | 73.95 |
| Mexico ......... | 3.3525 | 4.9154 | 2.3518 | 1.7585 | .... | .03249 | .00205 | 1.9752 | .5782 | 2.4024 |
| Netherlands .. | 1.9065 | 2.7953 | 1.3374 | .... | .56868 | .01847 | .00116 | 1.1233 | .32880 | 1.3662 |
| Switzerland ... | 1.4255 | 2.0901 | .... | .74771 | .42521 | .01381 | .00087 | .83986 | .24585 | 1.0215 |
| U.K. ............. | .68204 | .... | .47845 | .35774 | .20344 | .00661 | .00042 | .40184 | .11763 | .48874 |
| U.S. ............. | .... | 1.4662 | .70151 | .52452 | .29828 | .00969 | .00061 | .58917 | .17246 | .71659 |

Source: Dow Jones Telerate, Inc.

dollars to purchase one British pound; that it would cost 4.9154 Mexican pesos to obtain one British pound; and that the price of a British pound in U.S. dollars is $1.4662. The entries in the row marked "U.K." show that one British pound was worth .68204 U.S. dollars, .47845 Swiss francs, and .48874 Canadian dollars. Note that the quotes in the "U.S." row are price quotes in American terms for the nine currencies, while the entries in the "Dollar" column are price quotes in European terms for the nine currencies.

The forward quotes for the major currencies, presented in Figure 7-1, reflect the currencies' prices in the foreign exchange forward market. Recall from Chapter One that a forward market is characterized by trading activity between individual buyers and sellers (counterparties), where all contract terms are negotiable and no cash changes hands until the contract matures. These markets were cumbersome for agricultural commodities, and thus paved the way for the development of the U.S. futures exchanges. The same cannot be said for the foreign exchange forward market. This is an extremely liquid market which operates 24 hours a day where the major participants are large money-center banks who deal in denominations of $1,000,000 or more.

Given these large transaction amounts and the existence of counterparty risk, there was a need for a foreign currency futures market. This need became more acute in 1971 when the United States abandoned the gold standard and the dollar was permitted to float against the other major currencies. With currency values being determined by the forces of supply and demand, fluctuations in value increased dramatically for all market participants. Thus, in May of 1972 the Chicago Mercantile Exchange introduced foreign exchange futures contracts, which provided several advantages to nonbank market participants who had to manage the increased currency volatility. First, these contracts were denominated in much smaller amounts than those commonly traded in the spot and forward market, which made it easier for relatively small hedgers to transfer currency risk to equally small speculators. Furthermore, position gains and losses were taken daily via margin accounts by marking all positions to the market. Finally, since contract performance was guaranteed by the clearing corporation, counterparty risk was eliminated. These currency futures contracts were a phenomenal success and made acceptance much easier for the other financial futures contracts which were to follow.

Figure 7-3 presents *The Wall Street Journal* foreign exchange futures data for Monday, April 11, 1994. Information regarding the futures contracts of six major currencies is presented in a standardized format. This format conveys such information as the trading location of

*Figure 7-3*
*Currency*

**THE WALL STREET JOURNAL** TUESDAY, APRIL 12, 1994

|  | Open | High | Low | Settle | Change | Lifetime High | Low | Open Interest |
|---|---|---|---|---|---|---|---|---|
| **JAPAN YEN (CME) – 12.5 million yen; $ per yen (.00)** | | | | | | | | |
| June | .9541 | .9729 | .9540 | .9726 | + .0196 | .9945 | .8540 | 52,216 |
| Sept | .9610 | .9782 | .9610 | .9779 | + .0196 | .9900 | .8942 | 2,175 |
| Dec | .9802 | .9815 | .9802 | .9839 | + .0196 | .9930 | .9525 | 618 |
| Est vol 27,607; vol Fri 25,727; open int 55,009, – 1,165. | | | | | | | | |
| **DEUTSCHEMARK (CME) – 125,000 marks; $ per mark** | | | | | | | | |
| June | .5825 | .5844 | .5811 | .5822 | + .0003 | .6162 | .5607 | 89,493 |
| Sept | .5823 | .5823 | .5802 | .5807 | + .0003 | .6130 | .5600 | 2,604 |
| Dec | .5824 | .5824 | .5803 | .5806 | + .0003 | .5953 | .5590 | 119 |
| Mr95 | .5817 | .5817 | .5810 | .5815 | + .0003 | .5956 | .5805 | 611 |
| Est vol 32,383; vol Fri 26,120; open int 92,827, – 2,951. | | | | | | | | |
| **CANADIAN DOLLAR (CME) – 100,000 dlrs.; $ per Can $** | | | | | | | | |
| June | .7193 | .7195 | .7171 | .7181 | – .0024 | .7805 | .7113 | 39,423 |
| Sept | .7150 | .7154 | .7144 | .7148 | – .0024 | .7740 | .7068 | 1,977 |
| Dec | .7130 | .7130 | .7120 | .7125 | – .0024 | .7670 | .7038 | 1,223 |
| Mr95 | .7095 | .7110 | .7095 | .7106 | – .0024 | .7605 | .7020 | 606 |
| Est vol 3,562; vol Fri 4,913; open int 43,291, +95. | | | | | | | | |
| **BRITISH POUND (CME) – 62,500 pds.; $ per pound** | | | | | | | | |
| June | 1.4722 | 1.4754 | 1.4646 | 1.4676 | – .0050 | 1.5300 | 1.4350 | 46,323 |
| Sept | 1.4630 | 1.4650 | 1.4620 | 1.4642 | – .0048 | 1.4980 | 1.4440 | 925 |
| Est vol 11,022; vol Fri 10,082; open int 47,281, – 1,212. | | | | | | | | |
| **SWISS FRANC (CME) – 125,000 francs; $ per franc** | | | | | | | | |
| June | .6921 | .6958 | .6917 | .6933 | + .0022 | .7115 | .6590 | 33,798 |
| Sept | .6960 | .6966 | .6925 | .6942 | + .0022 | .7165 | .6590 | 320 |
| Est vol 16,670; vol Fri 17,052; open int 34,162, – 438. | | | | | | | | |
| **AUSTRALIAN DOLLAR (CME) – 100,000 dlrs.; $ per A.$** | | | | | | | | |
| June | .7205 | .7235 | .7200 | .7205 | – .0028 | .7269 | .6395 | 5,646 |
| Est vol 597; vol Fri 2,532; open int 5,703, +1,349. | | | | | | | | |
| **U.S. DOLLAR INDEX (FINEX) – 1,000 times USDX** | | | | | | | | |
| June | 95.15 | 95.40 | 94.90 | 95.19 | – .32 | 99.04 | 92.70 | 8,562 |
| Sept | 95.60 | 95.83 | 95.80 | 95.67 | – .32 | 98.55 | 94.46 | 2,018 |
| Est vol 1,250; vol Fri 1,426; open int 10,687, – 136. | | | | | | | | |
| The index: High 94.93; Low 94.49; Close 94.71 – .22 | | | | | | | | |

the futures contracts; the quantity of foreign currency controlled by the contract; the terms of the price quote (all Chicago Mercantile Exchange foreign currency contracts are quoted in American terms); the contracts' price changes; and the quantity of contracts traded and held by market participants.

For example, the deutsche mark quotes show that deutsche mark futures contracts are traded on the Chicago Mercantile Exchange, where each contract controls 125,000 deutsche marks, prices are quoted in cents per deutsche mark, and maturities follow a quarterly cycle of December, March, June, and September. Trading is active in four deutsche mark futures contracts maturing between June of 1994 and March of 1995. The "Open" column shows that the June 1994 contract began the trading day at a price of .5825, or $.5825 per deutsche mark. During the day, the highest price for June 1994 deutsche marks was .5844, or $.5844 per deutsche mark, while the lowest price was .5811, or $.5811 per deutsche mark. These levels are indicated by the "High" and "Low" columns, respectively. The "Settle" column denotes that the June '94 deutsche mark futures contract closed, or settled, at a price of .5822, or $.5822 per deutsche mark, at the end of the trading day. The +.0003 entry in the "Change" column for the June '94 contract indicates that the price rose by three ticks, or $.003 per deutsche mark, relative to the settlement price of the prior day (Friday, April 8). The "Lifetime High and Low" columns show that since this contract began trading, it has ranged in value from $.6162 per deutsche mark to $.5607 per deutsche mark. The last column, "Open Interest," reveals that there are 89,493 long positions in June 1994 deutsche mark futures contracts which are outstanding. "Est vol 32,383" indicates that Friday's estimated trading volume was 32,383 for all deutsche mark futures contracts; while "vol Fri 26,120" shows that Friday's actual volume was 26,120 deutsche mark futures contracts. Finally, the total open interest for all deutsche mark futures contracts is 92,827, which is 2,951 contracts less than the previous trading day's open interest as indicated by "open int 92,827, –2,951."

## EXCHANGE RATE DETERMINATION

All exchange rates are determined by the forces of supply and demand. Two theories which attempt to explain these forces are the Theory of Interest Rate Parity and the Theory of Purchasing Power

Parity. Interest Rate Parity is short-term in nature and seeks to explain the relationship between spot exchange rates and forward exchange rates as determined by short-term interest rates. Purchasing Power Parity takes a longer view and attempts to explain the behavior of spot exchange rates over time as a function of inflation.

The underlying logic for Interest Rate Parity is straightforward: there should be no advantage to converting domestic funds to the currency of a country with a higher interest rate, investing the converted funds at the higher interest rate, and then converting the foreign funds back to the domestic currency. If it was possible to accumulate a greater amount of domestic funds via this strategy than by investing the funds in the domestic market, then market participants would pursue the more profitable conversion and foreign investment strategy. For example, suppose that one-year interest rates are 6% in the United States and 8% in Switzerland, and that the spot rate for the Swiss franc is $.6667/SF1, which implies a spot rate of SF1.5/$1, while the one-year forward rate for the Swiss franc is $.6600/SF1, which translates to SF1.5152/$1 in the forward market. If one has $1,000,000 to invest, then the preferred strategy will be to convert the dollars to francs in the spot market, ($1,000,000 SF1.5/$1 = SF1,500,000), invest the francs in Switzerland for one year at 8% to yield (SF1,500,000 (1.08) = SF1,620,000), convert the francs to dollars by selling the francs forward at the one-year rate ($.6600/SF1 SF1,620,000 = $1,069,200) or 6.9%. The alternative strategy is to invest the $1,000,000 in the United States for one year at 6% ($1,000,000 (1.06) = $1,060,000). Comparing the outcomes clearly shows that the foreign strategy is better. Thus, until the strategies provide identical outcomes, the foreign strategy will be preferred.

The continued activity in the two currencies, where Swiss francs are purchased for dollars in the spot market and sold for dollars in the forward market, will cause the exchange rates to adjust so that there will be no advantage to investing in Switzerland, the country with the higher interest rate. Continuing with the above example, suppose that the interest rates remain the same, but that the spot rate for the Swiss franc increases to $.6700/SF1, implying SF1.492537/$1, and the one-year forward rate falls to $.6576/SF1. Under these conditions, the strategies will have the same outcomes. Specifically, converting the dollars to francs results in ($1,000,000 SF1.492537/$1 = SF1,492,537). Investing the francs in Switzerland for one year at 8% will produce (SF1,492,537 (1.08) = SF1,611,940). These francs can be sold in the forward market for delivery in one year at $.6576/SF1 to yield (SF1,611,940 $.6576/SF1 = $1,060,011), or 6.0% on the original $1,000,000. Since this rate of return is identical to the one-year U.S. rate, the foreign advantage has been eliminated and the foreign exchange markets are in equilibrium.

It is important to note that the exchange rates adjusted to achieve equilibrium between the currencies and the interest rates of the two countries. Thus, equilibrium is attained when the currency's forward price equals the spot price adjusted for the interest rate differential between the two countries. This can be expressed exactly as:

$$F_t = S_t \; \frac{(1 + r_d)^t}{(1 + r_f)^t} \tag{1}$$

where $F_t$ is the forward rate, $S_t$ is the spot rate, and $r_d$ and $r_f$ are the domestic and foreign interest rates, respectively. While the approximate relationship between the exchange rates and the interest rate differential is:

$$F_t \approx S_t \; [1 + (r_d - r_f)] \tag{2}$$

Observe that this approximation is nothing more than the cost of carry model, introduced in Chapter Two, applied to foreign currencies where the carrying charges are expressed as the difference between the domestic and foreign interest rates. If the domestic rate is greater than the foreign rate, then the differential is positive, and the forward rate should be greater than the spot rate. Thus, the currency is said to be selling at a premium (i.e, premium to spot) in the forward market. Conversely, if the domestic rate is less than the foreign rate, then the differential is negative, and the forward exchange rate should be less than the spot rate. Under these conditions the currency is described as selling at a discount in the forward market; that is, the forward exchange rate is at a discount to the spot exchange rate. In general, countries with relatively high interest rates should have their currencies trading for discounts, while currencies from countries with relatively low interest rates should be selling at a premium in the forward market.

Consider the initial data from above: a spot rate of $.6700; a 6% U.S., or domestic, interest rate; and an 8% Swiss, or foreign, rate. Given the relationships expressed in the Interest Rate Parity equation, we should expect the Swiss franc to be trading at a discount to spot one year forward. Indeed, the one-year forward rate, $.6600, does exhibit a discount. However, the discount is not sufficiently deep since there is an opportunity for arbitrage profits. Taking these spot exchange and interest rate data and applying equation (1) will result in the equilibrium one-year forward rate of $.6576/SF1, while the approximation yields a forward exchange rate of $ .6566/SF1.

$$F_t = (\$.6700/SF1)\ \frac{(1.06)}{(1.08)}$$
$$= \$.6576/SF1$$
$$F_t \approx (\$.6700/SF1)\ [1 + (.06 - .08)]$$
$$\approx \$.6576/SF1$$

If the Swiss franc had been priced at $.6576/SF1 in the forward market, then the foreign strategy would have yielded a return identical to that of the domestic strategy, 6%. Proof: convert the $1,000,000 to Swiss francs in the spot market ($1,000,000 SF1.4925/$1 = SF1,492,537). Invest the francs in Switzerland for one year at the 8% rate to obtain (SF1,492,537 (1.08) = SF1,611,940). Then sell the francs in the forward market for one-year delivery (SF1,611,940 $.6566/SF1). Consider that it would be impossible to earn arbitrage profits by borrowing the funds domestically, converting to the foreign currency, investing in the foreign market, converting back to the domestic currency, and paying off the loan.

Purchasing Power Parity is based on the logic that spot exchange rates will adjust in response to the inflation rates of the two countries. As prices rise in a given country, its currency loses value since it takes more currency to purchase the same amount of goods. Thus, the currency becomes less attractive to hold as inflation erodes its purchasing power. The result will be a drop in demand for the currency, which will cause its price to decline *vis à vis* the other country's currency until it stabilizes at a value where market participants feel it accurately reflects the real purchasing power of the currency, relative to the other country's currency.

This relationship can be illustrated as follows. Consider the United States and Japan. Suppose that the United States experiences an inflation rate of 5% during the year, and that during the same time period Japan's inflation rate is 2%. If the spot exchange rate at the beginning of the year is ¥125/$1, or $.008/¥1, then one would expect the spot exchange rate to adjust to ¥119.485/$1, or $.00837/¥1, in one year to reflect the difference in the inflation rates and purchasing power between Japan and the United States. Observe that the dollar's value would decline about ¥5½, while the yen would rise by $.00037. These changes can be quantified as:

$$S_{t+1} = S_t \frac{(1 + I_d)}{(1 + I_f)} \qquad (3)$$

$$S_{t+1} \approx S_t \left[1 + (I_d - I_f)\right] \qquad (4)$$

where $S_{t+1}$ is the future spot rate, $S_t$ is the current spot rate, and $I_d$ and $I_f$ are the domestic and foreign inflation rates, respectively. Equation 3 shows the exact mathematical relationship, while the approximate relationship between the spot rates and inflation rates is given by the fourth expression. Notice the similarity between equations 1 and 3, and between approximations 2 and 4. Once again, the future value concept is being used to determine foreign exchange prices.

The theory of Purchasing Power Parity is straightforward; however, when applied, its results leave much to be desired. For example, in December of 1992 the spot exchange rate between the Japanese yen and the U.S dollar was ¥124.95/$1, or $.008003/¥1; during 1993, the U.S. inflation rate was 2.7%, while Japan's inflation rate was .9% for the same period. Purchasing Power Parity based forecasts for the December 1993 spot exchange rate can be obtained via expressions 3 and 4. Applying equation 3 yields a December 1993 spot rate forecast of:

$$S_{t+1} = ¥124.95 \frac{(1.009)}{(1.027)}$$

$$= ¥122.76$$

while the approximation, expression 4, generates a spot exchange rate forecast of:

$$S_{t+1} = ¥124.95 \left[1 + (.009 - .027)\right]$$

$$= ¥122.70$$

However, the actual value for the U.S. dollar in December of 1993 was ¥108.55, far below the forecasts.

This difference between the Purchasing Power Parity based spot exchange rate forecast, and the actual spot rate that occurred can be due to a variety of factors. The most likely reason for the divergence is that governments will attempt to use foreign exchange rates as tools to implement economic policy. When governments impose frictions on the foreign exchange market, or follow an intervention policy designed to achieve a certain exchange rate level, then the resulting foreign exchange rates can deviate significantly from their theoretical values.

## EXCHANGE RATE SYSTEMS

Exchange rate systems define the structure that determines exchange rate behavior. Broadly speaking, exchange rate systems can be characterized by the amount of governmental intervention that is used to influence the foreign exchange rates. At one end of the spectrum there is no government intervention in the foreign exchange market and rates are permitted to fluctuate freely in response to the market forces of supply and demand. This type of system is defined as a freely floating exchange rate system. At the opposite end of the spectrum there is continuous government intervention in the foreign exchange market so that the currency is not permitted to deviate from the desired exchange rate. This system is known as a fixed exchange rate system. Exchange rate systems that have varying degrees of intervention are classified as managed float systems.

One version of the managed float system is the pegged rate system, where the exchange rates of several currencies are set at an agreed-upon rate in relation to a central currency. These systems can require much government intervention to maintain the agreed-upon relationships among the various currencies.

The advantages of the freely floating exchange rate system are that exchange rates are set at market-determined values, and no government intervention is required. Thus, the exchange rates reflect the market's confidence in a country's underlying economy by the willingness of market participants to hold the country's currency. In a freely floating system it is very difficult for governments to follow ill-conceived economic policies without having their currencies suffer accordingly. Therefore, it is virtually impossible for a country to export its economic ills, such as inflation and unemployment, in a freely floating exchange rate system. However, the major disadvantage of the freely floating system is that exchange rates are subject to much volatility.

Conversely, a fixed-rate system offers the advantage of virtually no exchange rate volatility. However, the price for such stability is constant government intervention in the foreign exchange market. Moreover, if exchange rates are not permitted to fluctuate in accordance with market expectations regarding the underlying economy, then poorly conceived economic policies that result in unemployment and inflation can be transmitted to other countries.

Generally speaking, the values of the world's major currencies are determined in a relatively freely floating system. Some intervention occurs, but not enough to eliminate all volatility. This exchange rate volatility and associated foreign exchange risk are the reasons why foreign exchange futures contracts exist. The Chicago Mercantile Exchange foreign currency futures contracts on the Canadian dollar, the Japanese yen, the German deutsche mark, the Swiss franc, the British pound, and Australian dollar permit hedgers to transfer exchange rate risk to speculators.

In 1979 the European Community implemented the European Monetary System. This system was designed to promote price stability throughout the European Common Market countries and established the European Currency Unit (ECU). The ECU is a unit of account that is composed of a weighted average of the exchange rates of 10 European currencies. The focal point of this system was the Exchange Rate Mechanism (ERM), where each member was permitted to establish an exchange rate for its currency relative to the ECU. Each currency was permitted to rise or fall a given percentage from the ECU value. If a currency's fluctuations carried its value outside the permitted range, then central bank intervention would follow until the currency's value was once again within the prescribed limits.

Although each ERM member's currency is supposed to be pegged to the ECU, the reality is that since the reunification of Germany in 1990, the Exchange Rate Mechanism has evolved into a system where the Western European countries have adopted the German mark as the central currency. This meant that the Western European currencies' exchange rates with the rest of the world were being determined by the deutsche mark's exchange rate. Because the German central bank, the Bundesbank, was pursuing an anti-inflationary policy to mitigate the economic consequences of the reunification, German interest rates were kept at relatively high levels. This resulted in a steadily rising deutsche mark throughout 1991 and 1992. Therefore, the other European countries were forced to raise interest rates to maintain relative values for their currencies with the mark. Figures 7-4 and 7-5 graphically portray how the British pound was linked to the deutsche mark during this time.

Relatively high exchange rates made Western European goods expensive to the rest of the world. Consequently, exports diminished, and for countries like Britain that were suffering from high unemployment and economic recession, a stronger currency and higher interest rates meant an even worse domestic economic situation. Moreover, as long as the mark's value remained high relative to the rest of the world, the other Western European countries saw little chance of lowering their unemployment levels and ending their recessions. The situation became untenable for Britain in the late summer of 1992.

The Bundesbank policies had resulted in a steadily rising deutsche mark, and therefore a corresponding increase in the British pound, from June of 1991 through September of 1992. The pound marched relentlessly upward from its $1.75/£1 value in March to its $2.00/£1 value on September 8, 1992—a value that the British economy could not support. One week later, on September 16th, Britain and Italy left the ERM. Thus, the pound was free to float against the deutsche mark as well as against the rest of the world. By the end of September, the pound had fallen to $1.78/£1, and by the end of the year it had stabilized at approximately $1.50/£1 against the dollar, a 28% decline in three months.

## SPECULATING

The conditions in Western Europe during 1991 and 1992 provided great opportunities for reaping speculative profits in foreign exchange. Consider the situation of a small retail investor who was able to commit $15,000 to a speculative British pound strategy in September of 1992. Given the state of the British economy, this speculator believes that the pound is overvalued and anticipates a drop in the exchange rate. Thus, she plans to short the pound by selling British pound futures contracts as traded on the Chicago Mercantile Exchange. If this investor's broker requires speculators to post an initial margin of $1,750 per contract, and then maintain a margin of at least $1,300 per contract, then a trading worksheet like that of Figure 7-6 is

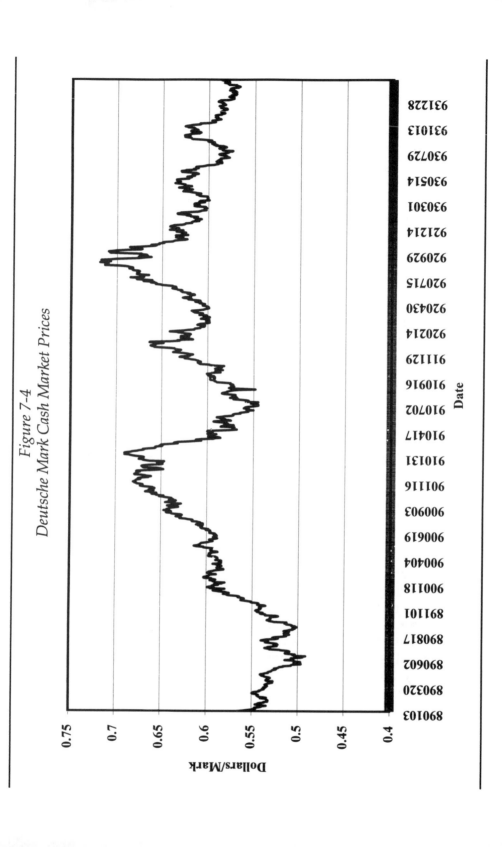

Figure 7-4
Deutsche Mark Cash Market Prices

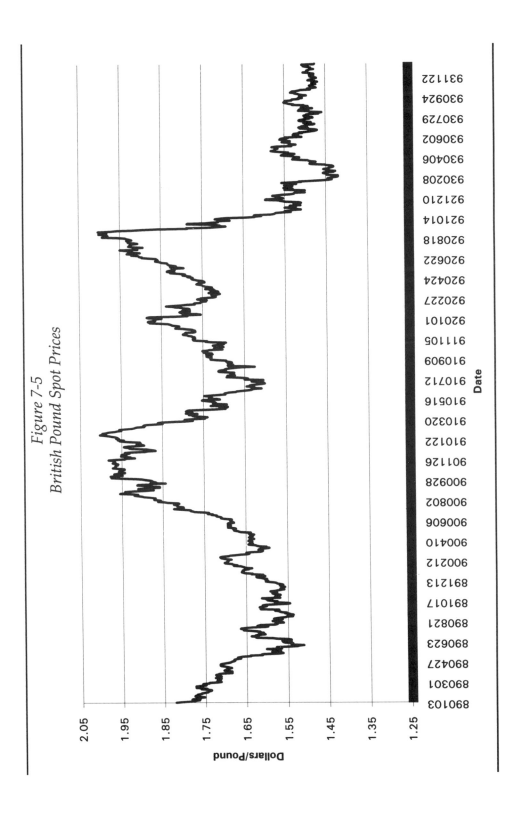

Figure 7-5
British Pound Spot Prices

a good representation of this speculator's British pound position between September 1st and October 1st of 1992.

Figure 7-6, the Speculative Worksheet, is divided into three sections, with the columns in each section being numbered appropriately. Section I provides a listing of the speculative position's overall activity. Section II gives a detailed account of the margin activity that occurs during the time that the position is open. Finally, the third section provides a record of the amount of cash that was invested and withdrawn from the position.

Columns 1 and 2 in the first section show that the speculator opened the position on September 1st in the December British pound contract traded at the Chicago Mercantile Exchange. Column 3 shows that the December pound contract was purchased for a price of $1.957/£1. The fourth column shows that £62,500 comprises a single futures contract, and the fifth column shows that the speculator's initial short position was two contracts. The position's value of $244,625 in the sixth column is obtained by first multiplying the unit price, column 3, by the number of units in the contract, column 4, to get the contract value; and then multiplying the result by the number of contracts in the position, column 5. The seventh column simply provides the position's daily gains and losses. The remaining columns must be interpreted in reference to the other two sections of the worksheet.

Column 8 in Section I shows exactly how much of the speculator's money remains. This balance is composed of the amount that has been posted with the broker as margin and the amount of cash that can be used to fund the position if the market moves against the speculator. As stated previously, this speculative cash does not have to be put on deposit with the broker, but should be held in a highly liquid, easily accessible account. The amount in Section I, column 8, must equal the sum of the day's ending margin account balance, Section II, column 8, and the day's ending speculative cash balance, Section III, column 5. The amount of cash plus margin available to the speculator will fluctuate each day as the position gains or loses value. The next column in Section I, column 9, shows the total amount of money that the speculator has invested in the position. This is composed of the initial margin, Section II, column 3, plus the amount of cash that has been held in reserve to fund the position in the event of adverse market movements, Section III, column 2. Column 10 is reserved for commissions. Since commissions can vary

## Figure 7-6
### British Pound Speculative Worksheet

I. Overall Futures Activity

| (1) Date | (2) Contract | (3) Unit Price | (4) Number of Units per Contract | (5) Number of Contracts +Long/-Short | (6) Position Value | (7) Position +Gain/-Loss | (8) Total Cash+Margin | (9) Invested Cash+Margin | (10) Commission | (11) Cumulative +Gain/-Loss |
|---|---|---|---|---|---|---|---|---|---|---|
| 9/1/92 | Dec B.Pound | 1.9570 | 62500 | -2 | ($244,625) | $0 | $15,000 | $15,000 | | $0 |
| 9/4/92 | Dec B.Pound | 1.9602 | 62500 | -2 | ($245,025) | ($400) | $14,600 | $15,000 | | ($400) |
| 9/8/92 | Dec B.Pound | 1.9688 | 62500 | -2 | ($246,100) | ($1,075) | $13,525 | $15,000 | | ($1,475) |
| 9/9/92 | Dec B.Pound | 1.9354 | 62500 | -2 | ($241,925) | $4,175 | $17,700 | $15,000 | | $2,700 |
| 9/10/92 | Dec B.Pound | 1.9292 | 62500 | -2 | ($241,150) | $775 | $18,475 | $15,000 | | $3,475 |
| 9/11/92 | Dec B.Pound | 1.8866 | 62500 | -2 | ($235,825) | $5,325 | $23,800 | $15,000 | | $8,800 |
| 9/14/92 | Dec B.Pound | 1.8558 | 62500 | -2 | ($231,975) | $3,850 | $27,650 | $15,000 | | $12,650 |
| 9/15/92 | Dec B.Pound | 1.8276 | 62500 | -2 | ($228,450) | $3,525 | $31,175 | $15,000 | | $16,175 |
| 9/16/92 | Dec B.Pound | 1.7476 | 62500 | -2 | ($218,450) | $10,000 | $41,175 | $15,000 | | $26,175 |
| 9/17/92 | Dec B.Pound | 1.7466 | 62500 | -2 | ($218,325) | $125 | $41,300 | $15,000 | | $26,300 |
| 9/18/92 | Dec B.Pound | 1.7090 | 62500 | -2 | ($213,625) | $4,700 | $46,000 | $15,000 | | $31,000 |
| 9/21/92 | Dec B.Pound | 1.6840 | 62500 | -2 | ($210,500) | $3,125 | $49,125 | $15,000 | | $34,125 |
| 9/22/92 | Dec B.Pound | 1.6772 | 62500 | -2 | ($209,650) | $850 | $49,975 | $15,000 | | $34,975 |
| 9/23/92 | Dec B.Pound | 1.6920 | 62500 | -2 | ($211,500) | ($1,850) | $48,125 | $15,000 | | $33,125 |
| 9/24/92 | Dec B.Pound | 1.6858 | 62500 | -2 | ($210,725) | $775 | $48,900 | $15,000 | | $33,900 |
| 9/25/92 | Dec B.Pound | 1.6916 | 62500 | -2 | ($211,450) | ($725) | $48,175 | $15,000 | | $33,175 |
| 9/28/92 | Dec B.Pound | 1.7088 | 62500 | -2 | ($213,600) | ($2,150) | $46,025 | $15,000 | | $31,025 |
| 9/29/92 | Dec B.Pound | 1.7608 | 62500 | -2 | ($220,100) | ($6,500) | $39,525 | $15,000 | | $24,525 |
| 9/30/92 | Dec B.Pound | 1.7556 | 62500 | -2 | ($219,450) | $650 | $40,175 | $15,000 | | $25,175 |
| 10/1/92 | Dec B.Pound | 1.7136 | 62500 | -2 | ($214,200) | $5,250 | $45,425 | $15,000 | | $30,425 |

## Figure 7-6
### British Pound Speculative Worksheet (continued)

II. Margin Activity
Initial Margin Requirement $1,750 per Contract
Maintenance Margin Requirement $1,300 per Contract

| (1) Date | (2) Beginning # of Maintenance Contracts | (3) Margin Account Beginning Balance | (4) Unit Price Change | (5) Position +Gain/-Loss | (6) Interim Margin Balance | (7) Cash Account +From Cash -To Cash | (8) Margin Account Ending Balance | (9) Ending Number of Contracts | (10) Maintenance Requirement |
|---|---|---|---|---|---|---|---|---|---|
| 9/1/92 | -2 | $3,500 | 0 | $0 | $3,500 | $0 | $3,500 | -2 | $2,600 |
| 9/4/92 | -2 | $3,500 | 0.0032 | ($400) | $3,100 | $0 | $3,100 | -2 | $2,600 |
| 9/8/92 | -2 | $3,100 | 0.0086 | ($1,075) | $2,025 | $1,475 | $3,500 | -2 | $2,600 |
| 9/9/92 | -2 | $3,500 | -0.0334 | $4,175 | $7,675 | $0 | $7,675 | -2 | $2,600 |
| 9/10/92 | -2 | $7,675 | -0.0062 | $775 | $8,450 | $0 | $8,450 | -2 | $2,600 |
| 9/11/92 | -2 | $8,450 | -0.0426 | $5,325 | $13,775 | $0 | $13,775 | -2 | $2,600 |
| 9/14/92 | -2 | $13,775 | -0.0308 | $3,850 | $17,625 | $0 | $17,625 | -2 | $2,600 |
| 9/15/92 | -2 | $17,625 | -0.0282 | $3,525 | $21,150 | $0 | $21,150 | -2 | $2,600 |
| 9/16/92 | -2 | $21,150 | -0.0800 | $10,000 | $31,150 | $0 | $31,150 | -2 | $2,600 |
| 9/17/92 | -2 | $31,150 | -0.0010 | $125 | $31,275 | $0 | $31,275 | -2 | $2,600 |
| 9/18/92 | -2 | $31,275 | -0.0376 | $4,700 | $35,975 | $0 | $35,975 | -2 | $2,600 |
| 9/21/92 | -2 | $35,975 | -0.0250 | $3,125 | $39,100 | $0 | $39,100 | -2 | $2,600 |
| 9/22/92 | -2 | $39,100 | -0.0068 | $850 | $39,950 | $0 | $39,950 | -2 | $2,600 |
| 9/23/92 | -2 | $39,950 | 0.0148 | ($1,850) | $38,100 | $0 | $38,100 | -2 | $2,600 |
| 9/24/92 | -2 | $38,100 | -0.0062 | $775 | $38,875 | $0 | $38,875 | -2 | $2,600 |
| 9/25/92 | -2 | $38,875 | 0.0058 | ($725) | $38,150 | $0 | $38,150 | -2 | $2,600 |
| 9/28/92 | -2 | $38,150 | 0.0172 | ($2,150) | $36,000 | $0 | $36,000 | -2 | $2,600 |
| 9/29/92 | -2 | $36,000 | 0.0520 | ($6,500) | $29,500 | $0 | $29,500 | -2 | $2,600 |
| 9/30/92 | -2 | $29,500 | -0.0052 | $650 | $30,150 | $0 | $30,150 | -2 | $2,600 |
| 10/1/92 | -2 | $30,150 | -0.0420 | $5,250 | $35,400 | ($35,400) | $0 | 0 | $0 |

## Figure 7-6
## British Pound Speculative Worksheet (continued)

III. Cash Activity

| (1) Date | (2) Speculative Cash Beginning Balance | (3) Cash Account Flows + Invested - Withdrawn | (4) Margin Account Flows + From Margin - To Margin | (5) Speculative Cash Ending Balance |
|---|---|---|---|---|
| 9/1/92 | $11,500 | | | $11,500 |
| 9/4/92 | $11,500 | | | $11,500 |
| 9/8/92 | $11,500 | | ($1,475) | $10,025 |
| 9/9/92 | $10,025 | | | $10,025 |
| 9/10/92 | $10,025 | | | $10,025 |
| 9/11/92 | $10,025 | | | $10,025 |
| 9/14/92 | $10,025 | | | $10,025 |
| 9/15/92 | $10,025 | | | $10,025 |
| 9/16/92 | $10,025 | | | $10,025 |
| 9/17/92 | $10,025 | | | $10,025 |
| 9/18/92 | $10,025 | | | $10,025 |
| 9/21/92 | $10,025 | | | $10,025 |
| 9/22/92 | $10,025 | | | $10,025 |
| 9/23/92 | $10,025 | | | $10,025 |
| 9/24/92 | $10,025 | | | $10,025 |
| 9/25/92 | $10,025 | | | $10,025 |
| 9/28/92 | $10,025 | | | $10,025 |
| 9/29/92 | $10,025 | | | $10,025 |
| 9/30/92 | $10,025 | | | $10,025 |
| 10/1/92 | $10,025 | | $35,400 | $45,425 |

widely throughout the industry, I do not even attempt to include them in the various examples. Make sure that you have a thorough understanding of your broker's commission schedule. The final column in Section I, column 11, shows the strategy's cumulative gain or loss. It is computed by subtracting column 9, the amount invested in cash and margin, from column 8, the total cash and margin balance. When appropriate, commissions should also be subtracted from the total cash plus margin amount in column 8. The amount in column 11 of Section I must agree with the position gains and losses and any cash flows reflected in the margin account, Section II, column 8. The second section of the speculative worksheet provides information about the speculator's margin activity, and begins with a listing of the margin requirements. In this example the speculator must post an initial margin of $1,750 per British pound contract sold, and the margin account must have a minimum balance equal to $1,300 per contract at all times. If the margin balance falls below the minimum requirement, then the speculator is required to restore the margin account to a level that is consistent with the initial margin requirement. This can be accomplished in one of two ways: either more cash can be added to the margin account or enough of the position can be liquidated so that the remaining margin balance is greater than or equal to the initial margin requirement for the remaining contracts.

The remainder of Section II is divided into 10 columns that provide daily data about the margin account. Columns 1 and 2 of Section II are self-explanatory and correspond to columns 1 and 5 of Section I. Column 3 shows the margin account balance at the beginning of each day. The figures in column 4 represent the change in value of the futures contract on a per-unit basis. Column 5, the amount of gain or loss in the futures position, is obtained by multiplying the unit price change, column 4, by the total number of units in the position. The number of units in the position is determined by multiplying the number of units per contract, Section I, column, 4 by the number of contracts in the position at the beginning of the day, Section II, column 2. Column 6 gives the interim margin balance amount. This reflects the gains or losses posted to the margin account as the price changes during the day and alerts the speculator to the possibility of a margin call. Column 7 provides information about any cash additions to the margin account or withdrawals from the margin account. The figures in the margin account ending balance column, column 8, represent the cumulative effect of the changes in the futures contract price, any cash inflows or outflows that have occurred, and any change in the number of contracts in the position. Column 9 shows the number of futures contracts in the position at the end of the day. This column is particularly important because it reflects any change in the number of contracts that constitute the position. Finally, the position's maintenance requirement is shown in column 10.

Section III is the last section of the speculative worksheet and deals with the speculator's cash activity. As mentioned above, this cash does not have to be put on deposit with the broker, but it should be kept in an account that is extremely liquid and easily accessible so that the wide price swings in the financial futures markets can be withstood. Financial futures contracts are no different from their physical commodity counterparts in terms of price volatility, price limits, and margin. It is extremely important that the small retail customer be aware of these attributes, since they have an impact on how much cash should be kept in reserve. The rule of thumb that the small investor should keep enough in the margin and cash accounts to withstand five days worth of limit moves still applies. In Figure 7-6, the $15,000 total cash and margin amount is adequate for a $3,000 daily limit move per contract for a one-lot, or one-contract position. This amount is consistent with the five-day rule of thumb: $3,000 times five days times one contract.

When the small retail speculator established her position by selling two December British pound contracts on Tuesday, September 1st, the December pounds were selling at $1.9570/£1. She deposited $5,500 with her broker to satisfy the initial margin requirement, and kept an additional $11,500 in her reserve account. By Friday, 9/4/92, the price of December pounds had risen by $.0032 per pound, or $200 per contract, for a $400 position loss, Section II, columns 4 and 5, to $1.9602/£1, Section I, column 3. Both the speculator's short position and margin account decreased in value by $400, Section I, column 7, and Section II, columns 5 and 6. At the end of the day the margin account balance had fallen by $400, Section II, column 8, and the total cash and margin amount decreased to $14,600, Section I, column 8. Furthermore, the position showed a cumulative loss of $400, Section I, column 11.

At the beginning of the second week, 9/8/92, the speculator was short two December pound contracts and she had $3,100 in her margin account. During the day December British pounds rose $.0086/£1 to $1.9688/£1, for a $1,075 loss to the speculator, Section II, columns 4 and 5, and Section I, column 7. This $1,075 loss to the position resulted in the margin account falling to the $2,025 level, Section II, column 6: the $3,100 margin balance at the beginning of the day less the $1,075 loss. Since the margin account had fallen below the $2,600 maintenance requirement, Section II, column 10, $1,475 was transferred into the margin account from the speculative cash account, Section II, column 7, and Section III, column 4, to restore the account to the initial margin requirement, Section II, column 8.

When trading opened on 9/9/92 the speculator was short two December pound contracts, Section II, column 2; had $3,500 in her margin account, Section II, column 3; had a total cash and margin balance of $13,525, Section I, column 8; and had suffered a cumulative loss of $1,475, Section I, column 11. During the day's trading the British pound suffered a large drop, and fell by $.0334/£1, which resulted in a $4,175 gain to the position and an interim margin balance of $7,675, Section II, columns 4, 5, and 6, and Section I, columns 3 and 7. At the end of the day her margin and total cash and margin accounts had grown to $17,700 and $7,675, Section I, column 8, and Section II, column 8; and the position's cumulative gain had risen to +$2,700, Section I, column 11.

The British pound continued to experience huge price declines in the ensuing week—the week that the ERM disintegrated. On Friday, 9/11/92, the pound dropped more than $.04/£, from $1.9292/£1 to $1.8866/£1, resulting in a $5,325 gain to the position, Section II, column 5, and an ending margin balance of $13,775, Section II, column 8. On Monday, 9/14/92, and Tuesday 9/15/92, the December British pound futures contract continued its decline by posting losses of $.0308/£1 and $.0282/£1, respectively. The next day, 9/16/92, the day that Britain left the ERM, the pound collapsed, and the December British pound futures contract fell by $.0800/£1—to $1.7476/£1 from $1.8866/£1—which translated to a $10,000 gain, Section I, column 7, and Section II, column 5. This caused the speculator's margin account to rise by another $10,000 and boosted the cumulative gain to $26,175, Section I, column 11. Thursday was relatively quiet, with the pound closing at $1.7466/£1, but on Friday, 9/18/92, the pound fell by another $.0376/£1 to $1.7090/£1, Section I, column 3, and Section II, column 4, yielding another $4,700 in gain to the speculator, Section II, column 5.

During the third week of September this speculator's margin account increased from a balance of $13,775 to a level of $35,975, a $22,200 increase in just five trading days.

A strong argument can be made for closing out the position and taking the profits. However, an equally persuasive argument can be made for leaving the position intact since there seemed to be tremendous profit potential because of the confusion in the foreign exchange markets resulting from the political turmoil in Europe. It is worth noting that this uncertainty is a two-edged sword, and that the speculator must be prepared to withstand the intervention of central banks. In this case the speculator felt it was worth the risk and decided to leave her short position intact.

The next week, between September 21 and September 25, the British pound fluctuated wildly, suffering further declines on Monday, Tuesday, and Thursday, but posting increases on Wednesday and Friday. The net effect was a small decline in the pound's value between the $1.7090/£1 close on Friday, 9/18/92, and the $1.6916/£1 close on Friday, 9/25/92, one week later, Section I, column 3, and a $2,175 increase in the margin account from $35,975 to $38,150, Section II, column 8.

During the last week of September, the British pound rose in value. On Monday, 9/28/92, it increased by $.0172/£, resulting in a $2,150 loss, while on Tuesday, 9/29/92, the pound posted a $.0520/£ gain which translated to a $6,500 loss for the speculator Section II, columns 4 and 5. Finally, the pound resumed its decline on Wednesday and Thursday, which permitted the speculator to recoup some of the losses that she suffered on the previous trading days.

This latest surge prompted her to close out her short position in the British pound on Thursday, October 1st. Thus, she withdrew all the funds in her margin account, $35,400, and put them into her speculative account, Section II, columns 7 and 8, and Section III, columns 4 and 5. After covering her short position by purchasing two pound contracts, she had no open position at the end of the day and there was no margin required, Section II, columns 9 and 10. Finally, this speculator accumulated $30,425 between 9/1/92 and 10/1/92, a well-deserved reward for her willingness to bear the risks associated with the foreign exchange market.

## HEDGING

Recall that hedging is defined as risk transference. When hedging foreign exchange positions, the hedger is transferring the risk associated with open foreign currency positions which were created in the normal course of business. These positions can be characterized as being either long or short. A long position represents an asset position, while a short position is characterized as a liability position. Long positions are subject to the risk of declining currency values, since the asset position will decline in value. Conversely, short positions are at risk from rising currency values because the liability will increase as the currency's value rises. This section will examine two hedgers who have exposure in British pounds during the first quarter of 1994, just after the ERM disintegration in September of 1993. In the three months that had elapsed since the turmoil in the foreign exchange markets, the British pound had stabilized at approximately $1.45/£1. The first hedger has incurred a liability in British pounds, and is at risk from an increasing pound. This risk can be managed by purchasing British pound futures contracts. The second hedger is carrying an asset denominated in British pounds and faces the risk of a falling pound. Such risk can be minimized by selling British pound futures contracts.

Both hedgers' worksheets are composed of five sections and are identical to the worksheets displayed in earlier chapters. Section I presents data relating to the activity in the hedger's spot market position. Section II shows the behavior of the basis during the hedge's life. The third section displays the hedger's futures market position, while the fourth and fifth sections show the hedger's margin account and cash account activity. Sections I and II are unique to the hedger's worksheet, and are explained in detail in the following paragraphs. The remaining three sections of the worksheet, Section III, "Overall Futures Activity;" Section IV, "Margin Activity;" and Section V, "Cash Activity;" carry the exact same interpretation as in the speculator's worksheet in Figure 7-6.

Section II of the hedger's worksheet, Figures 7-7 and 7-8, depicts the basis, its incremental change and its cumulative change. The foreign exchange hedgers, like the bond and equity managers, are trading the relatively higher price volatility of either the cash or the futures market for the more stable and less volatile combined spot and futures position. In each case, the hedger is willing to bear a lower amount of price risk, i.e., the basis volatility, because the effective price of the spot commodity being hedged is much more predictable than if no hedge had been created. It is worth repeating that the convergence of the spot and futures prices means that the basis becomes zero at maturity. However, prior to maturity the basis can be either positive or negative, thereby creating some opportunities for the hedger to earn a small profit during the life of the hedge as the basis fluctuates. A strengthening basis will be profitable if one is long the cash commodity and short the futures contract. A weakening basis will be profitable if one is short the cash commodity and long the futures contract.

The first hedger is assumed to be a U.S. retailer who has purchased £1,000,000 worth of merchandise from a British supplier. The contract was negotiated on January 3rd, 1994, with delivery and payment due on February 25th, 1994; the account payable to the supplier means that the retailer is short £1,000,000. Since the objective is to minimize the liability and obtain British pounds for the lowest possible price, the retailer must guard against an increase in the value of the British pound during the nine-week period from January 3rd to February 25th. Therefore the retailer will buy 16 British pound March futures contracts to hedge the liability. The number of contracts to include in the hedge is determined by computing the ratio of the liability's size to the British pound futures contract size (£1,000,000/£62,500). The March contract was chosen for its liquidity, and since its maturity was close to the February 25th delivery date.

In Figure 7-7 the long hedger's, or retailer's, spot market position in British pounds is shown as of 1/3/94, in Section I columns 1, 2, and 4. The cash, or spot, price of the British pound on that day was $1.4745/£1, which translates to a position value of $1,474,500, columns 3 and 5. Column 6 lists the commodity's unit price change in the cash market, and column 7 expresses the price change as either a gain or loss to the spot position. Column 8 is reserved for any commissions that might be incurred as a result of cash market activity. Column 9 accumulates the gains and losses that accrue to the spot position.

The basis, column 2 of Section II, is computed by subtracting the futures price, Section III, column 3, from the spot price, Section I, column 3. The positive basis of .0049 for 1/3/94 is consistent with a $1.4745/£1 spot price and a $1.4696/£1 March British pound futures price. Moreover, the positive basis implies that the retailer should reap some profits as maturity approaches and the basis shrinks. By the end of the hedge's first week, 1/7/94, the pound's spot price had risen by $.0188/£1, to $1.4933/£1, Section I, columns 3 and 6, while the March British pound futures contract price rose by $.0180/£1 to $1.4876/£1, Section III, column 3, and Section IV, column 4. This caused the basis to strengthen and rise to $.0008/£1 for a position

## Figure 7-7
### British Pound Long Hedger Worksheet

**I. Overall Spot Activity**

| (1) Date | (2) Spot Commodity | (3) Unit Price | (4) Amount of Spot Commodity | (5) Spot Position Value | (6) Unit Price Change | (7) Spot Position +Gain/-Loss | (8) Commission | (9) Spot Cumulative +Gain/-Loss |
|---|---|---|---|---|---|---|---|---|
| 1/3/94 | British Pound | 1.4745 | -1,000,000 | ($1,474,500) | $0.0000 | $0 | | ($18,800) |
| 1/7/94 | British Pound | 1.4933 | -1,000,000 | ($1,493,300) | $0.0188 | ($18,800) | | ($18,100) |
| 1/14/94 | British Pound | 1.4926 | -1,000,000 | ($1,492,600) | ($0.0007) | $700 | | ($17,600) |
| 1/21/94 | British Pound | 1.4921 | -1,000,000 | ($1,492,100) | ($0.0005) | $500 | | ($20,000) |
| 1/28/94 | British Pound | 1.4945 | -1,000,000 | ($1,494,500) | $0.0024 | ($2,400) | | ($1,700) |
| 2/4/94 | British Pound | 1.4762 | -1,000,000 | ($1,476,200) | ($0.0183) | $18,300 | | $12,300 |
| 2/11/94 | British Pound | 1.4622 | -1,000,000 | ($1,462,200) | ($0.0140) | $14,000 | | ($6,300) |
| 2/18/94 | British Pound | 1.4808 | -1,000,000 | ($1,480,800) | $0.0186 | ($18,600) | | ($13,000) |
| 2/25/94 | British Pound | 1.4875 | -1,000,000 | ($1,487,500) | $0.0067 | ($6,700) | | |

**II. Basis Activity**

| (1) Date | (2) Basis Unit Value Spot Futures | (3) Basis Change | (4) Basis Cumulative +Gain/-Loss |
|---|---|---|---|
| 1/3/94 | 0.0049 | 0 | $0.00 |
| 1/7/94 | 0.0057 | 0.0008 | ($800.00) |
| 1/14/94 | 0.0048 | -0.0009 | $100.00 |
| 1/21/94 | 0.0049 | 0.0001 | $0.00 |
| 1/28/94 | 0.0035 | -0.0014 | $1,400.00 |
| 2/4/94 | 0.0040 | 0.0005 | $900.00 |
| 2/11/94 | 0.0018 | -0.0022 | $3,100.00 |
| 2/18/94 | -0.0010 | -0.0028 | $5,900.00 |
| 2/25/94 | -0.0001 | 0.0009 | $5,000.00 |

## Figure 7-7
### British Pound Long Hedger Worksheet (continued)

**III. Overall Futures Activity**

| (1) Date | (2) Contract | (3) Unit Price | (4) Number of Units per Contract | (5) Number of Contracts +Long/-Short | (6) Futures Position Values | (7) Futures Position +Gain/-Loss | (8) Total Cash+Margin | (9) Invested Cash+Margin | (10) Commission | (11) Futures Cumulative +Gain/-Loss |
|---|---|---|---|---|---|---|---|---|---|---|
| 1/3/94 | March B.Pound | 1.4696 | 62,500 | 16 | $1,469,600 | $0 | $75,000 | $75,000 | | $0 |
| 1/7/94 | March B.Pound | 1.4876 | 62,500 | 16 | $1,487,600 | $18,000 | $93,000 | $75,000 | | $18,000 |
| 1/14/94 | March B.Pound | 1.4878 | 62,500 | 16 | $1,487,800 | $200 | $93,200 | $75,000 | | $18,200 |
| 1/21/94 | March B.Pound | 1.4872 | 62,500 | 16 | $1,487,200 | ($600) | $92,600 | $75,000 | | $17,600 |
| 1/28/94 | March B.Pound | 1.4910 | 62,500 | 16 | $1,491,000 | $3,800 | $96,400 | $75,000 | | $21,400 |
| 2/4/94 | March B.Pound | 1.4722 | 62,500 | 16 | $1,472,200 | ($18,800) | $77,600 | $75,000 | | $2,600 |
| 2/11/94 | March B.Pound | 1.4604 | 62,500 | 16 | $1,460,400 | ($11,800) | $65,800 | $75,000 | | ($9,200) |
| 2/18/94 | March B.Pound | 1.4818 | 62,500 | 16 | $1,481,800 | $21,400 | $87,200 | $75,000 | | $12,200 |
| 2/25/94 | March B.Pound | 1.4876 | 62,500 | 16 | $1,487,600 | $5,800 | $93,000 | $75,000 | | $18,000 |

**IV. Margin Activity**
Initial Margin Requirement   $1,750 per Contract
Maintenance Margin Requirement   $1,300 per Contract

| (1) Date | (2) Beginning # of Maintenance Contracts | (3) Margin Account Beginning Balance | (4) Unit Price Change | (5) Position +Gain/-Loss | (6) Interim Margin Balance | (7) Cash Account +From Cash -To Cash | (8) Margin Account Ending Balance | (9) Ending Number of Contracts | (10) Maintenance Requirement |
|---|---|---|---|---|---|---|---|---|---|
| 1/3/94 | 16 | $28,000 | 0 | $0 | $28,000 | $0 | $28,000 | 16 | $20,800 |
| 1/7/94 | 16 | $28,000 | 0.0180 | $18,000 | $46,000 | $0 | $46,000 | 16 | $20,800 |
| 1/14/94 | 16 | $46,000 | 0.0002 | $200 | $46,200 | $0 | $46,200 | 16 | $20,800 |
| 1/21/94 | 16 | $46,200 | -0.0006 | ($600) | $45,600 | $7,400 | $53,000 | 16 | $20,800 |
| 1/28/94 | 16 | $53,000 | 0.0038 | $3,800 | $56,800 | $0 | $56,800 | 16 | $20,800 |
| 2/4/94 | 16 | $56,800 | -0.0188 | ($18,800) | $38,000 | $15,000 | $53,000 | 16 | $20,800 |
| 2/11/94 | 16 | $53,000 | -0.0118 | ($11,800) | $41,200 | $11,800 | $53,000 | 16 | $20,800 |
| 2/18/94 | 16 | $53,000 | 0.0214 | $21,400 | $74,400 | $0 | $74,400 | 16 | $20,800 |
| 2/25/94 | 16 | $74,400 | 0.0058 | $5,800 | $80,200 | ($80,200) | $0 | 16 | $20,800 |

## Figure 7-7
### British Pound Long Hedger Worksheet (continued)

V. Cash Activity

| (1)<br>Date | (2)<br>Carrying<br>Cash Beginning<br>Balance | (3)<br>Cash Account<br>Flows<br>+Invested<br>-Withdrawn | (4)<br>Margin<br>Account Flows<br>+From Margin<br>-To Margin | (5)<br>Carrying<br>Cash Ending<br>Balance |
|---|---|---|---|---|
| 1/3/94 | $47,000 | $0 | $0 | $47,000 |
| 1/7/94 | $47,000 | $0 | $0 | $47,000 |
| 1/14/94 | $47,000 | $0 | $0 | $47,000 |
| 1/21/94 | $47,000 | $0 | ($7,400) | $39,600 |
| 1/28/94 | $39,600 | $0 | $0 | $39,600 |
| 2/4/94 | $39,600 | $0 | ($15,000) | $24,600 |
| 2/11/94 | $24,600 | $0 | ($11,800) | $12,800 |
| 2/18/94 | $12,800 | $0 | $0 | $12,800 |
| 2/25/94 | $12,800 | $0 | $80,200 | $93,000 |

loss of $800. Over the next week the spot price fell to $1.4926/£1, while the futures price rose to $1.4878/£1 from $1.4876/£1, which shrunk the basis to $.0048/£ resulting in a $100 gain to the position by 1/14/94, Section II, columns 2 and 4. By the end of the next week, 1/21/94, the basis had returned to its 1/3/94 level of $.0049/£1 and the position was even. Thus, with approximately one month until the hedge had to be liquidated, there was no relative change in the hedger's position, Section II, column 4, and Section I, column 3. However, during the next five weeks the pound would experience large price swings and the basis would decline rapidly, providing some profits to the hedger.

In January's final week, the basis shrunk to $.0035/£1, even though the pound's value rose to $1.4921/£1. In the first week of February the pound declined precipitously, to $1.4762/£1; the retailer's short spot position improved by $18,300 but the long futures position deteriorated by $18,800. Yet the basis rose to $.0040/£1 by 2/4/94. The next week, 2/11/94, the pound fell again to $1.4622/£1, the short spot position enjoyed another $14,000 gain, the futures position suffered an $11,800 loss, and the basis fell to $.0018/£1. This latest loss brought the interim margin balance down to $18,800, Section IV, column 6, and forced the retailer to transfer $9,200 from the cash account to the margin account, Section V, column 4, and Section IV, column 7. This restored the margin account to its $28,000 initial level. Then, in the final two weeks of the hedge's life, the March British pound futures price rose more rapidly than the spot price and the basis turned negative, Section II, column 2. On the day the hedge was to be liquidated, 2/25/94, the pound's spot price was $1.4875/£1, the March futures price was $1.4875/£1, and the basis stood at −$.0001/£1.

This change in basis from a positive $.00049/£1 on 1/3/94 to a −$.0001/£1 on 2/25/94 resulted in a $5,000 gain to the hedger and a reduction in the liability. Furthermore, the retailer's effective exchange rate was $1.4695/£1: the $1.4745/£1 spot price in effect when the hedge was constructed adjusted for the $.005/£1 basis gains. Thus, instead of paying $1,474,500 for the merchandise, the retailer was able to reduce the cost to $1,469,500, despite the fact that the British pound rose in value from $1.4745/£1 to $1.4875/£1 between 1/3/94 and 2/25/94.

The second hedger is assumed to be a U.S. manufacturer who has sold £1,000,000 worth of merchandise to a British customer. As with the retailer in the previous example, the contract was negotiated on January 3rd 1994, with delivery and payment due on February 25th, 1994; the account receivable means that the manufacturer is long £1,000,000. Since the objective is to maximize the value of the asset, the account receivable, and sell British pounds for the highest possible price, the manufacturer must protect against a decrease in the value of the British pound during the nine-week period from January 3rd to February 25th. Therefore the manufacturer will sell 16 British pound March futures contracts to hedge the account asset. The same procedure used to determine the hedge's size for the retailer is used here as well. The number of contracts to include in the hedge is determined by computing the ratio of the asset's size to the British pound futures contract size (£1,000,000/£62,500). As before, the March contract was chosen for its liquidity and its maturity.

Figure 7-8, the short hedger's worksheet, is quite similar to the long hedger's worksheet, Figure 7-7; however, there are some differences. The basic difference between the two worksheets is that the short hedger is long the spot commodity (British pounds) and is short the futures contract, while the long hedger is short the spot commodity and long the futures contract. This can be seen quite clearly by comparing the signs that precede the spot market positions and futures market positions: Section I, column 4; Section III, column 5; and Section IV, columns 2 and 9. The most interesting differences between the worksheets are in Sections II, IV, and V, the basis activity, margin activity, and cash activity sections, respectively.

The most significant difference between the two worksheets is shown in Section II, column 3, the cumulative gain or loss to the basis. Observe that the long hedger's basis activity in Figure 7-8 highlights the adverse effects of a narrowing basis when one is long the spot and short the futures. This contrasts sharply with the short hedger's basis activity (Figure 7-7), which shows the advantage to being short the basis as it shrinks. The margin activity section shows that the short hedger was forced to transfer $18,000 from the cash account to the margin account early in the hedge's life, 1/7/94, to restore the margin balance to its $28,000 required level. Note that the short hedger suffered a margin call despite an $800 gain in the basis, Section II, column 4. After the margin call on 1/7/94, the short hedger's margin balance remained above the maintenance requirement until the position was liquidated on 2/25/94. Recall that the long hedger did not sustain a margin call until 2/11/94.

## Figure 7-8
### British Pound Short Hedger Worksheet

**I. Overall Spot Activity**

| (1) Date | (2) Spot Commodity | (3) Unit Price | (4) Amount of Spot Commodity | (5) Spot Position Value | (6) Unit Price Change | (7) Spot Position +Gain/-Loss | (8) Commission | (9) Spot Cummulative +Gain/-Loss |
|---|---|---|---|---|---|---|---|---|
| 1/3/94 | British Pound | 1.4745 | 1,000,000 | $1,474,500 | $0.0000 | $0 | | |
| 1/7/94 | British Pound | 1.4933 | 1,000,000 | $1,493,300 | $0.0188 | $18,800 | | $18,800 |
| 1/14/94 | British Pound | 1.4926 | 1,000,000 | $1,492,600 | ($0.0007) | ($700) | | $18,100 |
| 1/21/94 | British Pound | 1.4921 | 1,000,000 | $1,492,100 | ($0.0005) | ($500) | | $17,600 |
| 1/28/94 | British Pound | 1.4945 | 1,000,000 | $1,494,500 | $0.0024 | $2,400 | | $20,000 |
| 2/4/94 | British Pound | 1.4762 | 1,000,000 | $1,476,200 | ($0.0183) | ($18,300) | | $1,700 |
| 2/11/94 | British Pound | 1.4622 | 1,000,000 | $1,462,200 | ($0.0140) | ($14,000) | | ($12,300) |
| 2/18/94 | British Pound | 1.4808 | 1,000,000 | $1,480,800 | $0.0186 | $18,600 | | $6,300 |
| 2/25/94 | British Pound | 1.4875 | 1,000,000 | $1,487,500 | $0.0067 | $6,700 | | $13,000 |

**II. Basis Activity**

| (1) Date | (2) Basis Unit Value Spot Futures | (3) Basis Change | (4) Basis Cumulative +Gain/-Loss |
|---|---|---|---|
| 1/3/94 | 0.0049 | 0 | 0 |
| 1/7/94 | 0.0057 | 0.0008 | 0.0008 |
| 1/14/94 | 0.0048 | -0.0009 | -0.0001 |
| 1/21/94 | 0.0049 | 0.0001 | 0.0000 |
| 1/28/94 | 0.0035 | -0.0014 | -0.0014 |
| 2/4/94 | 0.0040 | 0.0005 | -0.0009 |
| 2/11/94 | 0.0018 | -0.0022 | -0.0031 |
| 2/18/94 | -0.0010 | -0.0028 | -0.0059 |
| 2/25/94 | -0.0001 | 0.0009 | -0.0050 |

## Figure 7-8
### British Pound Short Hedger Worksheet (continued)

**III. Overall Futures Activity**

| (1) Date | (2) Contract | (3) Unit Price | (4) Number of Units per Contract | (5) Number of Contracts +Long/-Short | (6) Futures Position Values | (7) Futures Position +Gain/-Loss | (8) Total Cash+Margin | (9) Invested Cash+Margin | (10) Commission | (11) Futures Cumulative +Gain/-Loss |
|---|---|---|---|---|---|---|---|---|---|---|
| 1/3/94 | March B.Pound | 1.4696 | 62,500 | -16 | ($1,469,600) | $0 | $75,000 | $75,000 | | $0 |
| 1/7/94 | March B.Pound | 1.4876 | 62,500 | -16 | ($1,487,600) | ($18,000) | $57,000 | $75,000 | | ($18,000) |
| 1/14/94 | March B.Pound | 1.4878 | 62,500 | -16 | ($1,487,800) | ($200) | $56,800 | $75,000 | | ($18,200) |
| 1/21/94 | March B.Pound | 1.4872 | 62,500 | -16 | ($1,487,200) | $600 | $57,400 | $75,000 | | ($17,600) |
| 1/28/94 | March B.Pound | 1.4910 | 62,500 | -16 | ($1,491,000) | ($3,800) | $53,600 | $75,000 | | ($21,400) |
| 2/4/94 | March B.Pound | 1.4722 | 62,500 | -16 | ($1,472,200) | $18,800 | $72,400 | $75,000 | | ($2,600) |
| 2/11/94 | March B.Pound | 1.4604 | 62,500 | -16 | ($1,460,400) | $11,800 | $84,200 | $75,000 | | $9,200 |
| 2/18/94 | March B.Pound | 1.4818 | 62,500 | -16 | ($1,481,800) | ($21,400) | $62,800 | $75,000 | | ($12,200) |
| 2/25/94 | March B.Pound | 1.4876 | 62,500 | -16 | ($1,487,600) | ($5,800) | $57,000 | $75,000 | | ($18,000) |

**IV. Margin Activity**

Initial Margin Requirement    $1,750 per Contract
Maintenance Margin Requirement    $1,300 per Contract

| (1) Date | (2) Beginning # of Maintenance Contracts | (3) Margin Account Beginning Balance | (4) Unit Price Change | (5) Position +Gain/-Loss | (6) Interim Margin Balance | (7) Cash Account +From Cash -To Cash | (8) Margin Account Ending Balance | (9) Ending Number of Contracts | (10) Maintenance Requirement |
|---|---|---|---|---|---|---|---|---|---|
| 1/3/94 | -16 | $28,000 | 0 | $0 | $28,000 | $0 | $28,000 | -16 | $20,800 |
| 1/7/94 | -16 | $28,000 | 0.0180 | ($18,000) | $10,000 | $0 | $10,000 | -16 | $20,800 |
| 1/14/94 | -16 | $10,000 | 0.0002 | ($200) | $9,800 | $0 | $9,800 | -16 | $20,800 |
| 1/21/94 | -16 | $9,800 | -0.0006 | $600 | $10,400 | $0 | $10,400 | -16 | $20,800 |
| 1/28/94 | -16 | $10,400 | 0.0038 | ($3,800) | $6,600 | $0 | $6,600 | -16 | $20,800 |
| 2/4/94 | -16 | $6,600 | -0.0188 | $18,800 | $25,400 | $0 | $25,400 | -16 | $20,800 |
| 2/11/94 | -16 | $25,400 | -0.0118 | $11,800 | $37,200 | $0 | $37,200 | -16 | $20,800 |
| 2/18/94 | -16 | $37,200 | 0.0214 | ($21,400) | $15,800 | $0 | $15,800 | -16 | $20,800 |
| 2/25/94 | -16 | $15,800 | 0.0058 | ($5,800) | $10,000 | ($10,000) | $0 | -16 | $20,800 |

*Figure 7-8*
*British Pound Short Hedger Worksheet (continued)*

V. Cash Activity

| (1) | (2) | (3) | (4) | (5) |
|---|---|---|---|---|
| | Carrying Cash Beginning Balance | Cash Account Flows + Invested - Withdrawn | Margin Account Flows + From Margin - To Margin | Carrying Cash Ending Balance |
| Date | | | | |
| 1/3/94 | $47,000 | $0 | $0 | $47,000 |
| 1/7/94 | $47,000 | $0 | $0 | $47,000 |
| 1/14/94 | $47,000 | $0 | $0 | $47,000 |
| 1/21/94 | $47,000 | $0 | $0 | $47,000 |
| 1/28/94 | $47,000 | $0 | $0 | $47,000 |
| 2/4/94 | $47,000 | $0 | $0 | $47,000 |
| 2/11/94 | $47,000 | $0 | $0 | $47,000 |
| 2/18/94 | $47,000 | $0 | $0 | $47,000 |
| 2/25/94 | $47,000 | $0 | $10,000 | $57,000 |

Observe that this change in basis from a positive $.00049/£1 on 1/3/94 to a –$.0001/£1 on 2/25/94 resulted in a $5,000 loss to the manufacturer. Therefore, the manufacturer's effective exchange rate was $1.4695/£1: the $1.4745/£1 spot price in effect when the hedge was constructed minus the $.005/£1 basis loss. Thus, instead of obtaining $1,474,500 for the British pounds, the manufacturer was able to obtain only $1,469,500 for the £1,000,000, even though the British pound rose in value from $1.4745/£1 to $1.4875/£1 between 1/3/94 and 2/25/94.

Even though both the retailer and the manufacturer hedged their spot market positions, the retailer had superior results. The reason for the long hedger's superior performance is that the short spot market position decreased by $13,000, while the long futures position rose by $18,000. Although the retailer had to purchase the 1,000,000 British pounds in the spot market for $1.4875/£1, or $1,487,500, on February 25th, the cost was reduced by $18,000, the amount of the futures position gain, for an effective cost of $1,469,500, or $1.4695/£1. Conversely, the short hedger (the manufacturer) suffered the effects of the increase in the pound's price since the short futures position lost $18,000 while the long spot position gained $13,000. Despite the fact that the manufacturer was able to sell the £1,000,000 on February 25th in the spot market for $1.4875/£1, or $1,487,500, this revenue was reduced by the $18,000 loss suffered in the short position in the futures market. Therefore, the manufacturer collected $1,469,500 for the £1,000,000 for an effective sale price of $1.4695/£1.

## SUMMARY

This chapter has examined the foreign exchange market. The chapter began with a discussion of the spot, forward, and futures markets for foreign currencies and included an explanation of foreign exchange price quotes as reported in *The Wall Street Journal*. Next, the theories of exchange rate determination, Interest Rate Parity and Purchasing Power Parity were discussed. It was shown how exchange rates and interest rates form an integrated system where exchange rate equilibrium is maintained by arbitrage activity. The chapter continued with a discussion of speculators and hedgers, and examined long and short speculative positions and long and short hedged positions in the British pound. Worksheets were developed for each type of strategy, and were used to explain and illustrate clearly how profits are made and losses incurred in the foreign exchange futures market.

# Appendix A

# ANNOTATED BIBLIOGRAPHY

Chance, Don M., *An Introduction to Options and Futures,* 2d ed. Chicago, IL: The Dryden Press, 1991.
This book is written for university students, and is used in many undergraduate business programs. It provides good theoretical explanations of options and futures, and augments the theory with many practical examples. Most of the futures-related discussion focuses on financial instruments, however. This book is for those investors who want to expand their theoretical knowledge of options and futures contracts.

Chicago Board of Trade, *Commodity Trading Manual.* Chicago, IL: Board of Trade of the City of Chicago, 1994.
This is the latest version of the Chicago Board of Trade's own publication. It provides an extremely good overview of all aspects of the futures markets: their development, regulation, operations, and trading strategies. Many different agricultural and financial futures contracts are discussed and utilized in the numerous trading examples. This book is worth having as a basic reference on the United States futures markets.

Kolb, Robert W., *Understanding Futures Markets,* 4th ed. Miami, FL: Kolb Publishing Company, 1994.
This book is written for the more sophisticated investor who wants to learn how the futures markets fit within the more general

framework of Capital Market Theory. Thus, it is not surprising that this book is used in many graduate business programs. Since considerable attention is devoted to the theory underlying the futures markets in general, this book makes extensive use of the concepts of equilibrium and arbitrage. A large number of examples employing both agricultural and financial futures contracts accompany the theoretical discussions.

Leuthold, Raymond M., Joan C. Junkus, and Jean E. Cordier, *The Theory and Practice of Futures Markets.* Lexington, MA: Lexington Books, D.C. Heath and Company, 1989.
As the name implies, this is a textbook written for university students. It discusses the underlying theory of both agricultural and financial futures markets in great detail, and provides more examples of agricultural-based hedging and trading strategies than either the Chance or Kolb books.

Siegel, Daniel R., and Diane F. Siegel, *The Futures Markets.* Chicago, IL: Probus Publishing Company, 1990.
This is an excellent book written for the serious futures trader. It combines the theory and practice of futures markets in its clear explanation of an extremely wide variety of futures contracts. It is more sophisticated than the Chicago Board of Trade's manual, but is just as valuable a reference.

# Appendix B

# GLOSSARY

**Arbitrage:** Simultaneous purchase of cash commodities or futures in one market against the sale of cash commodities or futures in the same or a different market to profit from a discrepancy in prices.

**At-the-Market:** An order to buy or sell a futures contract at whatever price is obtainable when the order reaches the trading floor. Also called a Market Order.

**Basis:** The difference between the spot or cash price of a commodity and the price of the nearest futures contract for the same or a related commodity. Basis is usually computed in relation to the near futures contract and may reflect different time periods, product forms, qualities, or locations.

**Basis Point:** The measurement of a change in the yield of a debt security. One basis point equals 1/100 of one percent.

**Basis Risk:** The risk associated with an unexpected widening or narrowing of basis between the time a hedging position is established and the time that it is lifted.

**Bear:** One who expects a decline in prices. The opposite of "bull." A news item is considered bearish if it is expected to bring lower prices.

**Bear Market:** A market in which prices are declining.

**Bear Spread:** The simultaneous purchase and sale of two futures contracts in the same or related commodities with the intention of profiting from a decline in prices but at the same time limiting the potential loss if this expectation is wrong.

**Bid:** An offer to buy a specific quantity of a commodity at a stated price.

**Broker:** A person paid a fee or commission for executing buy or sell orders of a customer. In commodity futures trading, the term may refer to (1) Floor Broker—a person who actually executes orders on the trading floor of an exchange; (2) Account Executive, Associated Person, Registered Commodity Representative, or Customer's Man—the person who deals with customers in the offices of futures commission merchants; and (3) the futures Commission Merchant.

**Bull:** One who expects a rise in prices; the opposite of "bear." A news item is considered bullish if it portends higher prices.

**Bull Market:** A market in which prices are rising.

**Bull Spread:** The simultaneous purchase and sale of two futures contracts in the same or related commodities with the intention of profiting from a rise in prices but at the same time limiting the potential loss if this expectation is wrong. In the agricultural commodities, this is accomplished by buying the nearby delivery and selling the deferred.

**Buying Hedge (or Long Hedge):** Hedging transaction in which futures contracts are bought to protect against possible increased cost commodities.

**Carrying Charges:** Cost of storing a physical commodity or holding a financial instrument over a period of time. Includes insurance, storage, and interest on the invested funds as well as other incidental costs. It is a carrying charge market when there are higher futures prices for each successive contract maturity.

**Cash Commodity:** The physical or actual commodity as distinguished from the futures contract. Sometimes called spot commodity or actuals.

**Cash Market:** The market for the cash commodity (as contrasted to a futures contract), taking the form of (1) an organized, self-regulated central market (e.g., a commodity exchange); (2) a decentralized over-the-counter market; or (3) a local organization, such as grain elevator or meat processor, which provides a market for a small region.

**Cash Price:** The price in the marketplace for actual cash or spot commodities to be delivered via customary market channels.

**Cash Settlement:** A method of settling certain futures or option contracts whereby the seller (or short) pays the buyer (or long) the cash value of the commodity traded according to a procedure specified in the contract.

**Charting:** The use of graphs and charts in the technical analysis of futures markets to plot trends of price movements, average movements of price, volume of trading open interest.

**Chartist:** Technical trader who reacts to signals read from graphs of price movements.

**Clearing:** The procedure through which the clearinghouse or association becomes buyer to each seller of a futures contract, and seller to each buyer, and assumes responsibility for protecting buyers and sellers from financial loss by assuring performance on each contract.

**Clearinghouse:** An adjunct to a commodity exchange through which transactions executed on the floor of the exchange are settled. Also charged with assuring the proper conduct of the exchange's delivery procedures and the adequate financing of the trading.

**Clearing Member:** A member of the Clearinghouse or Association. All trades of a nonclearing member must be registered and eventually settled through a clearing member.

**Closing-Out:** Liquidating an existing long or short futures or option position with an equal and opposite transaction. Also known as Offset.

**Commodity Futures Trading Commission (CFTC):** The federal regulatory agency established by the CFTC Act of 1974 to administer the Commodity Exchange Act.

**Contract:** (1) A term of reference describing a unit of trading for a commodity future option; (2) An agreement to buy or sell a specified commodity, detailing the amount and grade of the product and the date on which the contract will mature and become deliverable.

**Convergence:** The tendency for prices of physicals and futures to approach one another, usually during the delivery month. Also called a "narrowing of the basis."

**Corner:** (1) To corner is to secure such relative control of a commodity or security that its price can be manipulated; (2) In the extreme situation, obtaining contracts requiring delivery of more commodities or securities than are available for delivery.

**Coupon (Coupon Rate):** A fixed dollar amount of interest payable per annum, stated as a percentage of principal value, usually payable in semiannual installments.

**Cover:** (1) Purchasing futures to offset a short position. Same as Short Covering. *See* Offset, Liquidation; (2) To have in hand the physical commodity when a short futures or leverage sale is made, or to acquire the commodity that might be deliverable on a short sale.

**Crop Year:** The time period from one harvest to the next, varying according to the commodity (i.e., July 1 to June 30 for wheat; September 1 to August 31 for soybeans).

**Crush:** In the soybean futures market, the simultaneous purchase of soybean futures and the sale of soybean meal and soybean oil futures to establish a processing margin.

**Day Order:** An order that expires automatically at the end of each day's trading session. There may be a day order with time contingency. For example, an "off at a specific time" order is an order that remains in force until the specified time during the session is reached. At such time, the order is automatically cancelled.

**Day Traders:** Commodity traders, generally members of the exchange on the trading floor, who take positions in commodities and then offset them prior to the close of trading on the same trading day.

**Day Trading:** Establishing and offsetting the same futures market position within one day.

**Deck:** The orders for purchase or sale of futures and option contracts held in the hands of a floor broker.

**Delivery:** The tender and receipt of the actual commodity, the cash value of the commodity, or of a delivery instrument covering the commodity (e.g., warehouse receipts or shipping certificates), used to settle a futures contract.

**Delivery Date:** The date on which the commodity or instrument of delivery must be delivered to fulfill the terms of a contract.

**Delivery Instrument:** A document used to effect delivery on a futures contract, such as a warehouse receipt or shipping certificate.

**Delivery Month:** The specified month within which a futures contract matures and can be settled by delivery.

**Fill or Kill Order:** An order which demands immediate execution or cancellation.

**Financial Instruments:** Currency, securities, and indices of their value. Examples include shares, mortgages, commercial paper, and Treasury Bills and Bonds.

**Fixed-Income Security:** A security whose nominal (or currency dollar) yield is fixed or determined with certainty at the time of purchase.

**Floor Broker:** Any person who, in or surrounding any pit, ring, post, or other place provided by a contract market for the meeting of persons similarly engaged, executes for another person any orders for the purchase or sale of any commodity for future delivery.

**Floor Trader:** An exchange member who usually executes his own trades by being personally present in the pit or place for futures trading.

**Forced Liquidation:** The situation in which a customer's account is liquidated (open positions are offset) by the brokerage firm holding the account, or, in the case of leverage accounts, by the leverage transaction merchant, usually after notification (margin calls), because the account is undercapitalized.

**Foreign Exchange:** Foreign currency. On the foreign exchange market, foreign currency is bought and sold for immediate or future delivery.

**Forward Contracting:** A cash transaction common in many industries, including commodity merchandising, in which the buyer and seller agree upon delivery on a specified quality and quantity of goods at a specified future date. A price may be agreed upon in advance, or there may be agreement that the price will be determined at the time of delivery.

**Forward Market:** Refers to informal (nonexchange) trading of commodities to be delivered at a future date. Contracts for forward delivery are "personalized" (i.e., delivery time and amount are as determined between seller and customer).

**Forward Months:** Futures contracts, currently trading, calling for later or distant delivery.

**Forward Purchase or Sale:** A purchase or sale of an actual commodity for deferred delivery.

**Fundamental Analysis:** Study of basic, underlying factors which will affect the supply and demand of the commodity being traded in futures contracts.

**Futures Contract:** An agreement to purchase or sell a commodity for delivery in the future: (1) at a price that is determined at initiation of the contract; (2) which is normally traded on a board of trade by members of the exchange; (3) which is used to assume or shift price risk; and (4) which obligates each party to the contract either to fulfill the terms of the contract or offset the contract by entering into an opposite transaction (by far the more commonly chosen alternative).

**Futures Price:** (1) Commonly held to mean the price of a commodity for future delivery that is traded on a futures exchange; (2) The price of any futures contract.

**Good This Week (GTW) Order:** Order which is valid only for the week in which it is placed.

**Good Till Cancelled (GTC) Order:** Order which is valid at any time during market hours until executed or cancelled.

**Gross Processing Margin (GPM):** Refers to the difference between the cost of a commodity and the combined sales income of the finished products which result from processing the commodity. Various industries have formulas to express the relationship of raw material costs to sales income from finished products.

**Hedging:** Taking a position in a futures market opposite to a position held in the cash market to minimize the risk of financial loss from an adverse price change; a purchase or sale of futures as a temporary substitute for a cash transaction that will occur later.

**Initial Margin:** Customers' funds put up as security for a guarantee of contract fulfillment at the time a futures market position is established.

**Intercommodity Spread:** A spread in which the long and short legs are in two different but generally related commodity markets. Also called an intermarket spread.

**Interest Rate Futures:** Futures contracts traded on fixed-income securities such as GNMAs, U.S. Treasury issues, or CDs. Currency is excluded from this category, even though interest rates are a factor in currency values.

**Inverted Market:** A futures market in which the nearer months are selling at prices higher than the more distant months; a market displaying "inverse carrying charges," characteristic of markets with supply shortages.

**Limit Move:** A price that has advanced or declined the permissible limit during one trading session, as fixed by the rules of a contract market.

**Limit Order:** An order in which the customer specifies a price limit or other condition, such as time of an order, as contrasted with a market order, which implies that the order, should be filled as soon as possible.

**Liquidation:** The closing out of a long position. The term is sometimes used to denote closing out a short position, but this is more often referred to as covering.

**Liquid Market:** A market in which selling and buying can be accomplished with minimal price change.

**Long:** (1) One who has bought a futures contract to establish market position; (2) a market position which obligates the holder to take delivery; (3) one who owns an inventory of commodities.

**Long Hedge:** Purchase of futures against the fixed price forward sale of a cash commodity.

**Long the Basis:** A person or firm that has bought the spot commodity and hedged with sale of futures is said to be long the basis.

**Margin:** The amount of money or collateral deposited by a customer with his broker, by a broker with a clearing member, or by a clearing member with the clearinghouse, for the purpose of insuring the broker or clearinghouse against loss on open futures contracts. The margin is not partial payment on a purchase. (1) Original or initial margin is the total amount of margin per contract required by the broker when a futures position is opened; (2) Maintenance margin is a sum which must be maintained on deposit at all times. If a customer's equity in any futures position drops to or under the level because of adverse price movement, the broker must issue a margin call to restore the customer's equity. *See* Variable Limit Margin.

**Margin Call:** (1) A request from a brokerage firm to a customer to bring margin deposits up to original levels; (2) a request by the clearinghouse to a clearing member to bring clearing margins back to minimum levels required by the clearinghouse rules.

**Market-if-Touched (MIT) Order:** An order that becomes a market order when a particular price is reached. A sell MIT is placed above the market; a buy MIT is placed below the market.

**Market Maker:** A professional securities dealer who stands ready to buy when there is an excess of sell orders and to sell when there is excess of buy orders. By maintaining an offering price sufficiently higher than their buying price, these firms are compensated for the risk involved in allowing their inventory of securities to act as a buffer against temporary order imbalances. In the commodities industry, this term is sometimes loosely used to refer to a floor trader or local who, in speculating for his own account, provides a market for commercial users of the market.

**Market on Opening:** An order to buy or sell at the beginning of the trading session at a price within the opening range of prices.

**Mark-to-Market:** Daily cash flow system used by U.S. futures exchanges to maintain a minimum level of margin equity for a given futures or option contract position by calculating the gain or loss in each contract position resulting from changes in the price of the futures or option contracts at the end of each trading day.

**Maturity:** Period within which a futures contract can be settled by delivery of the actual commodity.

**Momentum:** In technical analysis, the relative change in price over a specific time interval. Often equated with speed or velocity and considered in terms of relative strength.

**Nearby Delivery Month:** The month of the futures contract closest to maturity.

**Negative Carry:** The cost of financing a financial instrument (the short-term rate of interest), when the cost is above the current return of the financial instrument.

**Net Position:** The difference between the open long contracts and the open short contracts held by a trader in any one commodity.

**Offer:** An indication of willingness to sell at a given price; opposite of bid.

**Offset:** Liquidating a purchase of futures contracts through the sale of an equal number of contracts of the same delivery month, or covering a short sale of futures through the purchase of an equal number of contracts of the same delivery month.

**Open Interest:** The total number of futures contracts long or short in a delivery month or market that have been entered into and not yet liquidated by an offsetting transaction or fulfilled by delivery.

**Open Order (or Orders):** An order that remains in force until it is cancelled or until the futures contracts expire.

**Open Outcry:** Method of public auction required to make bids and offers in the trading pits or rings of commodity exchanges.

**Out Trade:** A trade which cannot be cleared by a clearinghouse because the trade data submitted by the two clearing members involved in the trade differs in some respect (e.g., price and/or quantity). In such cases, the two clearing members or brokers involved must reconcile the discrepancy, if possible, and resubmit the trade for clearing. If an agreement cannot be reached by the two clearing members or brokers involved, the dispute would be settled by an appropriate exchange committee.

**Overbought:** A technical opinion that the market price has risen too steeply and too fast in relation to underlying fundamental factors. Rank-and-file traders who were bullish and long have turned bearish.

**Overnight Trade:** A trade which is not liquidated on the same trading day in which it was established.

**Oversold:** A technical opinion that the market price has declined too steeply and too fast in relation to underlying fundamental factors. Rank-and-file traders who were bearish and short have turned bullish.

**Paper Profit or Loss:** The profit or loss that would be realized if the open contracts were liquidated as of a certain time or at a certain price.

**Par:** (1) Refers to the standard delivery point(s) and/or quality of a commodity that is deliverable on a futures contract at contract price. Serves as a benchmark upon which to base discounts or premiums for varying quality and delivery locations; (2) In bond markets, an index (usually 100) representing the face value of a bond.

**Point-and-Figure:** A method of charting which uses prices to form patterns of movement without regard to time. It defines a price trend as a continued movement in one direction until a reversal of a predetermined criterion is met.

**Position:** An interest in the market, either long or short, in the form of one or more open contracts.

**Position Limit:** The maximum position, either net long or net short, in one commodity future (or option) or in all futures (or options) of one commodity combined which may be held or controlled by one person as prescribed by an exchange and/or by the CFTC.

**Position Trader:** A commodity trader who either buys or sells contracts and holds them for an extended period of time, as distinguished from the day trader, who will normally initiate and offset a futures position within a single trading session.

**Positive Carry:** The cost of financing a financial instrument (the short-term rate of interest), where the cost is less than the current return of the financial instrument.

**Price Discovery:** The process of determining the price level for a commodity based on supply and demand factors.

**Pyramiding:** The use of profits on existing positions as margin to increase the size of the position, normally in successively smaller increments.

**Quotation:** The actual price or the bid or asked price of either cash commodities or futures contracts.

**Resistance:** In technical trading, a price area where new selling will emerge to dampen a continued rise.

**Riding the Yield Curve:** Trading in an interest rate future according to the expectations of change in the yield curve.

**Roll-Over:** A trading procedure involving the shift of one month of a straddle into another future month while holding the other contract month. The shift can take place in either the long or short straddle month. The term also applies to lifting a near futures position and re-establishing it in a more deferred delivery month.

**Round Lot:** A quantity of a commodity equal in size to the corresponding futures contract for the commodity.

**Round Turn:** A completed transaction involving both a purchase and a liquidating sale, or a sale followed by a covering purchase.

**Scalper:** A speculator on the trading floor of an exchange who buys and sells rapidly, with small profits or losses, holding his positions for only a short time during a trading session. Typically, a scalper will stand ready to buy at a fraction below the last transaction price and to sell at a fraction above, thus creating market liquidity.

**Scalping:** The practice of trading in and out of the market on very small price fluctuations. A person who engages in this practice is known as a scalper.

**Selling Hedge (or Short Hedge):** Selling futures contracts to protect against possible decreased prices of commodities.

**Settlement:** The act of fulfilling the delivery requirements of a futures contract.

**Settlement or Settling Price:** The daily price at which the clearing house clears all trades and settles all accounts between clearing members for each contract month. Settlement prices are used to determine both margin calls and invoice prices for deliveries. The term also refers to a price established by the exchange to even up positions which may not be able to be liquidated in regular trading.

**Short:** (1) The selling side of an open futures contract; (2) a trader whose net position in the futures market shows an excess of open sales over open purchases.

**Short Selling:** Selling a contract with the idea of delivering or of buying to offset it at a later date.

**Short the Basis:** The purchase of futures as a hedge against a commitment to sell in the cash or spot markets.

**Speculator:** An individual who does not hedge, but who trades in commodity futures with the objective of achieving profits through the successful anticipation of price movements.

**Spot:** Market of immediate delivery of the product and immediate payment. Also refers to a maturing delivery month of a futures contract.

**Spot Commodity:** (1) The actual commodity as distinguished from a futures contract; (2) sometimes used to refer to cash commodities available for immediate delivery.

**Spot Price:** The price at which a physical commodity for immediate delivery is selling at a given time and place.

**Spread (or Straddle):** The purchase of one futures delivery month against the sale of another futures delivery month of the same commodity; the purchase of one delivery month of one commodity against the sale of that same delivery month of a different commodity; or the purchase of one commodity in one market against the sale of that commodity in another market, to take advantage of and profit from a change in price relationships.

**Squeeze:** A market situation in which the lack of supplies tends to force shorts to cover their positions by offset at higher prices.

**Stop Limit Order:** A stop limit order is an order that goes into force as soon as there is a trade at the specified price. The order, however, can only be filled at the stop limit price or better.

**Stop Order:** This is an order that becomes a market order when a particular price level is reached. A sell stop is placed below the market, a buy stop is placed above the market. Sometimes referred to as Stop Loss Order.

**Support:** In technical analysis, a price area where new buying is likely to come in and stem any decline. *See also* Resistance.

**Technical Analysis:** An approach to forecasting commodity prices which examines patterns of price change, rates of change, and changes in volume trading and open interest, without regard to underlying fundamental market factors.

**Tender:** To give notice to the clearinghouse of the intention to initiate delivery of the physical commodity in satisfaction of the futures contract.

**Tick:** Refers to a minimum change in price up or down.

**Treasury Bills (or T-Bills):** Short term U.S. government obligations generally issued with 13-, 26- or 52-week maturities.

**Treasury Bonds (or T-Bonds):** Long-term obligations of the U.S. government which pay interest semi-annually until they mature or are called, at which time the principal and the final interest payment is paid to the investor.

**Treasury Notes:** Same as Treasury Bonds except that Treasury Notes are medium-term and not callable.

**Underlying Commodity:** The commodity or futures contract on which a commodity option is based, and which must be accepted or delivered if the option is exercised.

**Variable Limit Margin:** The performance deposit required whenever the daily trading limits on prices of a commodity are raised in accordance with exchange rules. In periods of extreme price volatility, some exchanges permit trading at price levels that exceed regular daily limits. At such times, margins also are increased.

**Variable Price Limit:** A price limit schedule, determined by an exchange, that permits variations above or below the normally allowable price movements for any one trading day.

**Variation Margin:** Payment required upon margin call.

**Volume of Trade:** The number of contracts traded during a specified period of time. It may be quoted as the number of contracts traded or in the total of physical units, such as bales or bushels, pounds or dozens.

**Warehouse Receipt:** A document providing possession of a commodity by a licensed warehouse that is recognized for delivery purposes by many commodity futures exchanges.

**Yield Curve:** A graphic representation of market yield for a fixed-income security plotted against the maturity of the security.

# Appendix C

# FUTURES CONTRACT SPECIFICATIONS

**Chicago Board of Trade Soybeans**

| | |
|---|---|
| Contract Size: | 5,000 bushels |
| Unit Price Change, or "Tick": | 1/4 cent per bushel, or $12.50 per contract. |
| Daily Limit on Price Movement: | 30 cents per bushel, or $1,500 per contract, above or below the previous day's settlement price. There is no limit in the spot month. |
| Contract Maturity Months: | September, November, January, March, May, July, and August. |
| Trading Hours: | 9:30 a.m. until 1:15 p.m. central standard time, except on the final trading day of an expiring contract, when trading stops at noon. |
| Last Trading Day: | Seven business days before the last business day of the delivery month. |

Deliverable Grades:                     Number 2 yellow soybeans at
                                        par, and substitutions at
                                        differentials established by the
                                        exchange.

## Chicago Board of Trade Soybean Meal

| | |
|---|---|
| Contract Size: | 100 tons, or 200,000 lbs. |
| Unit Price Change, or "Tick": | 10 cents per ton, or $10.00 per contract. |
| Daily Limit on Price Movement: | $10 per ton, or $1,000 per contract, above or below the previous day's settlement price. There is no limit in the spot month. |
| Contract Maturity Months: | January, March, May, July, August, September, October, and December. |
| Trading Hours: | 9:30 a.m. until 1:15 p.m. central standard time, except on the final trading day of an expiring contract, when trading stops at noon. |
| Last Trading Day: | Seven business days before the last business day of the delivery month. |
| Deliverable Grades: | One grade of meal only with minimum protein of 44%. Consult the Chicago Board of Trade regulations for the exact specifications. |

## Chicago Board of Trade Soybean Oil

| | |
|---|---|
| Contract Size: | 60,000 pounds. |
| Unit Price Change, or "Tick": | $.0001 per pound, or $6 per contract. |
| Daily Limit on Price Movement: | $.01 per pound, or $600 per contract, above or below the previous day's settlement price. There is no limit in the spot month. |
| Contract Maturity Months: | January, March, May, July, August, September, October, and December. |
| Trading Hours: | 9:30 a.m. until 1:15 p.m. central standard time, except on the final trading day of an expiring contract, when trading stops at noon. |
| Last Trading Day: | Seven business days before the last business day of the delivery month. |
| Deliverable Grades: | One grade of crude soybean oil only. Consult the Chicago Board of Trade regulations for the exact specifications. |

## Chicago Board of Trade United States Treasury Bonds

| | |
|---|---|
| Contract Size: | $100,000 face value United States Treasury Bond. |
| Unit Price Change, or "Tick": | 1/32 of a point, or $31.25 per contract, since each point is equal to $10,000. |
| Daily Limit on Price Movement: | 3 points, or $3,000 per contract, above or below the previous day's settlement price. |
| Contract Maturity Months: | March, June, September, and December. |
| Trading Hours: | 7:20 a.m. until 2:00 p.m. central standard time, Monday through Friday. Evening trading hours are from 5:00 p.m. to 8:30 p.m. central standard time, or 6:00 p.m. until 9:30 p.m. central daylight saving time, Sunday through Thursday. |
| Last Trading Day: | Seven business days before the last business day of the delivery month. |
| Deliverable Grades: | United States Treasury Bonds maturing at least 15 years from the first business day of the delivery month, if not callable. If the bond is callable, then it cannot be called for at least 15 years from the first day of the delivery month. The coupon is based upon an 8% standard. |

## Chicago Mercantile Exchange Standard & Poor's 500 Stock Index

| | |
|---|---|
| Contract Size: | 500 times the Standard & Poor's 500 Stock Price Index. |
| Unit Price Change, or "Tick": | .05 index points, or $25 per contract. |
| Daily Limit on Price Movement: | Coordinated with trading halts of the underlying stocks listed for trading in the securities markets. Consult the Chicago Mercantile Exchange for exact price limits. |
| Opening Price Limit: | During the opening range, there shall be no trading at a price more than five index points above or below the previous day's settlement price. If the primary futures contract is limit bid or offered at the five index point limit at the end of the first ten minutes of trading, then trading shall cease for two minutes. After the two minutes have passed, trading will reopen with a new trading range. |
| Contract Maturity Months: | March, June, September, and December. |
| Trading Hours: | 8:30 a.m. until 3:15 p.m. central standard time. |
| Last Trading Day: | The business day immediately preceding the day of determination of the final settlement price. |

Delivery:                                    Cash settlement to the final
                                             settlement price, determined by
                                             a special quotation of the S&P
                                             Stock Price Index based on the
                                             opening prices of the component
                                             stocks in the index on the third
                                             Friday of the contract month.

# Appendix D

# PROBLEMS AND SOLUTIONS

## CHAPTER 4

### Problem 4-1

Assume soybean market conditions identical to those in Figure 4-2, the short speculator. Suppose that a small retail investor had $50,000 that she wanted to commit to a short speculative soybean strategy in June of 1993. This investor's broker requires all soybean speculators to post an initial margin of $1,475 per contract and maintain a margin of at least $1,100 per contract. Construct this speculator's worksheet given that she shorts five July soybean contracts, and wants to keep her margin account between the maintenance and initial levels. The July soybean futures contract prices are as follows:

| | | |
|---|---|---|
| 6/01/93 | Jul beans | 5.89 |
| 6/02/93 | Jul beans | 5.8875 |
| 6/03/93 | Jul beans | 5.90 |
| 6/04/93 | Jul beans | 5.8825 |
| 6/07/93 | Jul beans | 5.92 |
| 6/08/93 | Jul beans | 5.9025 |

## Solution 4-1

The trading worksheet labeled Problem 4-1 represents this speculator's soybean position between June 1st and June 8th of 1993. The
various sections in Problem 4-1, the overall futures activity, the margin activity, and the cash activity, carry the exact same meaning as
the sections in Figure 4-2. However, the cash flows are quite a bit
different. The short speculator established her position by selling five
July soybean contracts on 6/01/93, and then maintained this short
position. During the following week she experienced some gains and
losses. However, she liquidated her position at the end of the week
and transferred her ending margin balance from her margin account
to her cash account on 6/08/93. This short speculator lost a total of
$313 during the week.

## Problem 4-2

Assume soybean market conditions identical to those in Figure 4-3,
the short hedger. The farmer's soybean position in the cash market is
opposite the processor's cash market position. In this situation the
farmer is long the cash commodity, soybeans, and the processor is
short the commodity. It is assumed that the time is late May of 1993
and that the processor needs 10,000 bushels of soybeans in July and
intends to buy them in the spot market at the lowest available price.
At the same time, the farmer has possession of 10,000 bushels of
soybeans that have been stored and carried from the previous year's
harvest and plans to sell them in early July in the cash, or spot,
market at the highest price available. Thus, to offset his cash position,
the farmer needs to sell soybean futures contracts. The farmer has
budgeted a total of $15,000 to satisfy his broker's requirements of an
$1,475 per contract initial margin, and a maintenance margin of
$1,100 per contract, and to insure that he will have enough cash in
reserve to withstand the soybean market's price movement. Construct this short hedger's worksheet given that he wants his margin
account balance to remain within the initial and maintenance levels.
The relevant soybean spot and futures prices are as follows:

# Problem 4-1
## Short Speculation Solution

### I. Overall Futures Activity

| (1) | (2) | (3) | (4) | (5) | (6) | (7) | (8) | (9) | (10) | (11) |
|---|---|---|---|---|---|---|---|---|---|---|
| Date | Contract | Unit Price | Number of Units per Contract | Number of Contracts +Long/-Short | Position Value | Position +Gain/-Loss | Total Cash+Margin | Invested Cash+Margin | Commission | Cumulative +Gain/-Loss |
| 6/1/93 | July Beans | $5.8900 | 5000 | -5 | ($147,250) | $0.00 | $50,000 | $50,000 | | $0 |
| 6/2/93 | July Beans | $5.8875 | 5000 | -5 | ($147,188) | $62.50 | $50,063 | $50,000 | | $62 |
| 6/3/93 | July Beans | $5.9000 | 5000 | -5 | ($147,500) | ($312.50) | $49,750 | $50,000 | | ($250) |
| 6/4/93 | July Beans | $5.8825 | 5000 | -5 | ($147,063) | $437.50 | $50,188 | $50,000 | | $187 |
| 6/7/93 | July Beans | $5.9200 | 5000 | -5 | ($148,000) | ($937.50) | $49,250 | $50,000 | | ($750) |
| 6/8/93 | July Beans | $5.9025 | 5000 | -5 | ($147,563) | $437.50 | $49,688 | $50,000 | | ($313) |

### II. Margin Activity
Intitial Margin Requirement      $1,475   per Contract
Maintenance Margin Requirement      $1,100   per Contract

| (1) | (2) | (3) | (4) | (5) | (6) | (7) | (8) | (9) | (10) |
|---|---|---|---|---|---|---|---|---|---|
| Date | Beginning # of Maintenance Contracts | Margin Account Beginning Balance | Unit Price Change | Position +Gain/-Loss | Interim Margin Balance | Cash Account +From Cash -To Cash | Margin Account Ending Balance | Ending Number of Contracts | Maintenance Requirement |
| 6/1/93 | -5 | $7,375 | $0.0000 | $0 | $7,375 | $0 | $7,375 | -5 | $5,500 |
| 6/2/93 | -5 | $7,375 | ($0.0025) | $62 | $7,437 | $0 | $7,437 | -5 | $5,500 |
| 6/3/93 | -5 | $7,437 | $0.0125 | ($313) | $7,125 | $0 | $7,125 | -5 | $5,500 |
| 6/4/93 | -5 | $7,125 | ($0.0175) | $438 | $7,562 | $0 | $7,562 | -5 | $5,500 |
| 6/7/93 | -5 | $7,562 | $0.0375 | ($937) | $6,625 | $0 | $6,625 | -5 | $5,500 |
| 6/8/93 | -5 | $6,625 | ($0.0175) | $438 | $7,063 | ($7,063) | ($1) | 0 | $0 |

# Problem 4-1
## Short Speculation Solution (continued)

### III. Cash Activity

| (1) Date | (2) Speculative Cash Beginning Balance | (3) Cash Account Flows + Invested - Withdrawn | (4) Margin Account Flows + From Margin - To Margin | (5) Speculative Cash Ending Balance |
|---|---|---|---|---|
| 6/1/93 | $42,625 | $0 | $0 | $42,625 |
| 6/2/93 | $42,625 | $0 | $0 | $42,625 |
| 6/3/93 | $42,625 | $0 | $0 | $42,625 |
| 6/4/93 | $42,625 | $0 | $0 | $42,625 |
| 6/7/93 | $42,625 | $0 | $0 | $42,625 |
| 6/8/93 | $42,625 | $0 | $7,063 | $49,688 |

*Spot Prices*                                    *Futures Prices*

| 5/20/93 | soybeans | 590     | Jul beans | 603 1/2 |
|---------|----------|---------|-----------|---------|
| 5/21/93 | soybeans | 595 1/2 | Jul beans | 608     |
| 5/24/93 | soybeans | 594 1/2 | Jul beans | 606     |
| 5/25/93 | soybeans | 595 1/2 | Jul beans | 607 1/2 |
| 5/26/93 | soybeans | 599 1/2 | Jul beans | 612 3/4 |
| 5/27/93 | soybeans | 595 1/2 | Jul beans | 609     |
| 5/28/93 | soybeans | 595 1/2 | Jul beans | 608 1/2 |
| 6/01/93 | soybeans | 575 1/2 | Jul beans | 589     |

## Solution 4-2

The trading worksheet labeled Problem 4-2 represents this short hedger's soybean position between May 20th and June 1st of 1993. This worksheet differs from Figure 4-3 with regard to funds being invested into the cash account. In this problem the hedger did not have to invest any additional cash into the position. Note that the ending margin account balance was maintained between the initial and maintenance levels of $2,950 and $2,200 by transferring funds between the margin and cash accounts. Only one transfer was necessary—$925 on May 26th—because the interim margin balance had fallen below the maintenance level.

## Problem 4-3

Assume soybean market conditions identical to those in Figure 4-5, the spreader, and that on August 3rd, 1993, you observe that the September-November soybean spread is at zero. Suppose that you want to do a five lot and have $5,000 to commit to the spread. You feel that $5,000 is adequate to meet your broker's initial margin requirement of $400 per spread and maintenance requirement of $300 per spread, and still provide enough of a cushion to withstand any adverse market moves. However, to be on the safe side you want to maintain a minimum balance of $1,600 in your margin account. Construct a worksheet that satisfies your $1,600 minimum balance requirement, and shows the spread's behavior between August 3, 1993, and August 10, 1993. Prices for the September and November soybean futures contracts are as follows:

# Problem 4-2
## Soybean Short Hedger Worksheet

### I. Overall Spot Activity

| (1) Date | (2) Spot Commodity | (3) Unit Price | (4) Amount of Spot Commodity | (5) Spot Position Value | (6) Unit Price Change | (7) Spot Position +Gain/-Loss | (8) Commission | (9) Spot Cumulative +Gain/-Loss |
|---|---|---|---|---|---|---|---|---|
| 5/20/93 | Soybeans | $5.9100 | +10000 | $59,100 | $0.0000 | $0 | | $0 |
| 5/21/93 | Soybeans | $5.9550 | +10000 | $59,550 | $0.0450 | $450 | | $450 |
| 5/24/93 | Soybeans | $5.9450 | +10000 | $59,450 | ($0.0100) | ($100) | | $350 |
| 5/25/93 | Soybeans | $5.9550 | +10000 | $59,550 | $0.0100 | $100 | | $450 |
| 5/26/93 | Soybeans | $5.9950 | +10000 | $59,950 | $0.0400 | $400 | | $850 |
| 5/27/93 | Soybeans | $5.9550 | +10000 | $59,550 | ($0.0400) | ($400) | | $450 |
| 5/28/93 | Soybeans | $5.9550 | +10000 | $59,550 | $0.0000 | $0 | | $450 |
| 6/1/93 | Soybeans | $5.7550 | +10000 | $57,550 | ($0.2000) | ($2,000) | | ($1,550) |

### II. Basis Activity

| (1) Date | (2) Basis Unit Value Spot Futures | (3) Basis Change | (4) Basis Cumulative +Gain/-Loss |
|---|---|---|---|
| 5/20/93 | -0.1250 | 0 | $0 |
| 5/21/93 | -0.1250 | 0.0000 | $0 |
| 5/24/93 | -0.1150 | 0.0100 | $100 |
| 5/25/93 | -0.1200 | -0.0050 | $50 |
| 5/26/93 | -0.1325 | -0.0125 | ($75) |
| 5/27/93 | -0.1350 | -0.0025 | ($100) |
| 5/28/93 | -0.1300 | 0.0050 | ($50) |
| 6/1/93 | -0.1350 | -0.0050 | ($100) |

# Problem 4-2
## Soybean Short Hedger Worksheet (continued)

**III. Overall Futures Activity**

| (1) Date | (2) Contract | (3) Unit Price | (4) Number of Units per Contract | (5) Number of Contracts +Long/-Short | (6) Futures Position Values | (7) Futures Position +Gain/-Loss | (8) Total Cash+Margin | (9) Invested Cash+Margin | (10) Commission | (11) Futures Cumulative +Gain/-Loss |
|---|---|---|---|---|---|---|---|---|---|---|
| 5/20/93 | JLY Soybeans | $6.0350 | 5000 | -2 | ($60,350) | $0 | $17,950 | $17,950 | | $0 |
| 5/21/93 | JLY Soybeans | $6.0800 | 5000 | -2 | ($60,800) | ($450) | $17,500 | $17,950 | | ($450) |
| 5/24/93 | JLY Soybeans | $6.0600 | 5000 | -2 | ($60,600) | $200 | $17,700 | $17,950 | | ($250) |
| 5/25/93 | JLY Soybeans | $6.0750 | 5000 | -2 | ($60,750) | ($150) | $17,550 | $17,950 | | ($400) |
| 5/26/93 | JLY Soybeans | $6.1275 | 5000 | -2 | ($61,275) | ($525) | $17,025 | $17,950 | | ($925) |
| 5/27/93 | JLY Soybeans | $6.0900 | 5000 | -2 | ($60,900) | $375 | $17,400 | $17,950 | | ($550) |
| 5/28/93 | JLY Soybeans | $6.0850 | 5000 | -2 | ($60,850) | $50 | $17,450 | $17,950 | | ($500) |
| 6/1/93 | JLY Soybeans | $5.8900 | 5000 | -2 | ($58,900) | $1,950 | $19,400 | $17,950 | | $1,450 |

**IV. Margin Activity**
Initial Margin Requirement    $1,475 per Contract
Maintenance Margin Requirement    $1,100 per Contract

| (1) Date | (2) Beginning # of Maintenance Contracts | (3) Margin Account Beginning Balance | (4) Unit Price Change | (5) Position +Gain/-Loss | (6) Interim Margin Balance | (7) Cash Account +From Cash -To Cash | (8) Margin Account Ending Balance | (9) Ending Number of Contracts | (10) Maintenance Requirement |
|---|---|---|---|---|---|---|---|---|---|
| 5/20/93 | -2 | $2,950 | 0 | $0 | $2,950 | $0 | $2,950 | -2 | $2,200 |
| 5/21/93 | -2 | $2,950 | 0.0450 | ($450) | $2,500 | $0 | $2,500 | -2 | $2,200 |
| 5/24/93 | -2 | $2,500 | -0.0200 | $200 | $2,700 | $0 | $2,700 | -2 | $2,200 |
| 5/25/93 | -2 | $2,700 | 0.0150 | ($150) | $2,550 | $0 | $2,550 | -2 | $2,200 |
| 5/26/93 | -2 | $2,550 | 0.0525 | ($525) | $2,025 | $925 | $2,950 | -2 | $2,200 |
| 5/27/93 | -2 | $2,950 | -0.0375 | $375 | $3,325 | $0 | $3,325 | -2 | $2,200 |
| 5/28/93 | -2 | $3,325 | -0.0050 | $50 | $3,375 | $0 | $3,375 | -2 | $2,200 |
| 6/1/93 | -2 | $3,375 | -0.1950 | $1,950 | $5,325 | ($5,325) | $0 | 0 | $0 |

**V. Cash Activity**

| (1) Date | (2) Carrying Cash Beginning Balance | (3) Cash Account Flows + Invested - Withdrawn | (4) Margin Account Flows + From Margin - To Margin | (5) Carrying Cash Ending Balance |
|---|---|---|---|---|
| 5/20/93 | $15,000 | $0 | $0 | $15,000 |
| 5/21/93 | $15,000 | $0 | $0 | $15,000 |
| 5/24/93 | $15,000 | $0 | $0 | $15,000 |
| 5/25/93 | $15,000 | $0 | $0 | $15,000 |
| 5/26/93 | $15,000 | $0 | ($925) | $14,075 |
| 5/27/93 | $14,075 | $0 | $0 | $14,075 |
| 5/28/93 | $14,075 | $0 | $0 | $14,075 |
| 6/1/93 | $14,075 | $0 | $5,325 | $19,400 |

| 8/03/93 | Sep beans | $7.06 | Nov beans | $7.06 |
| 8/04/93 | Sep beans | $6.96 1/2 | Nov beans | $6.96 1/4 |
| 8/05/93 | Sep beans | $6.79 | Nov beans | $6.78 |
| 8/06/93 | Sep beans | $6.79 1/4 | Nov beans | $6.79 |
| 8/09/93 | Sep beans | $6.77 1/2 | Nov beans | $6.70 |
| 8/10/93 | Sep Beans | $6.69 3/4 | Nov beans | $6.73 1/4 |

## Solution 4-3

The trading worksheet labeled Problem 4-3 represents this spreader's position between August 3, 1993, and August 10, 1993. This worksheet differs from Figure 4-5 with regard to the funds being transferred between the margin and cash accounts. Note that the margin account balance never fell below the minimum requirement.

## Problem 4-3
### Soybean Spreader Worksheet

**I. Detailed Futures Activity**

| (1) Date | (2) Long Position | (3) Unit Price | (4) Long Units Price Change | (5) Number of Contracts Bought | (6) Short Position | (7) Unit Price | (8) Short Units Price Change | (9) Number of Contracts Sold | (10) Spread Unit Value | (11) Spread Unit Change | (12) Number of Units per Contract | (13) Spread Value |
|---|---|---|---|---|---|---|---|---|---|---|---|---|
| 8/3/93 | Nov Beans | $7.0600 | $0.0000 | +5 | Sep Beans | $7.0600 | $0.0000 | -5 | $0.0000 | 0 | 5000 | $0 |
| 8/4/93 | Nov Beans | $6.9625 | ($0.0975) | +5 | Sep Beans | $6.9650 | ($0.0950) | -5 | ($0.0025) | ($0.0025) | 5000 | ($62) |
| 8/5/93 | Nov Beans | $6.7800 | ($0.1825) | +5 | Sep Beans | $6.7900 | ($0.1750) | -5 | ($0.0100) | ($0.0075) | 5000 | ($250) |
| 8/6/93 | Nov Beans | $6.7900 | $0.0100 | +5 | Sep Beans | $6.7925 | $0.0025 | -5 | ($0.0025) | $0.0075 | 5000 | ($63) |
| 8/9/93 | Nov Beans | $6.7000 | ($0.0900) | +5 | Sep Beans | $6.6775 | ($0.1150) | -5 | $0.0225 | $0.0250 | 5000 | $562 |
| 8/10/93 | Nov Beans | $6.7325 | $0.0325 | +5 | Sep Beans | $6.6975 | $0.0200 | -5 | $0.0350 | $0.0125 | 5000 | $875 |

**II. Over All Spread Activity**

| (1) Date | (2) Spread | (3) Spread Unit Value | (4) Number of Units Per Lot | (5) Number of Lots | (6) Spread Value | (7) Spread + Gain / -Loss | (8) Total Cash + Margins | (9) Invested Cash + Margins | (10) Spread Commission | (11) Cummulative + Gain / -Loss |
|---|---|---|---|---|---|---|---|---|---|---|
| 8/3/93 | + Nov-Sep Beans | $0.0000 | 5000 | 5 | $0 | $0 | $5,000 | $5,000 | | $0 |
| 8/4/93 | + Nov-Sep Beans | ($0.0025) | 5000 | 5 | ($62) | ($62) | $4,938 | $5,000 | | ($62) |
| 8/5/93 | + Nov-Sep Beans | ($0.0100) | 5000 | 5 | ($250) | ($188) | $4,750 | $5,000 | | ($250) |
| 8/6/93 | + Nov-Sep Beans | ($0.0025) | 5000 | 5 | ($63) | $187 | $4,937 | $5,000 | | ($63) |
| 8/9/93 | + Nov-Sep Beans | $0.0225 | 5000 | 5 | $562 | $625 | $5,563 | $5,000 | | $562 |
| 8/10/93 | + Nov-Sep Beans | $0.0350 | 5000 | 5 | $875 | $313 | $5,875 | $5,000 | | $875 |

# Problem 4-3

## Soybean Spreader Worksheet (continued)

Initial Margin Requirement: $400 per Spread
Maintenance Margin Requirement: $300 per Spread

| (1) Date | (2) Beginning Number of Lots | (3) Margin Account Beginning Balance | (4) Spread Unit Price Change | (5) Position +Gain / –Loss | (6) Interim Margin Balance | (7) Ending Number of Lots | (8) Cash Account +From Cash / –To Cash | (9) Margin Account Ending Balance | (10) Maintenance Requirement |
|---|---|---|---|---|---|---|---|---|---|
| 8/3/93 | +5 | $2,000 | $0.0000 | $0 | $2,000 | 5 | $0 | $2,000 | $1,500 |
| 8/4/93 | +5 | $2,000 | ($0.0025) | ($62) | $1,938 | 5 | $0 | $1,938 | $1,500 |
| 8/5/93 | +5 | $1,938 | ($0.0075) | ($188) | $1,750 | 5 | $0 | $1,750 | $1,500 |
| 8/6/93 | +5 | $1,750 | $0.0075 | $187 | $1,937 | 5 | $0 | $1,937 | $1,500 |
| 8/9/93 | +5 | $1,937 | $0.0250 | $625 | $2,563 | 5 | $0 | $2,563 | $1,500 |
| 8/10/93 | +5 | $2,563 | $0.0125 | $313 | $2,875 | 0 | $2,875 | $5,750 | $0 |

## IV. Cash Activity

| (1) Date | (2) Reserve Cash Beginning Balance | (3) Cash Account Flows +Invested / –Withdrawn | (4) Margin Account Flows +From Margin / –To Margin | (5) Reserve Ending Balance |
|---|---|---|---|---|
| 8/3/93 | $3,000 | $0 | $0 | $3,000 |
| 8/4/93 | $3,000 | $0 | $0 | $3,000 |
| 8/5/93 | $3,000 | $0 | $0 | $3,000 |
| 8/6/93 | $3,000 | $0 | $0 | $3,000 |
| 8/9/93 | $3,000 | $0 | $0 | $3,000 |
| 8/10/93 | $3,000 | $0 | $2,875 | $5,875 |

## Problem 5-1

Assume Treasury Bond market conditions identical to those in Figure 5-4, the short speculator. Suppose that a small retail investor had $9,050 that she wanted to commit to a short speculative Treasury Bond strategy in January of 1994. This investor's broker requires all T-Bond speculators to post an initial margin of $2,025 per contract and maintain a margin of at least $1,500 per contract. Construct this speculator's worksheet given that she shorts two March T-Bond contracts on January 4th. The March T-Bond contract prices are as follows:

|  |  |  |
|---|---|---|
| 1/4/94 | Mar bonds | 114-7 |
| 1/5/94 | Mar bonds | 113-14 |
| 1/6/94 | Mar bonds | 114-17 |
| 1/7/94 | Mar bonds | 116-3 |
| 1/10/94 | Mar bonds | 116-11 |
| 1/11/94 | Mar bonds | 116-13 |

## Solution 5-1

The trading worksheet labeled Problem 5-1 represents this speculator's Treasury Bond position between January 4th and January 11th of 1994. The various sections in Problem 5-1, the overall futures activity, the margin activity, and the cash activity, carry the exact same meaning as the sections in Figure 5-4. The short speculator established her position by selling two September T-Bond contracts on 6/2/89, and then maintained this short position. During the following week she experienced some large losses. Thus, she was forced to transfer $3,750 on January 7th from the cash reserve account to the margin account. The next day her position continued to erode, and finally on January 11th her losses were such that she was forced to liquidate her position.

## Problem 5-2

Assume that Treasury Bond market conditions are identical to those in Figure 5-7, the long hedger. This portfolio manager wants to establish a long T-Bond futures position to hedge a $1,000,000 short cash position in U.S. government bonds. With the initial and maintenance

## Problem 5-1
### Short U.S. T-Bond Speculative Worksheet

**I. Overall Futures Activity**

| (1) Date | (2) Contract | (3) Unit Price Per $1000 Bond | (4) Number of Units per Contract | (5) Number of Contracts +Long/-Short | (6) Position Value | (7) Position +Gain/-Loss | (8) Total Cash+Margin | (9) Invested Cash+Margin | (10) Commission | (11) Cumulative +Gain/-Loss |
|---|---|---|---|---|---|---|---|---|---|---|
| 1/4/94 | March T-Bonds | $1,142.1880 | 100 | -2 | ($228,438) | $0.00 | $9,050 | $9,050 | | $0.00 |
| 1/5/94 | March T-Bonds | $1,138.1250 | 100 | -2 | ($227,625) | $812.60 | $9,863 | $9,050 | | $812.60 |
| 1/6/94 | March T-Bonds | $1,145.3130 | 100 | -2 | ($229,063) | ($1,437.60) | $8,425 | $9,050 | | ($625.00) |
| 1/7/94 | March T-Bonds | $1,160.9380 | 100 | -2 | ($232,188) | ($3,125.00) | $5,300 | $9,050 | | ($3,750.00) |
| 1/10/94 | March T-Bonds | $1,163.4480 | 100 | -2 | ($232,688) | ($500.00) | $4,800 | $9,050 | | ($4,250.00) |
| 1/11/94 | March T-Bonds | $1,164.0630 | 100 | -2 | ($232,813) | ($125.00) | $4,675 | $9,050 | | ($4,375.00) |

**II. Margin Activity**
Initial Margin Requirement    $2,025 per Contract
Maintenance Margin Requirement    $1,500 per Contract

| (1) Date | (2) Beginning # of Maintenance Contracts | (3) Margin Account Beginning Balance | (4) Unit Price Change | (5) Position +Gain/-Loss | (6) Interim Margin Balance | (7) Cash Account +From Cash -To Cash | (8) Margin Account Ending Balance | (9) Ending Number of Contracts | (10) Maintenance Requirement |
|---|---|---|---|---|---|---|---|---|---|
| 1/4/94 | -2 | $4,050 | 0.0000 | $0.00 | $4,050 | $0 | $4,050 | -2 | $3,000 |
| 1/5/94 | -2 | $4,050 | (4.0630) | $812.60 | $4,863 | $0 | $4,863 | -2 | $3,000 |
| 1/6/94 | -2 | $4,863 | 7.1880 | ($1,437.60) | $3,425 | $0 | $3,425 | -2 | $3,000 |
| 1/7/94 | -2 | $3,425 | 15.6250 | ($3,125.00) | $300 | $3,750 | $4,050 | -2 | $3,000 |
| 1/10/94 | -2 | $4,050 | 2.5000 | ($500.00) | $3,550 | $0 | $3,550 | -2 | $3,000 |
| 1/11/94 | -2 | $3,550 | 0.6250 | ($125.00) | $3,425 | ($3,425) | $0 | 0 | $0 |

III. Cash Activity

| (1) | (2) | (3) | (4) | (5) |
|---|---|---|---|---|
| | Speculative Cash Beginning Balance | Cash Account Flows +Invested -Withdrawn | Margin Account Flows +From Margin -To Margin | Speculative Cash Ending Balance |
| Date | | | | |
| 1/4/94 | $5,000 | $0 | $0 | $5,000 |
| 1/5/94 | $5,000 | $0 | $0 | $5,000 |
| 1/6/94 | $5,000 | $0 | $0 | $5,000 |
| 1/7/94 | $5,000 | $0 | ($3,750) | $1,250 |
| 1/10/94 | $1,250 | $0 | $0 | $1,250 |
| 1/11/94 | $1,250 | $0 | $3,425 | $4,675 |

margins for T-Bond futures contracts set at $2,025 and $1,500, respectively, the manager feels that $120,250 is sufficient to satisfy all margin requirements and insure the integrity of the long futures position in a volatile market. Construct this long hedger's worksheet given that he wants his margin account balance to remain within the initial and maintenance levels. Treasury Bond spot and futures are as follows:

| Spot Prices | | | Futures Prices | |
|---|---|---|---|---|
| 1/2/89 | T-Bonds | 98-20 | Mar bonds | 114-7 |
| 1/5/89 | T-Bonds | 97-30 | Mar bonds | 113-26 |
| 1/1/89 | T-Bonds | 98-27 | Mar bonds | 114-17 |
| 1/7/89 | T-Bonds | 100-8 | Mar bonds | 116-3 |
| 1/8/89 | T-Bonds | 99-31 | Mar bonds | 116-11 |
| 1/9/94 | T-Bonds | 100-4 | Mar bonds | 116-13 |

## Solution 5-2

The trading worksheet labeled Problem 5-2 represents this long T-Bond hedger's position between January 4th and January 11th of 1994. This worksheet is quite similar to the long T-Bond hedger worksheet. However, it differs in that this position is carried for only one week instead of six weeks. Note that the ending margin account balance was maintained between the initial and maintenance levels of $27,000 and $20,000 by transferring funds between the margin and cash accounts. Excess funds were moved from the margin account to the cash account on January 7th.

## Problem 5-3

Assume Treasury Bond market conditions identical to those in Figure 5-8, the T-Bond spreader, and that on February 1st, 1994, you anticipate that the March-June T-Bond spread will widen. Suppose that you want to do a 10 lot and have $14,500 to commit to the spread initially. You feel that $5,000 is adequate to meet your broker's initial margin requirements of $950 per spread and maintenance requirement of $700 per spread, and still provide enough of a cushion to withstand any adverse market moves. While the spread is in exist-

## Problem 5-2
## U.S. Treasury Bond Long Hedger Worksheet

### I. Overall Spot Activity

| (1) Date | (2) Spot Commodity | (3) Unit Price Per $1000 Bond | (4) Amount of Spot Commodity | (5) Spot Position Value | (6) Unit Price Change | (7) Spot Position +Gain/-Loss | (8) Commission | (9) Spot Cummulative +Gain/-Loss |
|---|---|---|---|---|---|---|---|---|
| 1/4/94 | US T-Bond | 986.2500 | -10.00 | ($986.250) | $0.0000 | $0 | | $0 |
| 1/5/94 | US T-Bond | 979.3750 | -10.00 | ($979.375) | ($6.8750) | $6,875 | | $6,875 |
| 1/6/94 | US T-Bond | 986.8750 | -10.00 | ($986.875) | $7.5000 | ($7,500) | | ($625) |
| 1/7/94 | US T-Bond | 1,002.5000 | -10.00 | ($1,002.500) | $15.6250 | ($15,625) | | ($16,250) |
| 1/10/94 | US T-Bond | 999.6875 | -10.00 | ($999.688) | ($2.8125) | $2,813 | | ($13,438) |
| 1/11/94 | US T-Bond | 1,001.2500 | -10.00 | ($1,001.250) | $1.5625 | ($1,563) | | ($15,000) |

### II. Basis Activity

| (1) Date | (2) Basis Unit Value Spot Futures | (3) Basis Change | (4) Basis Cumulative +Gain/-Loss |
|---|---|---|---|
| 1/4/94 | -155.9380 | 0 | $0 |
| 1/5/94 | -158.7500 | -2.8120 | $2,812 |
| 1/6/94 | -158.4380 | 0.3120 | $2,500 |
| 1/7/94 | -158.4380 | 0.0000 | $2,500 |
| 1/10/94 | -163.7505 | -5.3125 | $7,813 |
| 1/11/94 | -162.8130 | 0.9375 | $6,875 |

# Problem 5-2

## U.S. Treasury Bond Long Hedger Worksheet (continued)

### III. Overall Futures Activity

| (1)<br>Date | (2)<br>Contract | (3)<br>Unit Price Per<br>$1000 Bond | (4)<br>Number of<br>Units per<br>Contract | (5)<br>Number of<br>Contracts<br>+Long/-Short | (6)<br>Futures<br>Position<br>Values | (7)<br>Futures<br>Position<br>+Gain/-Loss | (8)<br>Total<br>Cash+Margin | (9)<br>Invested<br>Cash+Margin | (10)<br>Commission | (11)<br>Futures<br>Cumulative<br>+Gain/-Loss |
|---|---|---|---|---|---|---|---|---|---|---|
| 1/4/94 | US T-Bond | 1,142.1880 | 100 | +10 | $1,142,188 | $0.00 | $120,250 | $120,250 | | $0 |
| 1/5/94 | US T-Bond | 1,138.1250 | 100 | +10 | $1,138,125 | ($4,063.00) | $116,187 | $120,250 | | ($4,063) |
| 1/6/94 | US T-Bond | 1,145.3130 | 100 | +10 | $1,145,313 | $7,188.00 | $123,375 | $120,250 | | $3,125 |
| 1/7/94 | US T-Bond | 1,160.9380 | 100 | +10 | $1,160,938 | $15,625.00 | $139,000 | $120,250 | | $18,750 |
| 1/10/94 | US T-Bond | 1,163.4380 | 100 | +10 | $1,163,438 | $2,500.00 | $141,500 | $120,250 | | $21,250 |
| 1/11/94 | US T-Bond | 1,164.0630 | 100 | +10 | $1,164,063 | $625.00 | $142,125 | $120,250 | | $21,875 |

### IV. Margin Activity

Initital Margin Requirement   $2,025  per Contract
Maintenance Margin Requirement   $1,500  per Contract

| (1)<br>Date | (2)<br>Beginning #<br>of Maintenance<br>Contracts | (3)<br>Margin Account<br>Beginning<br>Balance | (4)<br>Unit Price<br>Change | (5)<br>Position<br>+Gain/-Loss | (6)<br>Interim Margin<br>Balance | (7)<br>Cash Account<br>+From Cash<br>-To Cash | (8)<br>Margin Account<br>Ending<br>Balance | (9)<br>Ending<br>Number<br>of Contracts | (10)<br>Maintenance<br>Requirement |
|---|---|---|---|---|---|---|---|---|---|
| 1/4/94 | +10 | $20,250 | 0.0000 | $0.00 | $20,250 | $0 | $20,250 | 10 | $15,000 |
| 1/5/94 | +10 | $20,250 | (4.0630) | ($4,063.00) | $16,187 | $0 | $16,187 | 10 | $15,000 |
| 1/6/94 | +10 | $16,187 | 7.1880 | $7,188.00 | $23,375 | $0 | $23,375 | 10 | $15,000 |
| 1/7/94 | +10 | $23,375 | 15.6250 | $15,625.00 | $39,000 | ($20,000) | $19,000 | 10 | $15,000 |
| 1/10/94 | +10 | $19,000 | 2.5000 | $2,500.00 | $21,500 | $0 | $21,500 | 10 | $15,000 |
| 1/11/94 | +10 | $21,500 | 0.6250 | $625.00 | $22,125 | ($22,125) | $0 | 0 | $0 |

## Problem 5-2
### U.S. Treasury Bond Long Hedger Worksheet (continued)

**V. Cash Activity**

| (1) Date | (2) Carrying Cash Beginning Balance | (3) Cash Account Flows + Invested - Withdrawn | (4) Margin Account Flows + From Margin - To Margin | (5) Carrying Cash Ending Balance |
|---|---|---|---|---|
| 1/4/94 | $100,000 | $0 | $0 | $100,000 |
| 1/5/94 | $100,000 | $0 | $0 | $100,000 |
| 1/6/94 | $100,000 | $0 | $0 | $100,000 |
| 1/7/94 | $100,000 | $0 | $20,000 | $120,000 |
| 1/10/94 | $120,000 | $0 | $0 | $120,000 |
| 1/11/94 | $120,000 | $0 | $22,125 | $142,125 |

ence, you want to maintain the margin account between the initial and maintenance levels. However, to be on the safe side you deposit an additional $5,000 in your cash account on February 2nd. The spread was liquidated on February 8, 1994. Construct a worksheet that shows the spread's behavior between February 1st and February 8th, 1994. The March and June Treasury Bond futures prices are as follows:

| 2/01/94 | Mar bonds | 116-6 | June bonds | 115-3 |
| 2/02/94 | Mar bonds | 116-14 | June bonds | 115-11 |
| 2/03/94 | Mar bonds | 115-31 | June bonds | 114-29 |
| 2/04/94 | Mar bonds | 114-28 | June bonds | 113-27 |
| 2/07/94 | Mar bonds | 114-26 | June bonds | 113-24 |
| 2/08/94 | Mar bonds | 114-9 | June bonds | 113-7 |

## Solution 5-3

The trading worksheet labeled Problem 5-3 represents this spreader's position between February 1st and 8th of 1994. This problem is virtually identical to the T-Bond spreader example discussed in Chapter Five.

## Problem 5-3
## U.S. Treasury Bond Spreader Worksheet

### I. Detailed Futures Activity

| (1) Date | (2) Long Position | (3) Unit Price Per $1000 Bond | (4) Long Units Price Change | (5) Number of Contracts Bought | (6) Short Position | (7) Unit Price | (8) Short Units Price Change | (9) Number of Contracts Bought | (10) Spread Unit Value | (11) Spread Unit Price Change | (12) Number of Units per Contract | (13) Spread Value |
|---|---|---|---|---|---|---|---|---|---|---|---|---|
| 2/1/94 | June Bonds | $1,150.9380 | 0 | +10 | Mar Bonds | $1,161.8750 | 0 | -10 | ($10.9370) | 0.0000 | 100 | ($10,937.00) |
| 2/2/94 | June Bonds | $1,153.4380 | $2.50 | +10 | Mar Bonds | $1,164.3750 | $2.50 | -10 | ($10.9370) | 0.0000 | 100 | ($10,937.00) |
| 2/3/94 | June Bonds | $1,149.0630 | ($4.38) | +10 | Mar Bonds | $1,159.6880 | ($4.69) | -10 | ($10.6250) | 0.3120 | 100 | ($10,625.00) |
| 2/4/94 | June Bonds | $1,138.4380 | ($10.63) | +10 | Mar Bonds | $1,148.7500 | ($10.94) | -10 | ($10.3120) | 0.3130 | 100 | ($10,312.00) |
| 2/7/94 | June Bonds | $1,137.5000 | ($0.94) | +10 | Mar Bonds | $1,148.1250 | ($0.63) | -10 | ($10.6250) | -0.3130 | 100 | ($10,625.00) |
| 2/8/94 | June Bonds | $1,132.1880 | ($5.31) | +10 | Mar Bonds | $1,142.8130 | ($5.31) | -10 | ($10.6250) | 0.0000 | 100 | ($10,625.00) |

### II. Over All Spread Activity

| (1) Date | (2) Spread | (3) Spread Unit Value | (4) Number of Units Per Contract | (5) Number of Contracts | (6) Spread Value | (7) Spread + Gain / -Loss | (8) Total Cash + Margins | (9) Invested Cash + Margins | (10) Spread Commission | (11) Cummulative + Gain / -Loss |
|---|---|---|---|---|---|---|---|---|---|---|
| 2/1/94 | + June-Mar Bonds | ($10.9370) | 100 | 10 | ($10,937.00) | $0.00 | $14,500.00 | $14,500 | | $0.00 |
| 2/2/94 | + June-Mar Bonds | ($10.9370) | 100 | 10 | ($10,937.00) | $0.00 | $19,500.00 | $19,500 | | $0.00 |
| 2/3/94 | + June-Mar Bonds | ($10.6250) | 100 | 10 | ($10,625.00) | $312.00 | $14,812.00 | $14,500 | | $312.00 |
| 2/4/94 | + June-Mar Bonds | ($10.3120) | 100 | 10 | ($10,312.00) | $313.00 | $15,125.00 | $14,500 | | $625.00 |
| 2/7/94 | + June-Mar Bonds | ($10.6250) | 100 | 10 | ($10,625.00) | ($313.00) | $14,812.00 | $14,500 | | $312.00 |
| 2/8/94 | + June-Mar Bonds | ($10.6250) | 100 | 10 | ($10,625.00) | $0.00 | $14,812.00 | $14,500 | | $312.00 |

# Problem 5-3
## U.S. Treasury Bond Spreader Worksheet (continued)

**III. Margin Activity**

Initial Margin Requirement:   $950 per Spread
Maintenance Margin Requirement:   $700 per Spread

| (1) Date | (2) Beginning Number of Contracts | (3) Margin Account Beginning Balance | (4) Spread Unit Price Change | (5) Position + Gain / -Loss | (6) Interim Margin Balance | (7) Ending Number of Contracts | (8) Cash Account + From Cash / -To Cash | (9) Margin Account Ending Balance | (10) Maintenance Requirement |
|---|---|---|---|---|---|---|---|---|---|
| 2/1/94 | 10 | $9,500.00 | 0.0000 | $0.00 | $9,500.00 | 10 | $0 | $9,500.00 | $7,000 |
| 2/2/94 | 10 | $9,500.00 | 0.0000 | $0.00 | $9,500.00 | 10 | $0 | $9,500.00 | $7,000 |
| 2/3/94 | 10 | $9,500.00 | 0.3120 | $312.00 | $9,812.00 | 10 | $0 | $9,812.00 | $7,000 |
| 2/4/94 | 10 | $9,812.00 | 0.3130 | $313.00 | $10,125.00 | 10 | $0 | $10,125.00 | $7,000 |
| 2/7/94 | 10 | $10,125.00 | -0.3130 | ($313.00) | $9,812.00 | 10 | $0 | $9,812.00 | $7,000 |
| 2/8/94 | 10 | $9,812.00 | 0.0000 | $0.00 | $9,812.00 | 0 | ($9,812) | $0.00 | $0 |

**IV. Cash Activity**

| (1) Date | (2) Reserve Cash Beginning Balance | (3) Cash Account Flows + Invested / -Withdrawn | (4) Margin Account Flows + From Margin / -To Margin | (5) Reserve Ending Balance |
|---|---|---|---|---|
| 2/1/94 | $5,000 | $0 | $0 | $5,000.00 |
| 2/2/94 | $5,000 | $5,000 | $0 | $10,000.00 |
| 2/3/94 | $10,000 | $0 | $0 | $10,000.00 |
| 2/4/94 | $10,000 | $0 | $0 | $10,000.00 |
| 2/7/94 | $10,000 | $0 | $0 | $10,000.00 |
| 2/8/94 | $10,000 | $0 | $9,812 | $19,812.00 |

## Problem 6-1

Assume market conditions identical to those facing the long S&P speculator. Suppose that a small retail investor had $50,000 that he wanted to commit to a long speculative S&P Index strategy in February of 1993. This investor's broker requires all S&P Index speculators to post an initial margin of $10,500 per contract, and then maintain a margin of at least $10,000 per contract. Construct this speculator's worksheet given that he shorts one March S&P 500 futures contract and must keep his margin account above the $10,000 maintenance level. The March S&P 500 Index futures contract prices are as follows:

| | | |
|---|---|---|
| 2/1/93 | Mar S&P | 442 |
| 2/2/93 | Mar S&P | 443 |
| 2/3/93 | Mar S&P | 447.3 |
| 2/4/93 | Mar S&P | 449.2 |
| 2/5/93 | Mar S&P | 449.1 |
| 2/8/93 | Mar S&P | 448.1 |
| 2/9/93 | Mar S&P | 446 |

## Solution 6-1

The trading worksheet labeled Problem 6-1 represents this speculator's long S&P 500 position between February 1st and February 9th of 1993. The various sections in Problem 6-1 carry the exact same meaning as the sections in the long speculator's worksheet, and the strategies are virtually identical.

## Problem 6-2

Assume market conditions identical to those facing the short S&P 500 Index hedger. This investor wants to establish a short futures position to hedge a $250,000 long cash position in a well diversified equity portfolio. With the initial and maintenance margins for S&P 500 Index futures contracts set at $10,000 and $10,000, respectively, the manager feels that $50,000 is sufficient to satisfy all margin requirements and insure the integrity of the short futures position in a volatile market. Construct this short hedger's worksheet. S&P 500 Index spot and futures values are as follows:

# Problem 6-1
## Standard & Poor's Long Speculation Worksheet

### I. Overall Futures Activity

| (1) Date | (2) Contract | (3) Unit Price | (4) Number of Units per Contract | (5) Number of Contracts +Long/-Short | (6) Position Value | (7) Position +Gain/-Loss | (8) Total Cash+Margin | (9) Invested Cash+Margin | (10) Commission | (11) Cumulative +Gain/-Loss |
|---|---|---|---|---|---|---|---|---|---|---|
| 2/1/93 | March S&P 500 | 442.00 | $500 | +1 | $221,000 | $0.00 | $20,000 | $20,000 | | $0 |
| 2/2/93 | March S&P 500 | 443.00 | $500 | +1 | $221,500 | $500.00 | $20,500 | $20,000 | | $500 |
| 2/3/93 | March S&P 500 | 447.30 | $500 | +1 | $223,650 | $2,150.00 | $22,650 | $20,000 | | $2,650 |
| 2/4/93 | March S&P 500 | 449.20 | $500 | +1 | $224,600 | $950.00 | $23,600 | $20,000 | | $3,600 |
| 2/5/93 | March S&P 500 | 449.10 | $500 | +1 | $224,550 | ($50.00) | $23,550 | $20,000 | | $3,550 |
| 2/8/93 | March S&P 500 | 448.10 | $500 | +1 | $224,050 | ($500.00) | $23,050 | $20,000 | | $3,050 |
| 2/9/93 | March S&P 500 | 446.00 | $500 | +1 | $223,000 | ($1,050.00) | $22,000 | $20,000 | | $2,000 |

### II. Margin Activity

Initial Margin Requirement    $11,250 per Contract
Maintenance Margin Requirement    $10,000 per Contract

| (1) Date | (2) Beginning # of Maintenance Contracts | (3) Margin Account Beginning Balance | (4) Unit Price Change | (5) Position +Gain/-Loss | (6) Interim Margin Balance | (7) Cash Account +From Cash -To Cash | (8) Margin Account Ending Balance | (9) Ending Number of Contracts | (10) Maintenance Requirement |
|---|---|---|---|---|---|---|---|---|---|
| 2/1/93 | +1 | $11,250 | 0 | $0 | $11,250 | $0 | $11,250 | +1 | $10,000 |
| 2/2/93 | +1 | $11,250 | 1.0000 | $500 | $11,750 | $0 | $11,750 | +1 | $10,000 |
| 2/3/93 | +1 | $11,750 | 4.3000 | $2,150 | $13,900 | $0 | $13,900 | +1 | $10,000 |
| 2/4/93 | +1 | $13,900 | 1.9000 | $950 | $14,850 | $0 | $14,850 | +1 | $10,000 |
| 2/5/93 | +1 | $14,850 | -0.1000 | ($50) | $14,800 | $0 | $14,800 | +1 | $10,000 |
| 2/8/93 | +1 | $14,800 | -1.0000 | ($500) | $14,300 | $0 | $14,300 | +1 | $10,000 |
| 2/9/93 | +1 | $14,300 | -2.1000 | ($1,050) | $13,250 | ($13,250) | $0 | 0 | $0 |

# Problem 6-1

## Standard & Poor's Long Speculation Worksheet (continued)

III. Cash Activity

| (1) | (2) | (3) | (4) | (5) |
|---|---|---|---|---|
| | Speculative Cash Beginning Balance | Cash Account Flows + Invested -Withdrawn | Margin Account Flows + From Margin -To Margin | Speculative Cash Ending Balance |
| Date | | | | |
| 2/1/93 | $8,750 | $0 | $0 | $8,750 |
| 2/2/93 | $8,750 | $0 | $0 | $8,750 |
| 2/3/93 | $8,750 | $0 | $0 | $8,750 |
| 2/4/93 | $8,750 | $0 | $0 | $8,750 |
| 2/5/93 | $8,750 | $0 | $0 | $8,750 |
| 2/8/93 | $8,750 | $0 | $0 | $8,750 |
| 2/9/93 | $8,750 | $0 | $13,250 | $22,000 |

*Spot Values*                                              *Futures Values*

| 2/1/93 | S&P 500 | 442.2 | Mar | S&P | 442 |
| 2/2/93 | S&P 500 | 442.2 | Mar | S&P | 443 |
| 2/3/93 | S&P 500 | 447 | Mar | S&P | 447.3 |
| 2/4/93 | S&P 500 | 449.2 | Mar | S&P | 449.2 |
| 2/5/93 | S&P 500 | 448.3 | Mar | S&P | 449.1 |
| 2/8/93 | S&P 500 | 447.3 | Mar | S&P | 448.1 |
| 2/9/93 | S&P 500 | 445.1 | Mar | S&P | 446 |

## Solution 6-2

The trading worksheet labeled Problem 6-2 represents this short S&P 500 hedger's position between February 1st and February 9th of 1993. This worksheet differs from Chapter Six's short hedger with regard to the amount being hedged ($250,000 as opposed to $20,000,000) and the funds being transferred between the margin and cash accounts to maintain the $10,000 minimum. The problem requires funds to be transferred three times during the week.

# Problem 6-2
## Standard & Poor's 500 Short Hedger Worksheet

### I. Overall Spot Activity

| (1) Date | (2) Spot Commodity | (3) Unit Price | (4) Amount of Spot Commodity | (5) Spot Position Value | (6) Unit Price Change | (7) Spot Position +Gain/-Loss | (8) Commission | (9) Spot Cummulative +Gain/-Loss |
|---|---|---|---|---|---|---|---|---|
| 2/1/93 | S&P 500 | 442.20 | +1.13 | $249,843 | 0.0000 | $0 | | $0 |
| 2/2/93 | S&P 500 | 442.20 | +1.13 | $249,843 | 0.0000 | $0 | | $0 |
| 2/3/93 | S&P 500 | 447.00 | +1.13 | $252,555 | 4.8000 | $2,712 | | $2,712 |
| 2/4/93 | S&P 500 | 449.20 | +1.13 | $253,798 | 2.2000 | $1,243 | | $3,955 |
| 2/5/93 | S&P 500 | 448.30 | +1.13 | $253,290 | (0.9000) | ($509) | | $3,447 |
| 2/8/93 | S&P 500 | 447.30 | +1.13 | $252,725 | (1.0000) | ($565) | | $2,882 |
| 2/9/93 | S&P 500 | 445.10 | +1.13 | $251,482 | (2.2000) | ($1,243) | | $1,639 |

### II. Basis Activity

| (1) Date | (2) Basis Unit Value Spot Futures | (3) Basis Change | (4) Basis Cumulative +Gain/-Loss |
|---|---|---|---|
| 2/1/93 | 0.2000 | 0 | $0 |
| 2/2/93 | -0.8000 | -1.0000 | ($500) |
| 2/3/93 | -0.3000 | 0.5000 | $62 |
| 2/4/93 | 0.0000 | 0.3000 | $355 |
| 2/5/93 | -0.8000 | -0.8000 | ($104) |
| 2/8/93 | -0.8000 | 0.0000 | ($169) |
| 2/9/93 | -0.9000 | -0.1000 | ($362) |

## Problem 6-2
## Standard & Poor's 500 Short Hedger Worksheet (continued)

### III. Overall Futures Activity

| (1) Date | (2) Contract | (3) Unit Price | (4) Number of Units per Contract | (5) Number of Contracts +Long/-Short | (6) Futures Position Values | (7) Futures Position +Gain/-Loss | (8) Total Cash+Margin | (9) Invested Cash+Margin | (10) Commission | (11) Futures Cumulative +Gain/-Loss |
|---|---|---|---|---|---|---|---|---|---|---|
| 2/1/93 | March S&P 500 | 442.00 | $500 | -1 | ($221,000) | $0 | $50,000 | $50,000 | | $0 |
| 2/2/93 | March S&P 500 | 443.00 | $500 | -1 | ($221,500) | ($500) | $49,500 | $50,000 | | ($500) |
| 2/3/93 | March S&P 500 | 447.30 | $500 | -1 | ($223,650) | ($2,150) | $47,350 | $50,000 | | ($2,650) |
| 2/4/93 | March S&P 500 | 449.20 | $500 | -1 | ($224,600) | ($950) | $46,400 | $50,000 | | ($3,600) |
| 2/5/93 | March S&P 500 | 449.10 | $500 | -1 | ($224,550) | $50 | $46,450 | $50,000 | | ($3,550) |
| 2/8/93 | March S&P 500 | 448.10 | $500 | -1 | ($224,050) | $500 | $46,950 | $50,000 | | ($3,050) |
| 2/9/93 | March S&P 500 | 446.00 | $500 | -1 | ($223,000) | $1,050 | $48,000 | $50,000 | | ($2,000) |

### IV. Margin Activity
Initial Margin Requirement    $10,000 per Contract
Maintenance Margin Requirement    $10,000 per Contract

| (1) Date | (2) Beginning # of Maintenance Contracts | (3) Margin Account Beginning Balance | (4) Unit Price Change | (5) Position +Gain/-Loss | (6) Interim Margin Balance | (7) Cash Account +From Cash -To Cash | (8) Margin Account Ending Balance | (9) Ending Number of Contracts | (10) Maintenance Requirement |
|---|---|---|---|---|---|---|---|---|---|
| 2/1/93 | -1 | $10,000 | 0 | $0 | $10,000 | $0 | $10,000 | 1 | $10,000 |
| 2/2/93 | -1 | $10,000 | 1.0000 | ($500) | $9,500 | $500 | $10,000 | 1 | $10,000 |
| 2/3/93 | -1 | $10,000 | 4.3000 | ($2,150) | $7,850 | $2,150 | $10,000 | 1 | $10,000 |
| 2/4/93 | -1 | $10,000 | 1.9000 | ($950) | $9,050 | $950 | $10,000 | 1 | $10,000 |
| 2/5/93 | -1 | $10,050 | -0.1000 | $50 | $10,050 | $0 | $10,050 | 1 | $10,000 |
| 2/8/93 | -1 | $10,050 | -1.0000 | $500 | $10,550 | $0 | $10,550 | 1 | $10,000 |
| 2/9/93 | -1 | $10,550 | -2.1000 | $1,050 | $11,600 | ($11,600) | $0 | 0 | $0 |

## Problem 6-2
### Standard & Poor's 500 Short Hedger Worksheet (continued)

V. Cash Activity

| (1) Date | (2) Carrying Cash Beginning Balance | (3) Cash Account Flows + Invested - Withdrawn | (4) Margin Account Flows + From Margin - To Margin | (5) Carrying Cash Ending Balance |
|---|---|---|---|---|
| 2/1/93 | $40,000 | $0 | $0 | $40,000 |
| 2/2/93 | $40,000 | $0 | ($500) | $39,500 |
| 2/3/93 | $39,500 | $0 | ($2,150) | $37,350 |
| 2/4/93 | $37,350 | $0 | ($950) | $36,400 |
| 2/5/93 | $36,400 | $0 | $0 | $36,400 |
| 2/8/93 | $36,400 | $0 | $0 | $36,400 |
| 2/9/93 | $36,400 | $0 | $11,600 | $48,000 |

## Problem 7-1

Assume market conditions identical to those facing the long currency speculator. Suppose that a small retail investor had $8,500 that he wanted to commit to a short speculative deutsche mark strategy in February of 1994. This investor's broker requires all foreign exchange speculators to post an initial margin of $1,750 per contract and maintain a margin of at least $1,300 per contract. Construct this speculator's worksheet given that he shorts two March D Mark futures contracts. The March deutsche mark futures contract prices are as follows:

| | | |
|---|---|---|
| 2/1/94 | Mar D Mark | .5750 |
| 2/2/94 | Mar D Mark | .5755 |
| 2/3/94 | Mar D Mark | .5727 |
| 2/4/94 | Mar D Mark | .5666 |
| 2/7/94 | Mar D Mark | .5669 |
| 2/8/94 | Mar D Mark | .5654 |

## Solution 7-1

The trading worksheet labeled Problem 7-1 represents this speculator's short D Mark futures position between February 1st and February 8th of 1994. The various sections in Problem 7-1 carry the exact same meaning as the sections in the British pound speculator worksheet.

## Problem 7-2

Assume market conditions identical to those facing the long foreign exchange hedger. This hedger is short, has a liability of DM1,000,000 and wants to protect the position against an increase in the deutsche mark during the first week of February 1994. With the initial and maintenance margins for foreign currency futures contracts set at $1,750 and $1,300, respectively, the manager feels that $50,000 is sufficient to satisfy all margin requirements and insure the integrity of the short futures position in a volatile market. Construct this long

## Problem 7-1
## Deutsche Mark Speculative Worksheet

### I. Overall Futures Activity

| (1) Date | (2) Contract | (3) Unit Price | (4) Number of Units per Contract | (5) Number of Contracts +Long/-Short | (6) Position Value | (7) Position +Gain/-Loss | (8) Total Cash+Margin | (9) Invested Cash+Margin | (10) Commission | (11) Cumulative +Gain/-Loss |
|---|---|---|---|---|---|---|---|---|---|---|
| 2/1/94 | Mar D Mark | 0.5750 | 125000 | -2 | ($143,750) | $0 | $8,500 | $8,500 | | $0 |
| 2/2/94 | Mar D Mark | 0.5755 | 125000 | -2 | ($143,875) | ($63) | $8,437 | $8,500 | | ($63) |
| 2/3/94 | Mar D Mark | 0.5727 | 125000 | -2 | ($143,175) | $350 | $8,788 | $8,500 | | $287 |
| 2/4/94 | Mar D Mark | 0.5666 | 125000 | -2 | ($141,650) | $762 | $9,550 | $8,500 | | $1,050 |
| 2/7/94 | Mar D Mark | 0.5669 | 125000 | -2 | ($141,725) | ($37) | $9,513 | $8,500 | | $1,013 |
| 2/8/94 | Mar D Mark | 0.5654 | 125000 | -2 | ($141,350) | $187 | $14,400 | $13,200 | | $1,200 |

### II. Margin Activity
Initial Margin Requirement   $1,750 per Contract
Maintenance Margin Requirement   $1,300 per Contract

| (1) Date | (2) Beginning # of Maintenance Contracts | (3) Margin Account Beginning Balance | (4) Unit Price Change | (5) Position +Gain/-Loss | (6) Interim Margin Balance | (7) Cash Account +From Cash -To Cash | (8) Margin Account Ending Balance | (9) Ending Number of Contracts | (10) Maintenance Requirement |
|---|---|---|---|---|---|---|---|---|---|
| 2/1/94 | -2 | $3,500 | 0 | $0 | $3,500 | $0 | $3,500 | -2 | $2,600 |
| 2/2/94 | -2 | $3,500 | 0.0005 | ($63) | $3,437 | $0 | $3,437 | -2 | $2,600 |
| 2/3/94 | -2 | $3,437 | -0.0028 | $350 | $3,788 | $0 | $3,788 | -2 | $2,600 |
| 2/4/94 | -2 | $3,788 | -0.0061 | $762 | $4,550 | $0 | $4,550 | -2 | $2,600 |
| 2/7/94 | -2 | $4,550 | 0.0003 | ($37) | $4,513 | $0 | $4,513 | -2 | $2,600 |
| 2/8/94 | -2 | $4,513 | -0.0015 | $187 | $4,700 | ($4,700) | $0 | 0 | $0 |

## Problem 7-1
### Deutsche Mark Speculative Worksheet (continued)

III. Cash Activity

| (1) Date | (2) Speculative Cash Beginning Balance | (3) Cash Account Flows + Invested - Withdrawn | (4) Margin Account Flows + From Margin - To Margin | (5) Speculative Cash Ending Balance |
|---|---|---|---|---|
| 2/1/94 | $5,000 | | $0 | $5,000 |
| 2/2/94 | $5,000 | | $0 | $5,000 |
| 2/3/94 | $5,000 | | $0 | $5,000 |
| 2/4/94 | $5,000 | | $0 | $5,000 |
| 2/7/94 | $5,000 | | $0 | $5,000 |
| 2/8/94 | $5,000 | | $4,700 | $9,700 |

hedger's worksheet. Deutsche mark spot and futures values are as follows:

| Spot Values | | | | Futures Values | | |
|---|---|---|---|---|---|---|
| 2/1/94 | D mark | .5774 | | Mar | D mark | .575 |
| 2/2/94 | D mark | .5767 | | Mar | D mark | .5755 |
| 2/3/94 | D mark | .5740 | | Mar | D mark | .5727 |
| 2/4/94 | D mark | .5684 | | Mar | D mark | .5666 |
| 2/7/94 | D mark | .5684 | | Mar | D mark | .5669 |
| 2/8/94 | D mark | .5667 | | Mar | D mark | .5654 |

## Solution 7-2

The trading worksheet labeled Problem 7-2 represents this long deutsche mark hedger's position between February 1st and February 8th in 1994. This worksheet shows that the hedger was able to capture some basis gains since the spot D mark declined by more than the March D mark futures. However, one funds transfer was required on 2/4/94 when the mark dropped dramatically.

## Problem 7-2
### Deutsche Mark Long Hedger Worksheet

**I. Overall Spot Activity**

| (1) Date | (2) Spot Commodity | (3) Unit Price | (4) Amount of Spot Commodity | (5) Spot Position Value | (6) Unit Price Change | (7) Spot Position +Gain/-Loss | (8) Commission | (9) Spot Cummulative +Gain/-Loss |
|---|---|---|---|---|---|---|---|---|
| 2/1/94 | Deutsche Mark | 0.5774 | -1,000,000 | ($577,400) | $0.0000 | $0 | | |
| 2/2/94 | Deutsche Mark | 0.5767 | -1,000,000 | ($576,700) | ($0.0007) | $700 | | $700 |
| 2/3/94 | Deutsche Mark | 0.574 | -1,000,000 | ($574,000) | ($0.0027) | $2,700 | | $3,400 |
| 2/4/94 | Deutsche Mark | 0.5684 | -1,000,000 | ($568,400) | ($0.0056) | $5,600 | | $9,000 |
| 2/7/94 | Deutsche Mark | 0.5684 | -1,000,000 | ($568,400) | $0.0000 | $0 | | $9,000 |
| 2/8/94 | Deutsche Mark | 0.5667 | -1,000,000 | ($566,700) | ($0.0017) | $1,700 | | $10,700 |

**II. Basis Activity**

| (1) Date | (2) Basis Unit Value Spot Futures | (3) Basis Change | (4) Basis Cumulative +Gain/-Loss |
|---|---|---|---|
| 2/1/94 | 0.0024 | 0 | $0.00 |
| 2/2/94 | 0.0012 | -0.0012 | $1,200.00 |
| 2/3/94 | 0.0013 | 0.0001 | $1,100.00 |
| 2/4/94 | 0.0018 | 0.0005 | $600.00 |
| 2/7/94 | 0.0015 | -0.0003 | $900.00 |
| 2/8/94 | 0.0013 | -0.0002 | $1,100.00 |

## Problem 7-2
### Deutsche Mark Long Hedger Worksheet (continued)

**III. Overall Futures Activity**

| (1) | (2) | (3) | (4) | (5) | (6) | (7) | (8) | (9) | (10) | (11) |
|---|---|---|---|---|---|---|---|---|---|---|
| Date | Contract | Unit Price | Number of Units per Contract | Number of Contracts +Long/-Short | Futures Position Values | Futures Position +Gain/-Loss | Total Cash+Margin | Invested Cash+Margin | Commission | Futures Cumulative +Gain/-Loss |
| 2/1/94 | March D Mark | 0.5750 | 125,000 | 8 | $575,000 | $0 | $50,000 | $50,000 | | $0 |
| 2/2/94 | March D Mark | 0.5755 | 125,000 | 8 | $575,500 | $500 | $50,500 | $50,000 | | $500 |
| 2/3/94 | March D Mark | 0.5727 | 125,000 | 8 | $572,700 | ($2,800) | $47,700 | $50,000 | | ($2,300) |
| 2/4/94 | March D Mark | 0.5666 | 125,000 | 8 | $566,600 | ($6,100) | $41,600 | $50,000 | | ($8,400) |
| 2/7/94 | March D Mark | 0.5669 | 125,000 | 8 | $566,900 | $300 | $41,900 | $50,000 | | ($8,100) |
| 2/8/94 | March D Mark | 0.5654 | 125,000 | 8 | $565,400 | ($1,500) | $40,400 | $50,000 | | ($9,600) |

**IV. Margin Activity**
Intitial Margin Requirement      $1,750 per Contract
Maintenance Margin Requirement      $1,300 per Contract

| (1) | (2) | (3) | (4) | (5) | (6) | (7) | (8) | (9) | (10) |
|---|---|---|---|---|---|---|---|---|---|
| Date | Beginning # of Maintenance Contracts | Margin Account Beginning Balance | Unit Price Change | Position +Gain/-Loss | Interim Margin Balance | Cash Account +From Cash -To Cash | Margin Account Ending Balance | Ending Number of Contracts | Maintenance Requirement |
| 2/1/94 | 8 | $14,000 | 0 | $0 | $14,000 | $0 | $14,000 | 8 | $10,400 |
| 2/2/94 | 8 | $14,000 | 0.0005 | $500 | $14,500 | $0 | $14,500 | 8 | $10,400 |
| 2/3/94 | 8 | $14,500 | -0.0028 | ($2,800) | $11,700 | $0 | $11,700 | 8 | $10,400 |
| 2/4/94 | 8 | $11,700 | -0.0061 | ($6,100) | $5,600 | $8,400 | $14,000 | 8 | $10,400 |
| 2/7/94 | 8 | $14,000 | 0.0003 | $300 | $14,300 | $0 | $14,300 | 8 | $10,400 |
| 2/8/94 | 8 | $14,300 | -0.0015 | ($1,500) | $12,800 | ($12,800) | $0 | 0 | $0 |

## Problem 7-2
### Deutsche Mark Long Hedger Worksheet (continued)

**V. Cash Activity**

| (1) Date | (2) Carrying Cash Beginning Balance | (3) Cash Account Flows +Invested -Withdrawn | (4) Margin Account Flows +From Margin -To Margin | (5) Carrying Cash Ending Balance |
|---|---|---|---|---|
| 2/1/94 | $36,000 | $0 | $0 | $36,000 |
| 2/2/94 | $36,000 | $0 | $0 | $36,000 |
| 2/3/94 | $36,000 | $0 | $0 | $36,000 |
| 2/4/94 | $36,000 | $0 | ($8,400) | $27,600 |
| 2/7/94 | $27,600 | $0 | $0 | $27,600 |
| 2/8/94 | $27,600 | $0 | $12,800 | $40,400 |

# Appendix E

# BLANK WORKSHEETS

## Short Hedger

### I. Overall Spot Activity

| (1) Date | (2) Spot Commodity | (3) Unit Price | (4) Amount of Spot Commodity | (5) Spot Position Value | (6) Unit Price Change | (7) Spot Position +Gain/−Loss | (8) Commission | (9) Spot Cumulative +Gain/−Loss |
|---|---|---|---|---|---|---|---|---|
| | | | | | | | | |
| | | | | | | | | |
| | | | | | | | | |
| | | | | | | | | |

### II. Basis Activity

| (1) Date | (2) Basis Unit Value Spot Futures | (3) Basis Change | (4) Basis Cumulative +Gain/−Loss |
|---|---|---|---|
| | | | |
| | | | |
| | | | |
| | | | |

### III. Overall Futures Activity

| (1) Date | (2) Contract | (3) Unit Price | (4) Number of Units per Contract | (5) Number of Contracts +Long/−Short | (6) Futures Position Value | (7) Futures Position +Gain/−Loss | (8) Total Cash+Margin | (9) Invested Cash+Margin | (10) Commission | (11) Futures Cumulative +Gain/−Loss |
|---|---|---|---|---|---|---|---|---|---|---|
| | | | | | | | | | | |
| | | | | | | | | | | |
| | | | | | | | | | | |
| | | | | | | | | | | |

## Short Hedger (continued)

### IV. Margin Activity

Initial Margin Requirement: _____ per Contract

Maintenance Margin Requirement: _____ per Contract

| (1) Date | (2) Beginning # of Maintenance Contracts | (3) Margin Account Beginning Balance | (4) Unit Price Change | (5) Position +Gain/–Loss | (6) Interim Margin Balance | (7) Cash Account +From Cash/ –To Cash | (8) Margin Account Ending Balance | (9) Ending Number of Contracts | (10) Maintenance Requirements |
|---|---|---|---|---|---|---|---|---|---|
| | | | | | | | | | |
| | | | | | | | | | |
| | | | | | | | | | |
| | | | | | | | | | |

### V. Cash Activity

| (1) Date | (2) Carrying Cash Beginning Balance | (3) Cash Account Flows +Invested/ –Withdrawn | (4) Margin Accounts Flows +From Margin/ –To Margin | (5) Carrying Cash Ending Balance |
|---|---|---|---|---|
| | | | | |
| | | | | |
| | | | | |
| | | | | |

## Short Hedger

### I. Overall Spot Activity

| (1) Date | (2) Spot Commodity | (3) Unit Price | (4) Amount of Spot Commodity | (5) Spot Position Value | (6) Unit Price Change | (7) Spot Position +Gain/−Loss | (8) Commission | (9) Spot Cumulative +Gain/−Loss |
|---|---|---|---|---|---|---|---|---|
| | | | | | | | | |
| | | | | | | | | |
| | | | | | | | | |
| | | | | | | | | |

### II. Basis Activity

| (1) Date | (2) Basis Unit Value Spot Futures | (3) Basis Change | (4) Basis Cumulative +Gain/−Loss |
|---|---|---|---|
| | | | |
| | | | |
| | | | |
| | | | |

### III. Overall Futures Activity

| (1) Date | (2) Contract | (3) Unit Price | (4) Number of Units per Contract | (5) Number of Contracts +Long/−Short | (6) Futures Position Value | (7) Futures Position +Gain/−Loss | (8) Total Cash+Margin | (9) Invested Cash+Margin | (10) Commission | (11) Futures Cumulative +Gain/−Loss |
|---|---|---|---|---|---|---|---|---|---|---|
| | | | | | | | | | | |
| | | | | | | | | | | |
| | | | | | | | | | | |
| | | | | | | | | | | |

## Short Hedger (continued)

### IV. Margin Activity

Initial Margin Requirement: _____ per Contract
Maintenance Margin Requirement: _____ per Contract

| (1) Date | (2) Beginning # of Maintenance Contracts | (3) Margin Account Beginning Balance | (4) Unit Price Change | (5) Position +Gain/–Loss | (6) Interim Margin Balance | (7) Cash Account +From Cash/ –To Cash | (8) Margin Account Ending Balance | (9) Ending Number of Contracts | (10) Maintenance Requirements |
|---|---|---|---|---|---|---|---|---|---|
| | | | | | | | | | |
| | | | | | | | | | |
| | | | | | | | | | |
| | | | | | | | | | |

### V. Cash Activity

| (1) Date | (2) Carrying Cash Beginning Balance | (3) Cash Account Flows +Invested/ –Withdrawn | (4) Margin Accounts Flows +From Margin/ –To Margin | (5) Carrying Cash Ending Balance |
|---|---|---|---|---|
| | | | | |
| | | | | |
| | | | | |
| | | | | |
| | | | | |
| | | | | |

# Long Hedger

## I. Overall Spot Activity

| (1)<br>Date | (2)<br>Spot<br>Commodity | (3)<br>Unit<br>Price | (4)<br>Amount<br>of Spot<br>Commodity | (5)<br>Spot<br>Position<br>Value | (6)<br>Unit<br>Price<br>Change | (7)<br>Spot<br>Position<br>+Gain/−Loss | (8)<br>Commission | (9)<br>Spot<br>Cumulative<br>+Gain/−Loss |
|---|---|---|---|---|---|---|---|---|
| | | | | | | | | |
| | | | | | | | | |
| | | | | | | | | |

## II. Basis Activity

| (1)<br>Date | (2)<br>Basis<br>Unit Value<br>Spot Futures | (3)<br>Basis<br>Change | (4)<br>Basis<br>Cumulative<br>+Gain/−Loss |
|---|---|---|---|
| | | | |
| | | | |
| | | | |

## III. Overall Futures Activity

| (1)<br>Date | (2)<br>Contract | (3)<br>Unit<br>Price | (4)<br>Number<br>of Units<br>per Contract | (5)<br>Number of<br>Contracts<br>+Long/−Short | (6)<br>Futures<br>Position<br>Value | (7)<br>Position<br>+Gain/−Loss | (8)<br>Total<br>Cash+Margin | (9)<br>Invested<br>Cash+Margin | (10)<br>Commission | (11)<br>Futures<br>Cumulative<br>+Gain/−Loss |
|---|---|---|---|---|---|---|---|---|---|---|
| | | | | | | | | | | |
| | | | | | | | | | | |
| | | | | | | | | | | |

## Long Hedger (continued)

### IV. Margin Activity

Initial Margin Requirement: _____ per Contract
Maintenance Margin Requirement: _____ per Contract

| (1) Date | (2) Beginning # of Maintenance Contracts | (3) Margin Account Beginning Balance | (4) Unit Price Change | (5) Position +Gain/–Loss | (6) Interim Margin Balance | (7) Cash Account +From Cash/ –To Cash | (8) Margin Account Ending Balance | (9) Ending Number of Contracts | (10) Maintenance Requirements |
|---|---|---|---|---|---|---|---|---|---|
|  |  |  |  |  |  |  |  |  |  |
|  |  |  |  |  |  |  |  |  |  |
|  |  |  |  |  |  |  |  |  |  |
|  |  |  |  |  |  |  |  |  |  |

### V. Cash Activity

| (1) Date | (2) Carrying Cash Beginning Balance | (3) Cash Account Flows +Invested/ –Withdrawn | (4) Margin Accounts Flows +From Margin/ –To Margin | (5) Carrying Cash Ending Balance |
|---|---|---|---|---|
|  |  |  |  |  |
|  |  |  |  |  |
|  |  |  |  |  |
|  |  |  |  |  |
|  |  |  |  |  |

# Long Hedger

## I. Overall Spot Activity

| (1)<br>Date | (2)<br>Spot<br>Commodity | (3)<br>Unit<br>Price | (4)<br>Amount<br>of Spot<br>Commodity | (5)<br>Spot<br>Position<br>Value | (6)<br>Unit<br>Price<br>Change | (7)<br>Spot<br>Position<br>+Gain/–Loss | (8)<br>Commission | (9)<br>Spot<br>Cumulative<br>+Gain/–Loss |
|---|---|---|---|---|---|---|---|---|
| | | | | | | | | |
| | | | | | | | | |
| | | | | | | | | |
| | | | | | | | | |

## II. Basis Activity

| (1)<br>Date | (2)<br>Basis<br>Unit Value<br>Spot Futures | (3)<br>Basis<br>Change | (4)<br>Basis<br>Cumulative<br>+Gain/–Loss |
|---|---|---|---|
| | | | |
| | | | |
| | | | |
| | | | |

## III. Overall Futures Activity

| (1)<br>Date | (2)<br>Contract | (3)<br>Unit<br>Price | (4)<br>Number<br>of Units<br>per Contract | (5)<br>Number of<br>Contracts<br>+Long/–Short | (6)<br>Futures<br>Position<br>Value | (7)<br>Position<br>+Gain/–Loss | (8)<br>Total<br>Cash+Margin | (9)<br>Invested<br>Cash+Margin | (10)<br>Commission | (11)<br>Futures<br>Cumulative<br>+Gain/–Loss |
|---|---|---|---|---|---|---|---|---|---|---|
| | | | | | | | | | | |
| | | | | | | | | | | |
| | | | | | | | | | | |
| | | | | | | | | | | |

## Long Hedger (continued)

**IV. Margin Activity**
Initial Margin Requirement: _____ per Contract
Maintenance Margin Requirement: _____ per Contract

| (1) Date | (2) Beginning # of Maintenance Contracts | (3) Margin Account Beginning Balance | (4) Unit Price Change | (5) Position +Gain/−Loss | (6) Interim Margin Balance | (7) Cash Account +From Cash/ −To Cash | (8) Margin Account Ending Balance | (9) Ending Number of Contracts | (10) Maintenance Requirements |
|---|---|---|---|---|---|---|---|---|---|
| | | | | | | | | | |
| | | | | | | | | | |
| | | | | | | | | | |
| | | | | | | | | | |

**V. Cash Activity**

| (1) Date | (2) Carrying Cash Beginning Balance | (3) Cash Account Flows +Invested/ −Withdrawn | (4) Margin Accounts Flows +From Margin/ −To Margin | (5) Carrying Cash Ending Balance |
|---|---|---|---|---|
| | | | | |
| | | | | |
| | | | | |
| | | | | |
| | | | | |

## Long Speculation

### I. Overall Futures Activity

| (1) Date | (2) Contract | (3) Unit Price | (4) Number of Units per Contract | (5) Number of Contracts +Long/−Short | (6) Position Value | (7) Position +Gain/−Loss | (8) Total Cash+Margin | (9) Invested Cash+Margin | (10) Commission | (11) Cumulative +Gain/−Loss |
|---|---|---|---|---|---|---|---|---|---|---|
|  |  |  |  |  |  |  |  |  |  |  |
|  |  |  |  |  |  |  |  |  |  |  |
|  |  |  |  |  |  |  |  |  |  |  |

### II. Margin Activity
Initial Margin Requirement: $____0____ per Contract
Maintenance Margin Requirement: $____0____ per Contract

| (1) Date | (2) Beginning Number of Contracts | (3) Margin Account Beginning Balance | (4) Unit Price Change | (5) Position +Gain/−Loss | (6) Interim Margin Balance | (7) Cash Account +From Cash/ −To Cash | (8) Margin Account Ending Balance | (9) Ending Number of Contracts | (10) Maintenance Requirements |
|---|---|---|---|---|---|---|---|---|---|
|  |  |  |  |  |  |  |  |  |  |
|  |  |  |  |  |  |  |  |  |  |
|  |  |  |  |  |  |  |  |  |  |
|  |  |  |  |  |  |  |  |  |  |

### III. Cash Activity

| (1) Date | (2) Speculative Cash Beginning Balance | (3) Cash Account Flows +Invested/ −Withdrawn | (4) Margin Accounts Flows +From Margin/ −To Margin | (5) Speculative Cash Ending Balance |
|---|---|---|---|---|
|  |  |  |  |  |
|  |  |  |  |  |
|  |  |  |  |  |
|  |  |  |  |  |

## Long Speculation

### I. Overall Futures Activity

| (1) Date | (2) Contract | (3) Unit Price | (4) Number of Units per Contract | (5) Number of Contracts +Long/−Short | (6) Position Value | (7) Position +Gain/−Loss | (8) Total Cash+Margin | (9) Invested Cash+Margin | (10) Commission | (11) Cumulative +Gain/−Loss |
|---|---|---|---|---|---|---|---|---|---|---|
| | | | | | | | | | | |
| | | | | | | | | | | |
| | | | | | | | | | | |

### II. Margin Activity

Initial Margin Requirement: $ ___0___ per Contract
Maintenance Margin Requirement: $ ___0___ per Contract

| (1) Date | (2) Beginning Number of Contracts | (3) Margin Account Beginning Balance | (4) Unit Price Change | (5) Position +Gain/−Loss | (6) Interim Margin Balance | (7) Cash Account +From Cash/ −To Cash | (8) Margin Account Ending Balance | (9) Ending Number of Contracts | (10) Maintenance Requirements |
|---|---|---|---|---|---|---|---|---|---|
| | | | | | | | | | |
| | | | | | | | | | |
| | | | | | | | | | |
| | | | | | | | | | |

### III. Cash Activity

| (1) Date | (2) Speculative Cash Beginning Balance | (3) Cash Account Flows +Invested/ −Withdrawn | (4) Margin Accounts Flows +From Margin/ −To Margin | (5) Speculative Cash Ending Balance |
|---|---|---|---|---|
| | | | | |
| | | | | |
| | | | | |
| | | | | |

# Short Speculation

## I. Overall Futures Activity

| (1) Date | (2) Contract | (3) Unit Price | (4) Number of Units per Contract | (5) Number of Contracts +Long/−Short | (6) Position Value | (7) Position +Gain/−Loss | (8) Total Cash+Margin | (9) Invested Cash+Margin | (10) Commission | (11) Cumulative +Gain/−Loss |
|---|---|---|---|---|---|---|---|---|---|---|
|  |  |  |  |  |  |  |  |  |  |  |
|  |  |  |  |  |  |  |  |  |  |  |
|  |  |  |  |  |  |  |  |  |  |  |

## II. Margin Activity

Initial Margin Requirement: $ \_\_\_\_ 0 \_\_\_\_ per Contract

Maintenance Margin Requirement: $ \_\_\_\_ 0 \_\_\_\_ per Contract

| (1) Date | (2) Beginning Number of Contracts | (3) Margin Account Beginning Balance | (4) Unit Price Change | (5) Position +Gain/−Loss | (6) Interim Margin Balance | (7) Cash Account +From Cash/ −To Cash | (8) Margin Account Ending Balance | (9) Ending Number of Contracts | (10) Maintenance Requirements |
|---|---|---|---|---|---|---|---|---|---|
|  |  |  |  |  |  |  |  |  |  |
|  |  |  |  |  |  |  |  |  |  |
|  |  |  |  |  |  |  |  |  |  |
|  |  |  |  |  |  |  |  |  |  |

## III. Cash Activity

| (1) Date | (2) Speculative Cash Beginning Balance | (3) Cash Account Flows +Invested/ −Withdrawn | (4) Margin Accounts Flows +From Margin/ −To Margin | (5) Speculative Cash Ending Balance |
|---|---|---|---|---|
|  |  |  |  |  |
|  |  |  |  |  |
|  |  |  |  |  |
|  |  |  |  |  |

## Short Speculation

### I. Overall Futures Activity

| (1) Date | (2) Contract | (3) Unit Price | (4) Number of Units per Contract | (5) Number of Contracts +Long/–Short | (6) Position Value | (7) Position +Gain/–Loss | (8) Total Cash+Margin | (9) Invested Cash+Margin | (10) Commission | (11) Cumulative +Gain/–Loss |
|---|---|---|---|---|---|---|---|---|---|---|
|  |  |  |  |  |  |  |  |  |  |  |
|  |  |  |  |  |  |  |  |  |  |  |
|  |  |  |  |  |  |  |  |  |  |  |

### II. Margin Activity

Initial Margin Requirement:     $ ___0___ per Contract
Maintenance Margin Requirement: $ ___0___ per Contract

| (1) Date | (2) Beginning Number of Contracts | (3) Margin Account Beginning Balance | (4) Unit Price Change | (5) Position +Gain/–Loss | (6) Interim Margin Balance | (7) Cash Account +From Cash/ –To Cash | (8) Margin Account Ending Balance | (9) Ending Number of Contracts | (10) Maintenance Requirements |
|---|---|---|---|---|---|---|---|---|---|
|  |  |  |  |  |  |  |  |  |  |
|  |  |  |  |  |  |  |  |  |  |
|  |  |  |  |  |  |  |  |  |  |
|  |  |  |  |  |  |  |  |  |  |

### III. Cash Activity

| (1) Date | (2) Speculative Cash Beginning Balance | (3) Cash Account Flows +Invested/ –Withdrawn | (4) Margin Accounts Flows +From Margin/ –To Margin | (5) Speculative Cash Ending Balance |
|---|---|---|---|---|
|  |  |  |  |  |
|  |  |  |  |  |
|  |  |  |  |  |
|  |  |  |  |  |

## Spreads

### I. Detailed Futures Activity

| (1) Date | (2) Long Position | (3) Unit Price | (4) Long Unit Price Change | (5) Number of Contracts Bought | (6) Short Position | (7) Unit Price | (8) Short Unit Price Change | (9) Number of Contracts Sold | (10) Spread Unit Value | (11) Spread Unit Change | (12) Number of Units per Contract | (13) Spread Value |
|---|---|---|---|---|---|---|---|---|---|---|---|---|
| | | | | | | | | | | | | |
| | | | | | | | | | | | | |
| | | | | | | | | | | | | |

### II. Overall Spread Activity

| (1) Date | (2) Spread | (3) Spread Unit Value | (4) Number of Units per Lot | (5) Number of Lots | (6) Spread Value | (7) Spread +Gain/−Loss | (8) Total Cash+Margin | (9) Invested Cash+Margin | (10) Spread Commission | (11) Cumulative +Gain/−Loss |
|---|---|---|---|---|---|---|---|---|---|---|
| | | | | | | | | | | |
| | | | | | | | | | | |
| | | | | | | | | | | |
| | | | | | | | | | | |
| | | | | | | | | | | |
| | | | | | | | | | | |

# Spreads (continued)

## III. Margin Activity

Initial Margin Requirement: $ _____ per Spread

Maintenance Margin Requirement: $ _____ per Spread

| (1) Date | (2) Beginning Number of Lots | (3) Margin Account Beginning Balance | (4) Spread Unit Price Change | (5) Position +Gain/−Loss | (6) Interim Margin Balance | (7) Ending Number of Lots | (8) Cash Account +From Cash/ −To Cash | (9) Margin Account Ending Balance | (10) Maintenance Requirements |
|---|---|---|---|---|---|---|---|---|---|
|  |  |  |  |  |  |  |  |  |  |
|  |  |  |  |  |  |  |  |  |  |
|  |  |  |  |  |  |  |  |  |  |
|  |  |  |  |  |  |  |  |  |  |

## IV. Cash Activity

| (1) Date | (2) Reserve Cash Beginning Balance | (3) Cash Account Flows +Invested/ −Withdrawn | (4) Margin Accounts Flows +From Margin/−To Margin | (5) Reserve Cash Ending Balance |
|---|---|---|---|---|
|  |  |  |  |  |
|  |  |  |  |  |
|  |  |  |  |  |
|  |  |  |  |  |

# Spreads

## I. Detailed Futures Activity

| (1) Date | (2) Long Position | (3) Unit Price | (4) Long Unit Price Change | (5) Number of Contracts Bought | (6) Short Position | (7) Unit Price | (8) Short Unit Price Change | (9) Number of Contracts Sold | (10) Spread Unit Value | (11) Spread Unit Change | (12) Number of Units per Contract | (13) Spread Value |
|---|---|---|---|---|---|---|---|---|---|---|---|---|
|  |  |  |  |  |  |  |  |  |  |  |  |  |
|  |  |  |  |  |  |  |  |  |  |  |  |  |
|  |  |  |  |  |  |  |  |  |  |  |  |  |

## II. Overall Spread Activity

| (1) Date | (2) Spread | (3) Spread Unit Value | (4) Number of Units per Lot | (5) Number of Lots | (6) Spread Value | (7) Spread +Gain/−Loss | (8) Total Cash+Margin | (9) Invested Cash+Margin | (10) Spread Commission | (11) Cumulative +Gain/−Loss |
|---|---|---|---|---|---|---|---|---|---|---|
|  |  |  |  |  |  |  |  |  |  |  |
|  |  |  |  |  |  |  |  |  |  |  |
|  |  |  |  |  |  |  |  |  |  |  |
|  |  |  |  |  |  |  |  |  |  |  |

*Spreads (continued)*

## III. Margin Activity

Initial Margin Requirement: $ _____ per Spread
Maintenance Margin Requirement: $ _____ per Spread

| (1) Date | (2) Beginning Number of Lots | (3) Margin Account Beginning Balance | (4) Spread Unit Price Change | (5) Position +Gain/–Loss | (6) Interim Margin Balance | (7) Ending Number of Lots | (8) Cash Account +From Cash/ –To Cash | (9) Margin Account Ending Balance | (10) Maintenance Requirements |
|---|---|---|---|---|---|---|---|---|---|
| | | | | | | | | | |
| | | | | | | | | | |
| | | | | | | | | | |
| | | | | | | | | | |

## IV. Cash Activity

| (1) Date | (2) Reserve Cash Beginning Balance | (3) Cash Account Flows +Invested/ –Withdrawn | (4) Margin Accounts Flows +From Margin/–To Margin | (5) Reserve Cash Ending Balance |
|---|---|---|---|---|
| | | | | |
| | | | | |
| | | | | |
| | | | | |

# INDEX

# About the Author

Carl F. Luft is an Assistant Professor of Finance at DePaul University. He earned an M.B.A. in international business from DePaul in 1977 and a Ph.D. in finance from Georgia State University in 1983. While completing his doctoral degree, Mr. Luft served as a consultant with the Atlanta branch of Cantor-Fitzgerald Brokerage House. Since returning to Chicago, he has consulted with Cargill Investor Services, Mercury Trading, and Hull Trading and taught at the Chicago Board Options Exchange's Options Institute and the Chicago Mercantile Exchange.